Using
Turbo
Prolog™

Using
Turbo
Prolog™

Phillip R. Robinson

With a Foreword
by Philippe Kahn

Osborne **McGraw-Hill**
Berkeley, California

Osborne **McGraw-Hill**
2600 Tenth Street
Berkeley, California 94710
U.S.A.

For information on translations and book distributors outside of the U.S.A., please write to Osborne **McGraw-Hill** at the above address.

A complete list of trademarks appears on page 329.

Using Turbo Prolog™

1234567890 DODO 89876

ISBN 0-07-881253-4

I'd like to dedicate this book to my eight-month-old daughter, Jamaica, who consistently offered her enthusiastic advice on which keys to hit on the PC keyboard. Although I enjoyed writing the book, I'm glad it's done so I'll have more time to spend with her.

Contents

Foreword

I am really excited about Phil's new book, and I am delighted to recommend it to anyone interested in Turbo Prolog. The growing interest in artificial intelligence (AI) and fifth-generation languages, including Turbo Prolog, is characteristic of the second part of the 1980s.

New programming languages and new implementations of those languages have always been the stimulus for the development of exciting new applications in areas previously untouched by computers and computer technology. These new developments will be particularly interesting as we see more implementations of AI technology in areas such as expert systems development and natural-language interfaces, which are not only representative of advancements in software programming, but which also work toward the goal of making computers and computer-stored knowledge available to everyone.

When we introduced Turbo Prolog, we made the tools of AI application development available to all interested programmers and would-be programmers, by providing a very easy-to-use yet highly advanced development environment that is also affordable. We also optimized the Prolog language for speed and efficiency. Our Turbo Prolog manual takes the first step toward introducing you to the language and providing you with reference information for its various functions and features.

Phil's book is designed to give you the next step. He goes beyond our tutorial of "how to" and gets into descriptions and examples of using Turbo Prolog. He also goes into details of the language's various features and how and when to use them.

I've know Phil for several years, and I have great respect for his abilities as a writer and reporter. During his career at *BYTE* magazine, he has covered the growth of the entire microcomputer industry. His understanding of the personal computer industry is second to none.

I know you will enjoy the book, and by combining the information in *Using Turbo Prolog* with our Turbo Prolog compiler and manual, I'm certain you will begin developing useful new software applications. We look forward to hearing about your Turbo Prolog programs and your personal contributions to the "brave new world of artificial intelligence."

Philippe Kahn
President
Borland International, Inc.

Preface

A knowledge of Prolog is important for anyone involved with computers because the language has become the premier programming environment for artificial intelligence (AI), one of the major emerging application areas for computers. AI is intimately linked to some of the most exciting areas of computer science: fifth-generation processors, expert systems, and natural-language processing.

Until recently, however, most implementations of Prolog were designed for minicomputers or workstations, making the language available only to those few programmers who had access to such computer hardware. Because Turbo Prolog is designed to be used with personal computers like the IBM PC (and PC-compatibles), the power and excitement of AI applications are available to virtually everyone. (And at less than $100, Turbo Prolog is also affordable for just about everyone.)

The Turbo Prolog package — which includes a compiler, a development environment, example programs, a manual, and a source-code application — provides a complete programming environment. Although these tools are powerful, Turbo Prolog is easy to use, even if you are a beginning programmer. Its windowing environment enables you to list, edit, compile, run, and debug programs quickly and efficiently. And once you begin writing Turbo Prolog programs, you will find that it is one of the fastest Prologs available. Benchmark (or standardized) tests show that in LIPS (Logical Inferences Per Second, the standard way to measure the thinking speed of a Prolog compiler), Turbo Prolog executes programs much faster than most PC-based Prolog compilers. In fact, Turbo Prolog competes favorably with some Prologs running on minicomputers.

The software developer responsible for Turbo Prolog, Borland International, is one of the most successful personal computer language companies in history. Borland's Turbo Pascal has become a standard in and of itself, not only because it has sold so many copies, but also because of the program's reputation for reliability, power, ease of use, and value. I predict that Turbo Prolog will set a new standard in the Prolog arena, just as Turbo Pascal set new standards for Pascal.

In designing Turbo Prolog, Borland made the decision to include most standard Prolog conventions, leave out a few others, and add many powerful features that are unique to Turbo Prolog. (Some of the additional features involve speed, graphics and sound support, and a simplified syntax.) The more you use Turbo Prolog, the more you'll find that it fulfills your programming requirements for many practical and fascinating applications.

About This Book

Using Turbo Prolog introduces you to the Prolog programming language in general and to Turbo Prolog in particular. This book will walk you through Turbo Prolog from the first time you put your System/Program disk into the disk drive. After learning how to load the program, you'll be introduced to the development environment (the windows and menus) and the Editor where you actually begin typing in programs. Then you'll proceed step by step through the workings of Prolog and Turbo Prolog's standard predicates. Each chapter uses demonstration programs to illustrate the predicates at work on the screen, so you'll see how the programs work at each stage in their development. These programs build from the simplest predicate to more advanced applications such as sound, graphics, and advanced compiler controls. Some of the nuts and bolts of GeoBase, the large application written in Turbo Prolog that Borland provides on the Library/Example disk, will also be described.

While you can learn the fundamentals of Prolog programming by simply reading *Using Turbo Prolog,* you'll gain the greatest understanding of how to program in Turbo Prolog by actually sitting down and working through the examples and discussions in this book. Actually tracing through programs is one of the most effective ways to assimilate the logical processes of Prolog.

If you do have Turbo Prolog, you may wonder why you should bother with another book when Borland ships you a combined tutorial and reference manual with the disks. For one thing, this book offers a different point of view and a different voice. For most computer users, learning Prolog is not as simple as learning another programming language. Most PC owners, for example, have been exposed to some version of BASIC or Pascal. These are procedural languages, and although Prolog has some procedural elements, it is an entirely different animal in that it is largely declarative, a difference that demands a different way of thinking for the programmer. Consequently, you'll probably need a panoply of sources to help you attack this new challenge in computer—human relations.

Another good reason to put *Using Turbo Prolog* on your desk along with the user's manual is that this book uses a large number of screen displays and example programs to explain abstract concepts. You don't have to wonder about what will happen on the screen or try to picture it in your mind: it is right there in front of you on the page. This should help ease you into the development environment. This book uses a variety of window placements and configurations to remind you that the development environment is malleable and that you can make the environment fit your needs. Your screen may not be identical to those shown in the book, especially with changes in the default configuration, but the displays should give you a handle on the way Turbo looks and works.

Furthermore, the example programs in this book are thoroughly explained. If you've ever attempted to learn a computer language before, you know that the more examples you look at —and work to modify — the better you'll know that language.

As you work through *Using Turbo Prolog*, you'll find that the Turbo Prolog user's manual is an excellent reference source. The example programs found in the manual are superb, and the technical details provided in the back will be invaluable as you begin writing your own sophisticated programs. If you didn't buy Turbo Prolog but copied it from someone else's disks, you should go out immediately and buy the compiler and the user's manual. Not only is the manual invaluable, but neither of the two reasons commonly offered for justifying software copying (or piracy) —expense and hard disk installation —is valid in the case of Turbo Prolog. Paying under $100 for a complete language with documentation, a windowing editor, scores of example programs on disk, a large sample application, and technical support is hard to beat. Furthermore, you shouldn't have any trouble installing Turbo Prolog on your hard disk or making as many backups as you need, because the program is not copy-protected.

The first release of Turbo Prolog was referred to as version 1.0. As with Turbo Pascal (or any other software package for that matter), subsequent versions and updates are always released. These versions are typically referred to as version 1.02, version 1.1, version 2.0, and so on. If you are using Turbo Prolog version 1.0, many of the screens in this book will not be identical to those on your computer display since *Using Turbo Prolog* is not based on both version 1.0 and version 1.02. Virtually all of the changes made in version 1.02 were changes to the *user interface*, which is what you see on the screen. (There may be, for example, a difference in the Editor window status line or an additional selection on the Options menu.) There are few, if any, operational changes. Borland may not release version 1.02 to the general public. The firm may choose to wait until version 1.1 is ready for release. All of the programs in this book will work with version 1.0 and subsequent releases of the Turbo Prolog program. Where applicable, the text describes the differences between version 1.0 and later releases. In addition, version 1.0 referred to the two Turbo Prolog disks as the "Program disk" and the "Utilities and Sample Program disk." These names were changed in later releases of the program to "System/Program disk" and "Library/Example disk" respectively and are referred to as such in this book.

—P.R.R.

Acknowledgments

It's only logical that I should thank the people who helped me write this book. They came in two varieties. Jon Erickson of Osborne/McGraw-Hill and Brenda McLaughlin of *BYTE* magazine held the outside world at bay so I could write a book while taking care of an eight-month-old daughter and working at a full-time magazine job. Robin Shepherd Tygh, Philippe Kahn, and Dan Kerman of Borland International introduced me to Turbo Prolog, kept me up to date with the latest version, and answered my technical questions about its workings.

Introduction

Prolog is an exciting topic at all levels of computing because artificial intelligence (AI) is an exciting topic and Prolog just happens to be one of the foremost programming languages used by AI researchers. For programmers investigating AI, Prolog offers a different approach to software than is employed by the more familiar languages, such as BASIC, COBOL, Pascal, and C — an approach that is much better suited to some of the problems AI researchers are trying to solve.

If you have been drawn to Turbo Prolog because of its association with AI, it is important to understand that the language will not turn your PC into a brain, nor will it offer you immediate avenues to superpowerful applications. Instead, it will let you learn how to design, and apply, some software methods that were first developed by AI researchers. As you work through this book and see how Turbo Prolog finds solutions to goals, you'll realize how the computer can be made to do some of the programmer's work and get a glimpse of how such methods can prod a computer into behaving slightly, very slightly, like human beings sometimes do.

A Short History of Prolog

Prolog stands for "PROgramming in LOGic" and is a computer programming language that was invented around 1970 by Alain Colmerauer and his colleagues at the University of Marseille. Prolog quickly became the leading AI language in Europe while LISP (another programming language used by AI researchers) was primarily used by programmers in the United States. By the late 1970s, versions of Prolog for microcomputers started to appear. One of the most popular microcomputer Prolog compilers was micro-Prolog, and many other Prolog books are devoted to it. But micro-Prolog does not offer the wealth of predicates that a language such as Turbo Prolog offers. It is also much slower than Turbo Prolog in that a micro-Prolog program takes far longer to make a logical decision than does Turbo Prolog.

There wasn't a lot of interest in Prolog until Japanese computer scientists launched their famous fifth-generation project with the goal of designing new computers and software that would reign supreme into the 1990s and beyond. It wasn't simply coincidental that the language they chose to base their work upon was Prolog. Suddenly, people began taking another look at Prolog and its capabilities.

What Is Prolog Good For?

Individual computer languages are rarely good for all types of problems. FORTRAN (short for "FORmula TRANslation"), for example, is used primarily by scientists and mathematicians while COBOL (short for "COmmon Business Oriented Language") is used mainly in the business world. Many implementations of Prolog lack the ability to handle "number crunching" or "text processing" problems; instead, Prolog is designed to handle "logical problems" (that is, problems for which decisions need to be made in an orderly fashion). Prolog tries to make the computer "reason" its way to a solution. It is particularly well suited to several types of artificial intelligence problems. The two most significant of these are *expert systems* and *natural-language processing*.

Expert Systems

Expert systems are computer programs that imitate a human expert. They contain information (that is, a database) and a tool for understanding questions and finding the right answers to those questions in the database (that is, an *inference engine*). Typical applications for expert systems include medicine (where computers are asked to diagnose diseases) and geology (where computers are asked where oil might be found).

Turbo Prolog has a built-in structure for creating databases and has a ready-to-run inference engine. All you have to do is tell the program the rules to run by, and it will discover its own path to the appropriate information. Many other programming languages would require that you write the rules, explain the rules, specify the paths, and generally work at a much more detailed level to create the inference engine before you ever began to retrieve the needed information. Also, Turbo Prolog's database is built with the same structures that are used to write the rules —learn one facet of the problem and you know how to deal with both.

Natural-Language Processing

Natural-language processing is the technique of forcing computers to understand human languages. Scientists who study natural-language processing hope to create hardware and software that would allow you to type **"Move the Turbo Prolog files to the prolog directory"** and have the computer follow your directions. Today you have to use a command such as **b: copy a:*.pro \prolog [v]** to meet that end. Turbo Prolog can use the idea of a database and an inference engine to divide human language into different parts and relationships and thus try to "understand" the meaning.

Logic

As its name implies, Prolog depends upon logical manipulations. As a computer language, it is not unique in this respect: there are a number of other languages in the general field of "logic programming." Such languages work with *propositional logic,* also known as *predicate logic* or *propositional calculus.* For instance, the following statements are facts:

People with baseball shoes play baseball.
Person #1 has baseball shoes.

What might be inferred, figured, deduced, calculated, computed, or determined from those facts is that Person #1 plays baseball.

Turbo Prolog makes the computer handle the inferring part. In fact, Turbo Prolog has a built-in inference engine that automatically hunts through facts and builds or tests logical conclusions. The problem just given might seem trivial, but if you had a technical database loaded with thousands of facts and rules, it would not be practical to hand that list to a human and ask for a quick answer. (In natural-language processing, the database would contain rules about parsing and understanding language.)

Resolution and Unification

Mathematical rules of logic that can reduce textual statements to symbolic representations have been around for years. But in 1965, J. Alan Robinson discovered the *resolution principle,* which showed how these representations could be cast in the right form and given to a computer for analysis.

Resolution is an inference rule—it lets the computer tell what proposition follows logically from what other propositions. Software that employs the resolution principle works with logical "clauses" (you'll see these throughout the book). It uses *unification* to try matching the right and left sides of clauses in a logical way by investigating the variable values that will allow a proper match.

If you want to know more about the theoretical basis of Prolog and about resolution and unification, the book *Programming in Prolog,* by W.F. Clocksin and C.S. Mellish, is an excellent source of information (see the bibliography in Appendix B). While there are many good books on logic and computers, Chapter 10 in the Clocksin and Mellish book does a particularly good, Prolog-style job of describing predicate logic.

Procedural Versus Declarative Languages

Since Prolog is a *declarative* language, it requires that you declare rules and facts about specific symbols, and then ask it to see if a particular goal follows logically from those rules and facts. The inference engine that does the checking is part of Prolog itself. Many of the unique features of Turbo Prolog involve procedural interactivities with the declarative kernel of Prolog. It lets you, for instance, logically handle features such as graphics and sound that are not typically part of Prolog or logic programming.

Pascal, BASIC, and other such languages are *procedural* in nature. Not only do you have to state facts and rules; you also have to use the language to tell the compiler how to look for a solution, where to look, when to stop, and so on. A few lines of a declarative language can do as much work as many more lines of a procedural language.

The distinction between declarative and procedural languages is one reason a language implementation like Turbo Prolog is such a fine tool for developing AI applications, especially when it is compared with other languages.

Using Turbo Prolog
Disk Offer

All of the programs in this book are available on a 5 1/4-inch IBM PC disk (PC-DOS format). You can receive this disk by sending a check or money order for $24.95 (which includes shipping and handling) to

Carrot Top Press
UTP Disk #1
2874 South Palisades Drive
Santa Cruz, CA 95062

California residents, add 6% sales tax; residents of BART counties, add 6 1/2%.

_____

Please send me the *Using Turbo Prolog* programs on disk. My $24.95 payment is enclosed. (California residents, add 6% sales tax; residents of BART counties, add 6 1/2%.)

_____ check   _____ money order

Name _____

Street Address or Box _____

City _____ State _____ ZIP _____

Carrot Top Press, UTP Disk #1, 2874 South Palisades Drive, Santa Cruz, CA 95062

I

Part I provides you with a basic introduction to Turbo Prolog, focusing on the tools you need to begin programming and on the unique characteristics of the Turbo Prolog environment. This section also describes the powerful Turbo Prolog Editor that allows you to write and debug programs quickly and efficiently.

1

Setting Up

This chapter gives details about the system you need in order to run Turbo Prolog and tells you how to make working disks from the originals. You will learn what to do and who to ask for help if things aren't working right. A program might not work as you expect for several reasons, and contrary to computer manufacturers' claims, these reasons are often computer problems, not human error. If you don't have the right system (both software and hardware) Turbo Prolog won't work, no matter how hard you try.

If you know how to back up your disks, if you know your system will run Turbo Prolog, and if you know how to get technical help from a software publisher, skip this chapter and proceed to Chapter 2.

What You Need to Run Turbo Prolog

If you have a working IBM PC, you've probably got a system that can run Turbo Prolog. The only difficult requirement is that your PC must have at least 384K of RAM. While many business machines now sport 512K or more, there are still plenty of PCs that have 256K or less. If you have such a system, consider increasing the RAM to 512K or to a full 640K. You won't be sorry, no matter what software you end up using, and you won't have to spend much to get the extra memory.

System Hardware

You will need an IBM PC, XT, AT, Portable, 3270 PC, or PCjr to run Turbo Prolog. You can also use any machine that is a *true compatible* of any of the systems just mentioned. Even the systems that are perfectly compatible —that is, those that will run all software written for the IBM systems and can connect directly to any hardware peripherals or enhancements made for the IBM systems —may still differ in some way from the actual IBM designs.

Because there are many levels of compatibility, some systems will run most of the software designed for IBM machines, and some will run all IBM software. Some compatible machines (or *clones*) can attach to any peripheral built for the IBM machines, and some can work only with particular devices.

If you know you have a true compatible, proceed to the next section of this chapter. If you don't know, ask your dealer for a compatibility guarantee before buying (you can then bring it back if Turbo Prolog won't run on it), or check reviews in computer magazines.

System Software

You will need to have DOS 2.0 or greater. PC-DOS, the most popular disk operating-system software for IBM PCs, has evolved along with the PC hardware. Each substantially new version of DOS receives a new version number: 1.0 was followed by the slightly enhanced 1.1; the greatly improved 2.0 was followed by 2.1, 3.0, 3.1, and so on. A few machines in Europe offer DOS 4.0. Microsoft, the designer of PC-DOS, is rumored to be planning an introduction of DOS 5.0.

Most IBM PC users have DOS 2.0 or an even newer version. When the revisions are made, new machines are sold with the new version of DOS. DOS 2.0 has many improved features over DOS 1.0 and 1.1, and you should get it even if you don't end up working much with Turbo Prolog.

Turbo Prolog won't work with DOS 1.0 or 1.1. It will work with any DOS that has a number greater than or equal to 2.0 (2.0, 2.1, 3.0, 3.1, 3.2, and so on). Each DOS revision is written so that all programs that ran on earlier versions will still run on the later versions. However, software that requires a later version of DOS will sometimes use features and utility programs that don't exist in the earlier version. If you have a compatible, your DOS may be called something like MS-DOS (the generic name), Z-DOS, or X-DOS. If your machine is IBM-compatible, these operating systems should work with Turbo Prolog. Still, you'll need version 2.0 or greater to run Turbo Prolog.

Memory

The programs that you run on your computer are held in the RAM memory chips. Borland's language designers are proud of making a Prolog that will run in only 384K of RAM. While many IBM PCs and compatibles are now selling with 512K of RAM, the typical IBM PC is more likely to have 256K. Many early systems had only 64K. The most common way to add memory to a PC is to plug an extra circuit board into the slots inside the central processing unit. The memory chips on the plug-in memory card add to the memory already in the system. Such cards can hold 256K, 384K, or even more. If you have more RAM, your Turbo Prolog will be able to do more work.

The maximum amount of RAM the IBM PC can use without special schemes is 640K. It isn't a bad idea to add right up to that limit. Even if most of your applications programs don't use that much, you can use the extra memory for *Terminate and Stay Resident (TSR)* —also called memory resident —programs or as a RAM disk. Many new programs are appearing in the TSR format. This type of software loads before your main program and then sits in memory, waiting to be called up at the touch of a special key combination. Borland had the first big TSR bestseller, SideKick. That program contained a notepad, a calculator, and other tools that were particularly useful because they were instantly available.

RAM disks emulate the activity of disk drives but do their work in RAM. This makes saving, loading, and running much faster for many programs. After you fill up your memory to 512K or 640K, get a RAM disk program, available commercially or free from many user groups, books, and magazines, and configure some of your leftover RAM into a RAM disk.

Disk Drives

You only need a single floppy disk drive to use Turbo Prolog. However, most systems have at least two floppy disk drives. If you have only a single drive, consider getting a partner for it. Having at least two disk drives helps you work with the sample Turbo Prolog programs, back up disks, and save your own programs more efficiently.

Although a hard disk is not required, the price of hard disks has decreased so significantly that it's a shame not to take advantage of their large storage capacity and their speed. Many computer users don't realize that hard disks aren't only 20 or more times larger (in storage space) than floppy disks, but that hard disk drives can read or write information much faster than floppy disks can.

Graphics Adapter Cards

An IBM monochrome display adapter like the one that comes with the standard IBM PC is adequate for most of Turbo Prolog. To take advantage of Turbo Prolog's color graphics, however, you'll need an IBM Color Graphics Adapter or a compatible board. There are some boards, such as the Hercules adapter, that Prolog won't work with. This may change in later versions of the program.

Making Copies of System Disks

Read the license agreement that comes with the program. Then make backup copies of each of the Turbo Prolog disks. Put the original Turbo Prolog disks away in a cool, dry, clean place. Use the copies as your working disks. You might want to make a second set of backup disks to keep in a separate disk file. You should follow these same rules with the disks you make to store your own programs.

Keep the various sets of backup disks in separate places. Unfortunately, some people who regularly back up their disks leave the backup disks in the same place as the working disks. That exposes the backup disks to the same conditions that could damage the working copies.

If you have a hard disk, you'll probably want to copy all of your Turbo Prolog files to a single directory on it. In that case, you should still take care to store the original floppy disks away in a safe place. Also, you should consider getting some sort of backup for your hard disk — either floppy disks (if your hard disk's not too big; for example, a 10-megabyte disk) with special fast-backup software, cartridge hard disks, or a streaming tape drive.

Legalities of Copying the Disks

Peel the plastic off your Turbo Prolog book. Inside you'll find two 5 1/4-inch disks: the Library/Example disk (also called the Utilities and Sample Program disk) and the System/Program disk (also called the Program disk). The System/Program disk has a serial number at the bottom right of the label. Write that number inside the front cover of your Borland manual.

While you're looking inside the front cover of the Borland book, notice the warranty and license agreement. The warranty is standard for microcomputer software makers these days. It promises only that the disk is a disk, the book is a book, and both are free of defects in materials and workmanship. If they aren't, Borland will replace them. The warranty specifically advises you that Borland isn't claiming the program is good for any particular purpose or use.

The license agreement, "Borland's No-Nonsense License Statement," is different from many others. The firm doesn't ask you not to make any copies of the software, loan it to a friend, or use it on a different computer. Instead, Borland just asks you to treat the software like a book: no matter how many copies you make as backups, make sure that only one copy of Turbo Prolog is being used at a time. Copying all of the files to a hard disk will be addressed later in this chapter.

Tear out the warranty card and send it off to Borland. Although you can get technical information and help without having the card on file at Borland, answering the questions on the card will help Borland's software designers improve Turbo Prolog and introduce other programs that you might like. Sending in the card will also put you on Borland's mailing list; you'll receive both technical information on Turbo Prolog and notice of newer versions.

Booting

Turn on your IBM PC and your monitor and slip your DOS disk into the A disk drive. If you have a hard disk system, you probably have DOS on the hard disk. In that case, just start the system. A standard system will then ask you for the date and time, which you should enter so that you'll have correct date and time stamps on your Turbo Prolog files. If you aren't asked to enter the date and time, it could be because you have a built-in clock and an AUTOEXEC.BAT file. When one of these files is on the startup disk, the system automatically executes the commands in the file.

If you use TSR programs (like SideKick or ProKey), you shouldn't have any problem loading them unless they eat up too much memory. Remember, you need at least 384K, which includes 20 or 30K for DOS and the rest for Turbo Prolog, free and clear. Since some of the newer TSR programs require more than 100K, it isn't too difficult to overload even a 512K system to the point that Turbo Prolog won't run. If that happens, you'll get an "Insufficient Memory" notice on the screen when you try to run Turbo Prolog.

Printing the README File

Turbo Prolog disks can be modified much more often than the manual can. For that reason, Borland puts on one of the disks a README file that includes corrections to the manual, new information, and other notes you might need to know. You can read this file on the screen or print it out. Borland includes a README.COM program that makes either option a breeze. Put the System/Program disk into the A drive, type

```
readme
```

and press RETURN. The README.COM program will tell you that it is reading the README file. Then it will display the first page of that file on the screen, along with a bottom-line menu of commands that manipulate the README file, as shown in Figure 1-1. To print the README file, make sure your printer is set up and turned on. Then press the F2 function key while you're inside the README.COM program.

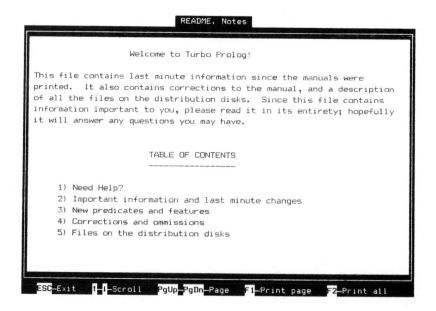

Figure 1-1. First screen of the README.COM program with the README file

Checking for All
Of the Files

Before you actually copy your disks, check to see that all the necessary files are on them. Slip out the DOS disk and put the Turbo Prolog System/Program disk in the A drive (or whatever drive you use for floppy disks if you have a hard disk system). Type

```
dir:
```

and press RETURN to get a directory of all the files on that disk. You should have the same files as those listed in Figure 1-2. Slip the System/Program disk out and replace it with the Library/Example disk. Use the same steps to get a directory for it, and compare that directory to the list in Figure 1-3. The list should be the same or there should be an explanation in the README file. The exact size and date aren't important, just the file name.

How to Copy Your Disks

There are two commands for disk copying: Diskcopy and Copy. Either way, you'll need two floppy disks that either are blank or contain files you no longer want. Find some disk labels and print "Turbo Prolog

```
READM       COM     17867    4-24-86     4:11p
PROLOG      EXE    237888    6-19-86     9:17a
PROLOG      SYS        92    4-28-86    12:02p
PROLOG      ERR      7131    5-15-86     9:26a
PROLOG      HLP      9962    4-25-86     6:27a
PLINK       BAT       510    5-09-86     9:05a
HANOI       PRO      2348    4-25-86    12:55p
INSTALL     COM     12308    4-28-86     1:58p
README              10843    6-23-86    11:15a
COMMAND     COM     17664    3-08-83    12:00p
        10 File(s)        39936 bytes free
```

Figure 1-2.   Directory of files on System/Program disk

```
PROLOG    LIB    155648    6-19-86     9:17a
INIT      OBJ      1079    6-12-86     6:54p
GEOBASE   PRO      6406    4-25-86     6:15p
GEOBASE   INC     22536    4-25-86    10:41a
GEOBASE   DBA     45237    4-28-86    10:55a
GEOBASE   HLP      3428    4-28-86    10:56a
EXAMPL1   PRO       293    4-01-86     1:35p
EXAMPL2   PRO       292    4-01-86     1:37p
EXAMPL3   PRO       214    4-01-86     1:37p
EXAMPL4   PRO       525    4-25-86    11:27a
EXAMPL5   PRO      1986    4-25-86    11:28a
EXAMPL6   PRO       318    4-25-86    11:28a
EXAMPL7   PRO       412    6-12-86    12:06p
EXAMPL8   PRO       174    4-01-86     1:39p
EXAMPL9   PRO       539    4-24-86     4:05p
EXAMPL10  PRO       278    5-22-86     4:10p
EXAMPL11  PRO       223    4-01-86     1:40p
EXAMPL12  PRO       393    4-24-86     4:29p
EXAMPL13  PRO       423    4-24-86     4:40p
EXAMPL14  PRO       426    5-19-86     5:01p
EXAMPL15  PRO       340    4-25-86    11:26a
EXAMPL16  PRO       790    4-01-86     1:41p
EXAMPL17  PRO       249    4-25-86    11:26a
```

Figure 1-3.   Sample directory of files on Library/Example disk

System/Program — Working Copy" on one and "Turbo Prolog Library/ Example — Working Copy" on the other. Then put the labels on the disks. Don't first put the labels on the disks and then write on them with a ballpoint pen, as this can damage the disks.

The Diskcopy command does more of the backup work for you than the Copy command can. To use it, put the DOS disk into the main drive and type

```
diskcopy a: b:
```

with just those single spaces between parts as shown. Then press RETURN. If the Diskcopy program is on your system disk, the computer will respond by asking you to put the source diskette in the A drive and the target diskette in the B drive. (If the Diskcopy command isn't on your DOS disk, either find it or try the Copy command method explained later.) Put the System/Program disk into A and a newly labeled disk into B. Then press any key. When the copying is finished, press Y (for "Yes, I want to copy another"). Then put the Library/Example disk into A and the second newly labeled disk into B. Press any key again, and wait for copying to finish. Then press N for "No," pull the disks out, and put the originals in a safe place.

Using the Copy Command

To use the Copy command instead of the Diskcopy command, you must first format the newly labeled disks (Diskcopy does that for you). Label your working disks as just described. Then put your DOS disk into the A drive, type

```
format b:/s
```

and press RETURN. The computer will prompt you to put a disk into the B drive. Use the first of the newly labeled disks. Then press any key, and the formatting will begin.

Formatting prepares a disk for information. Blank disks right out of the manufacturer's box don't have the signpost data on them that allows them to organize and therefore save information. Formatting posts those signs. The "/s" after the format command puts the basic operating-system information on the disk. A disk with the system information can be used as the first disk in the computer when it starts up. Add "/s" just for the disk you'll use to hold the Turbo Prolog program. You don't need to do it for the Library/Example working disk.

To format a working disk for utilities and sample programs, put the second newly labeled disk into the B drive, and with the DOS disk in the A drive, type

```
format b:
```

and press RETURN. The formatting program tells you to put the B disks in, but they're already there, so press any key. This procedure will format a blank disk without the system information. You don't really need both working disks to be system disks. Besides, the Library/Example disk is so full that the system information won't fit on it unless you get rid of some other files.

Now that both working, newly labeled disks are formatted, put the original System/Program disk into the A drive and the blank, working System/Program disk-to-be into the B drive. Type

```
copy a:*.* b:
```

and press RETURN. All of the files on the original disk will be copied to the working disk. When that's done, put the original disk away and put the working disk into your disk holder. Put the original Library/Example disk into the A drive and the blank Library/Example working disk into the B drive, and type the Copy command as before. Again, once the copying is finished, put the original away in a safe place. Use only the working copies of the System/Program disk and the Library/Example disk.

Hard Disk Systems

If your hard disk is labeled "C," put the System/Program disk into the A drive. From DOS on the C drive, type

```
copy a:*.* c:
```

and press RETURN. If you want to put Turbo Prolog in a particular directory, you'll have to include that information in the instructions. Hard disk directories are beyond the scope of this book. You should go to a computer store, purchase one of the books about PC-DOS or MS-DOS, and then bone up on the basic DOS commands, including "mkdir" and "chdir."

Table 1-1.   Description of Files on Original Disk

File	Description
README.COM	A program that presents a README file to you along with commands for printing it or scrolling within it.
README	A text file that holds updates and suggestions for Turbo Prolog. Because the disks can be changed much more frequently than the manual, the latest information —including corrections and additions to the manual —is put into this file.
PROLOG.EXE	The main Turbo Prolog compiler program. This one file comprises the editor, compiler, file handler, and run-time package.
PROLOG.SYS	A file containing information about color, window size and placement, and default directories.
PROLOG.ERR	The error-message file. The compiler will find errors and mention them by number without this file, but it won't be able to add an English description of what the error is.
PROLOG.HLP	The help-message file. Because this file is in ASCII text, you can modify it however you like.
PROLOG.LIB	The library file, vital to linking operations that create .EXE files (executable files) out of .OBJ files (object files).
INIT.OBJ	Another file involved in linking. It must be the first .OBJ file in all LINK commands for creating .EXE files. INIT.OBJ has the code for initializing the PC before you work on the Turbo Prolog program.
PLINK.BAT	Another linking file. This batch file links .OBJ code files.
*.PRO	A file that starts with letters and has the .PRO extension on the end. This is the form used for Turbo Prolog program files. Most of the files on the Library/Example disk have this form, as will any program file you save from inside Turbo Prolog.
GEOBASE.PRO	A file containing the source program code for the GeoBase natural-language geography information database.
GEOBASE.INC	This file contains more GeoBase program code.
GEOBASE.DBA	The GeoBase database.
GEOBASE.HLP	The help statements for the GeoBase program.
READ64.ME	Another file of extra information (like the main README). However, this file concerns only the EXAMPL64.PRO example program.

Minimum Files for Cramped Disks

All of the Turbo Prolog files that Borland sent you are not required for all uses of Turbo Prolog. Even most of the material on the System/Program disk is expendable at times. Table 1-1 details what the major files are and what they do.

The only files you need to start Turbo Prolog in most circumstances are PROLOG.EXE and PROLOG.SYS. To get error messages along with your error numbers, you'll need PROLOG.ERR in the same directory with PROLOG.EXE. Other files are necessary for certain kinds of compiling (as you'll see in Chapter 12).

2

The Turbo Environment: Menus and Windows

Learning to use a particular computer language is not just a matter of learning the general theory of that language: you also have to master a particular implementation. Compare it to driving a car, where knowledge of the functions of the steering wheel, the accelerator, and the brake pedal isn't enough. You don't really know your car until you've driven it in various conditions, learned the layout of its instruments and controls, gotten a feel for the gear shift, and know where to get it fixed.

Computers and computer languages aren't nearly as standardized as cars. No two Prologs are exactly alike. Turbo Prolog's set of instructions and commands differs from that of any other Prolog. In addition, Turbo comes with its own built-in windowing package and editor.

Turbo Prolog has a built-in system of menus and windows to help you write, compile, run, and debug programs. This chapter will brief you on those menus and windows so you'll be ready to take the next step in Chapter 3, where you learn to edit (write and modify) a program. If you know how to start a program from the DOS prompt, know what windows are, and know how to use multiple-level menus, and if you're also willing to learn Turbo Prolog's menu commands as you program, you don't need this chapter right away.

Two things will give you a basic handle on Turbo Prolog's menus: a familiarity with the major commands of Turbo Pascal —Edit, Compile, Run, Save, and the like —and experience with a program like Microsoft Word that uses multiple-level menus at the bottom of the screen. If you've worked with one of the languages on Apple's Macintosh that employs separate windows for listing, tracing, and so on, you'll be able to skip this chapter for now. Later, you can always come back for a closer look at some of the specific options within the multiple-level menus.

Starting the Program

Now that you've made copies of your disks and know what to do when trouble strikes (explained in Chapter 1), you're ready to start Turbo Prolog and take a look at the Turbo Prolog programming environment. Put your Turbo Prolog System/Program working disk into the A drive and the Turbo Prolog Library /Example disk into the B drive. If you have a hard disk system, get into the directory that contains your Turbo Prolog files. The most important file is the PROLOG.EXE file. This is the main Turbo Prolog program. Type

```
prolog
```

and press RETURN. After a few seconds, you'll see the initial status screen for Turbo Prolog, shown in Figure 2-1.

Initial Copyright Screen

Don't hit the space bar yet. First take a closer look at this screen, and notice a few things about the Turbo Prolog you're about to use. For one

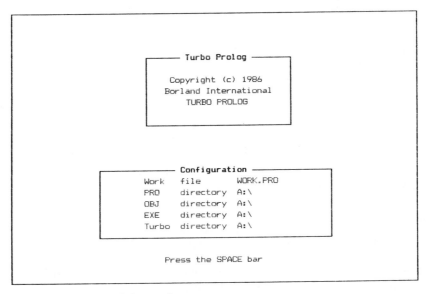

Figure 2-1.   Initial Copyright screen

thing, you can see which version you are working with. Corrections to bugs and additions to the language will probably prompt Borland to issue versions with numbers like 1.02, 1.1, and 2.0. (All programs have bugs, and the complexity of language programs usually means that they have more than their share.)

The area labeled "Configuration" tells you that the temporary name for whatever file you start working on is WORK.PRO. It also tells you that all of your directories are presently set to the A disk. That doesn't matter much now, but it will become more important as you advance further in Turbo Prolog.

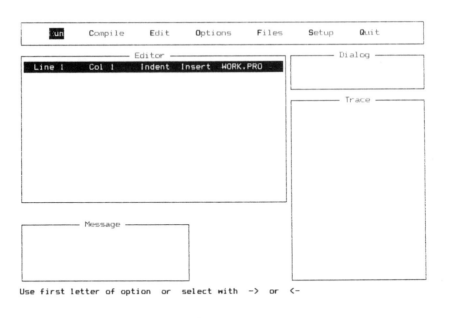

Figure 2-2.   Turbo Prolog Main screen

Main Screen

Now press the space bar on your keyboard. You will then see the screen shown in Figure 2-2. If you're an experienced computer user, chances are you've seen a screen with windows and menus like this. If you're new to the game, don't be intimidated. This will be a lot easier to work with than many older languages, such as the early version of Turbo Pascal.

Figure 2-3 shows the main screen for Turbo Pascal version 3.0. As Figure 2-4 shows, Turbo Pascal tells you which drive and directory are active, the name of the file you're working on, how much memory you have, and what your major command choices are. Once you have this screen in Turbo Pascal, you select one of the commands by typing the first letter of the command. Press E, for example, and you'll be in the editor.

Turbo Prolog's environment is a lot easier to grasp than dBASE's or even Turbo Pascal's because of the addition of multiple-level menus and windows. Borland has stated publicly that this environment will be used

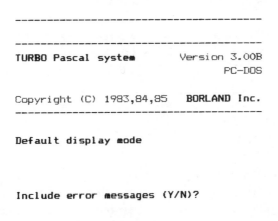

```
-----------------------------------------

-----------------------------------------

TURBO Pascal system        Version 3.00B
                                   PC-DOS

Copyright (C) 1983,84,85   BORLAND Inc.
-----------------------------------------

Default display mode



Include error messages (Y/N)?
```

Figure 2-3.   Turbo Pascal 3.0 main screen

```
Logged drive: B
Active directory: \

Work file:
Main file:

Edit      Compile  Run   Save

Dir       Quit  compiler Options

Text:     0 bytes
Free: 63485 bytes

>
```

Figure 2-4.   Turbo Pascal main menu display

on all of its future language products, including the new versions of Turbo Pascal. Learn it here, and you're ready for more than just Turbo Prolog.

On the main Turbo Prolog screen —referred to throughout this book as the main screen —you'll see four separate windows, a menu line at the top, and an information line at the bottom (see Figure 2-2).

Windows

Windows are portions of the full computer screen that act like complete screens by themselves. In a system without windows, switching from one task to another (for instance, switching from editing a program to running a program) often means erasing all elements of the Edit screen and replacing them with the Run screen. If you have a windowing system, you can choose to display both the Edit screen and the Run screen at the same time.

Getting Turbo Prolog isn't the only way to induce your PC to "do windows." You could also buy special windowing software that adds to your operating system and creates an environment with windows for other applications programs. With such a program, your PC would allocate a window to each separate program you run.

Turbo Prolog's windows are built into the compiler and are customized to handle the four major aspects of Turbo Prolog programming: editing, querying, tracing, and debugging. Each window can be moved, reduced, or enlarged.

Editor Window

The window you'll most frequently use is the Editor window. In Turbo Prolog's main screen, this window is the largest of the four and is at the top left of the screen (look again at Figure 2-2). Just beneath the title line of the Editor window is a line that will tell you the status of your editing work:

- The "Text:" message of version 1.0 tells you how many characters are in the file you are editing — the file that is displayed in the Editor window.

- The "Free:" message of version 1.0 tells you how much space you have left to fill. The limit is 64K characters.

- The "Line" and "Column" of versions 1.1 and later replaced "Text" and "Free." They tell you the line and column position of the cursor in the Editor window.

- The "Indent" message will be highlighted when the editor is in Auto Indent mode (explained in Chapter 3).

- The "Insert" message will be highlighted when the editor is in Insert mode instead of Overwrite mode.

- Finally, the last message on the right, after the "Insert" message, is the name of the file you are editing. Because the default name is WORK.PRO, that's what you'll see there. (Compilers take *source* files that you have written with an editor and compile them into *object* files. Any Turbo Prolog source file will have the .PRO extension on its name.) If the window isn't wide enough to show you the whole thing, all you'll see is "WORK." If you enlarged the window by stretching its right boundary farther toward the right edge of the screen, you'd see the whole file name.

Dialog Window

Prolog programs typically search through a list of rules and facts to try to answer questions, but they can also do anything that other programming languages can do: they can play games, draw graphics, or solve equations. You will ask questions and get answers in the Dialog window, at the top right of the main screen. Unless the program specifies otherwise, that's also where Turbo Prolog displays whatever else the program tells it to do.

Message Window

Some varieties of Prolog don't tell you when something is going wrong. If you make a typing mistake or if there is a problem with your program, the Prolog interpreter or compiler will give you at best a cryptic error message.

Turbo Prolog uses the Message window (lower left on the main screen) to tell you what's happening, right or wrong. When you instruct it to compile something, it will make a note in the message window of what it is doing. The Turbo Prolog compiler also includes a thorough syntax checker that will alert you to the location and substance of mistakes in your programs.

Turbo Prolog isn't smart enough to tell you when a program isn't going to do what you want it to. It is only able to find mistakes that will stop it from doing anything at all. Errors and error messages will be addressed in greater detail later. You might flip to the back of the Borland *Owner's Handbook* and take a quick look at the error messages. You'll certainly see them again while you're learning to program.

Trace Window

Even if your program adheres to the official Turbo Prolog syntax rules, it might not accomplish exactly what you want. If it does perform as you planned, you still might want to know how it got from start to finish. That's the purpose of the Trace window (lower right in the main screen).

You can add *trace* commands to Turbo Prolog programs to force the program to work step by step instead of in one big rush. After each step, the program will stop and the Trace window will tell you where logic has taken your PC. Tracing will be discussed later in the book.

Main Menu

A *menu* is a list of possible commands or functions. Menus are popular in a lot of computer programs because they relieve programmers and users of the burden of remembering all permissible command choices. There are several kinds of menus; there can even be menus within menus, called *submenus*, when powerful commands contain more specialized options. Turbo Prolog uses a line at the top of the main screen to show you the seven fundamental commands: Run, Compile, Edit, Options, Files, Setup, and Quit.

If there is a submenu of more specialized options when you choose a command, Turbo Prolog will display that submenu and wait for you to make a further choice. If there are no more choices for you to make, Turbo Prolog will try to execute your program. If it runs into any problems with the compilation, it will let you know in the Message window.

Selection in a Menu

You can choose one of the main commands, and later one of the submenu options, in either of the following two ways.

- Type the first letter of your chosen function. For example, if you type F you'll select the Files command, and you'll see a submenu appear beneath the word "Files" on the menu line.

- Use the arrow keys (directional cursor keys) to move the highlighting to the command of your choice. This also works within submenus, though you'll need the up and down keys instead of the right and left keys. Once you have your chosen command highlighted, press the RETURN key.

Escape

Use the Escape key (ESC, to the left of the alphabetical section, just beyond the 1 key on the PC keyboard) whenever you don't like where you are. If you're working inside a window, pressing ESC will get you back to the main menu line. You can see the menu line while you're in a window, but you can't choose any of the menu commands. If you're in a submenu, pressing the ESC key will return you to the main menu command above that submenu.

Commands Without Pull-down Menus

Four of the seven fundamental commmands have no special submenus. They are Quit, Edit, Compile, and Run.

Quit Command

The Quit command will quit Turbo Prolog. It will stop the program and return you to the DOS prompt (A>, if that's the disk you started on). Pressing Q will get you out of the Turbo Prolog "fast-lane" and back into the leisurely world of DOS. There are two exceptions to this rule. If the file you're working on has been edited since you loaded it, or if it is brand new, Turbo Prolog will ask if you want to save the file. If you answer

"Yes," it will help you do so. If you answer "No," it will disappear and send you back to DOS.

Edit Command

When you press E in the main menu, you'll leap into the Editor window. Once you're there, you can write a new program or modify an old one (if you've already loaded it using the Files command and submenu).

Compile Command

Once you have successfully edited (written and rewritten) a program to the point where you're ready to try it, you'll want the Compile command. Type C while you're in the main menu, and the program file in the Editor window will be compiled into a ready-to-run program stored in the computer's main memory.

Compiling can be very simple. However, for more complex programs, Turbo Prolog does contain several compilation options (in the Options command submenu) for compiling a program into different sorts of disk files. It also contains some powerful compiler directives.

Run Command

When you have written or edited a program and have compiled it, the next thing to do is to run it. The Run command will start the program that is in the computer's memory — usually the program you just compiled into memory. If you had compiled a program into memory, but had since gone into the Editor and modified the source file for that program, the Run command would first compile that program (automatically, without you having to touch the C key) and then run it.

The Run command recognizes two different types of Turbo Prolog programs: those with internal goals and those without. If a program has an internal goal, it will run completely through to that goal when you issue the Run command. Once the program has run its course, all you have to do is press the space bar to return to the main menu. If a program has no internal goal, the program will begin to run and will then wait for you to enter a goal in the Dialog window. Some of the function keys have the special commands assigned to them while a program runs.

Using the Run command is easy. Just press the ESC key as many times as necessary to jump from wherever you are to the main menu. Then press the R key. When you decide to use the Trace window, using Run will be a little more complicated.

Commands With Pull-down Menus

The Options, Files, and Setup commands have submenus. You'll discover them when you select the associated main command. The submenu will unroll beneath —or pull down from —the main command.

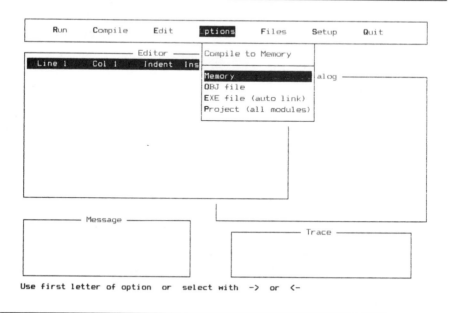

Figure 2- 5.   Options command submenu

Options Command and Submenu

Figure 2-5 shows the submenu that pulls down when you select the
Options command. The choices under Options all concern program
compilation. They are put under "Options" instead of under "Compile"
because they aren't frequently used, whereas the Compile command is.

Files Command and Submenu

The Files command includes many of the functions you might use DOS
for outside of Turbo Prolog. In fact, it even lets you get out to DOS and
back without erasing Turbo Prolog from memory. Figure 2-6 shows the
submenu beneath the Files command. Remember, Files won't do anything until you select one of the submenu choices. To do that, you either
press the key of the first letter of the command or use the arrow keys to

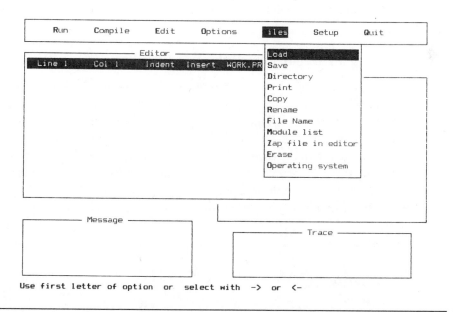

Figure 2-6.   Files command submenu

highlight the command and then press RETURN. If at any point Turbo Prolog cannot find a file that you ask for, it will notify you in the Message window.

Load Command

The Load command lets you bring files in from a disk and put them into the Editor window for modification or execution. Choose the Load command and you'll be asked for a file name. There are two ways to specify the name of the file you want to load:

- You can type the full name of the file and press RETURN. If you don't put the period and file-type extension at the end of the file name, Turbo Prolog will assume that you are working with a standard Turbo Prolog file and will attach a .PRO onto the name you provide.

- You can choose the file you want from a directory. The Load, Save, Directory, Rename, and Erase commands all offer this directory capability.

Getting a Directory With the Load Command

Once you have chosen the Load command, if you press the RETURN key without listing a file name, you'll see a directory of all of the files with .PRO extensions (see Figure 2-7 for an example). This list will come from the default disk drive and directory. You can change that default permanently with the Directory choice in the Files submenu (described later in this chapter), or you can present the Load command with a pattern containing wildcards and then press RETURN.

For instance, if you answer the file-name question by typing

```
a: e*.pro
```

and pressing RETURN, you will see a directory of all files on the A drive

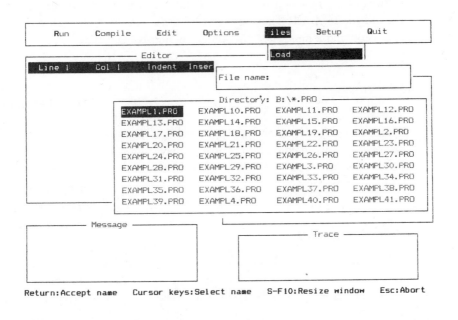

Figure 2-7.   Example of a directory obtained through the Load command

that start with the letter "e," have from one to seven other letters appended to the "e," and end with a .PRO extension. Consult a DOS manual for a more thorough description of wildcards.

Once you have a directory, highlight the file you want by using the arrow keys along with HOME, END, PGUP, and PGDN, and then press RETURN to get that file. You can also press the ESC key from any directory to return to the file-name question.

Save Command

Choose the Save command to save the Editor window file to a disk. If there is another file on the disk that has the same name as the file you are trying to save (this usually would be the file that you loaded a copy of before beginning to edit) the Save command will change the extension on the old file to .BAK. That way, you'll have a new version with a .PRO extension and a one-generation-older version backup file.

Directory

This command lets you get a directory of what's on your disk without going through the Load or Save command. Use it as you use the Directory option of the Load command. The disk drive and pathname you choose will become the default (the standard selection unless you change it) for all Files commands.

Print Command

The Print command will use your printer to make a hard copy of the file in the Editor window. Unlike most of the other Files commands, this command can be used only on the file in the Editor window, and not on disk files.

Copy Command

If you want to copy one disk file to another, use this command. All you have to do is specify the name of the file to copy from and the name of the file to copy to.

Rename Command

To change the name of any file on the disk, use the Rename command. Type the old name and press RETURN. Then type the new name and press RETURN.

File Name

The File Name command will change the name of the file in the Editor window. This is useful if, for example, you want to load a program, trim away a lot of it, and then build a new program on what's left. If you kept the old program name, the new program would be saved over it, relegating the old program to a .BAK file. Then you'd have to use the Rename command to give the new program a more appropriate moniker. Use File Name to change the active name and then when you choose the Save command, you won't disturb the old program.

Module List

Modular programming, or breaking a large piece of software into smaller, independent modules, is a fundamental tool in modern software engineering. Turbo Prolog can handle programs that are broken into modules. This command lets you tell the compiler the name of the project file that lists all of the module names.

Zap File in Editor

This command lets you quickly and completely erase the file in the Editor window. Don't worry about accidentally pressing it. Before the file is actually "zapped," you have to confirm that you really do want to lose it. The name of the zapped file will still be the working file name.

Erase Command

Erase is another file-manipulation command that works like Load, Save, or Rename. You'll need to specify the name of the file you want to erase from the disk either by typing its name or by using a directory, just as you do with the Load command.

Operating System

This command will let you use DOS commands without wiping Turbo Prolog from the PC's memory. Once you choose it, you can type DOS commands just as if you didn't have Turbo Prolog in resident memory. When you're done with DOS, type

`exit`

and press RETURN to return to Turbo Prolog. The DOS that you started your computer with must be available on the disk when you use this command, or you'll just get an error message and have to return to Turbo Prolog.

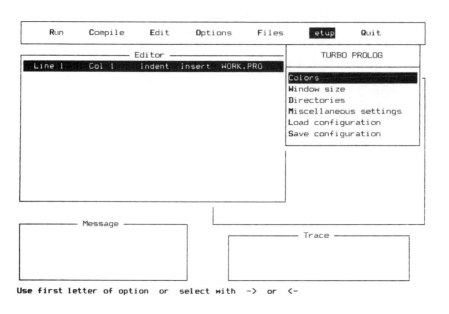

Figure 2-8.   Setup command submenu

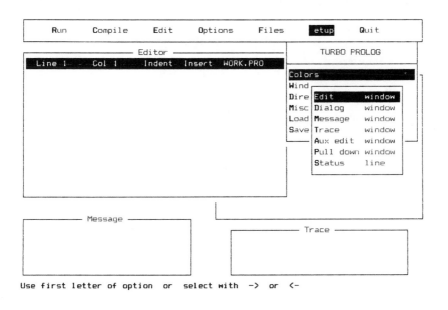

Figure 2-9.   Setup Colors menu

Setup Command and Menu

The submenu beneath the Setup command allows you to inspect, temporarily modify, or permanently change the configuration of your Turbo Prolog. Figure 2-8 shows the submenu that appears once you tap the S key in the main menu. The submenu choices you'll see detail how Turbo Prolog displays and receives its information.

Colors

Here, for the first time, you'll find another menu beneath a submenu (see Figure 2-9). You can use this command to define the background and foreground colors of your system windows. Once again, press the key of the first letter of the window you want to affect. Then look at the

Table 2-1. Color Attribute Values for Both Monochrome and Color Displays

Monochrome Display Adapter

Characters (Foreground)	Background	Description	Attribute Value
Black	Black	Blank	0
White	Black	Normal video	7
Black	White	Inverse video	112

Notes: 1. Add 1 to underline character in foreground color.

   2. Add 8 to change all white to high-intensity white.

   3. Add 128 to make the character blink.

Color Graphics Adapter

Foreground Color	Attribute	Background Color	Attribute
Black	0	Black	0
Gray	8	Blue	16
Blue	1	Green	32
Light blue	9	Cyan	48
Green	2	Red	64
Light green	10	Magenta	80
Cyan	3	Brown	96
Light Cyan	11		
Red	4	White	112
Light red (pink)	12		
Magenta	5		
Light magenta	13		
Brown	6		
Yellow	14		
White	7		
High-intensity white	15		

Notes: 1. Choose one foreground and one background color and add the numbers together.

   2. Add 128 to make the displayed object blink.

bottom line of the screen to see the key commands for altering the window colors. The arrow keys let you step through the color selections. Table 2-1 shows you what colors the numeric attributes represent.

Window Size

Press W from the Setup command's submenu, and you'll be ready to alter the size, position, or shape of your Turbo Prolog windows. Choose the window you want to work with (see Figure 2-10) and then use the commands listed across the bottom of the screen to alter the window's perimeter. Use the arrow keys alone to change window size. Press the CTRL key at the same time to make larger changes in a hurry. Use the arrow keys with the SHIFT key to move the window.

Information won't disappear if a window is too narrow to display it all. Instead, it will either wrap around to the next line of that window, or

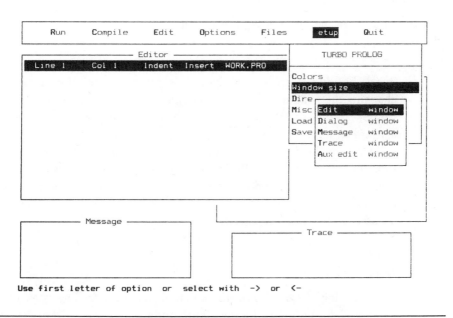

Figure 2-10.   Setup Window Size menu

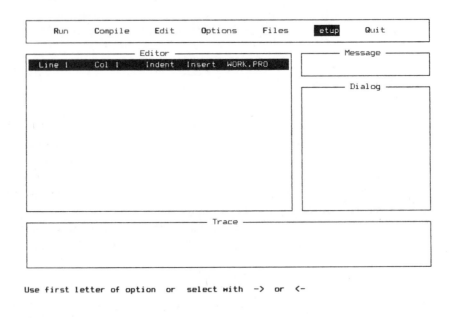

| Run | Compile | Edit | Options | Files | etup | Quit |

```
┌─────────────────── Editor ───────────────────┐   ┌── Message ──┐
│ Line 1     Col 1      Indent  Insert  WORK.PRO│   │             │
│                                               │   └─────────────┘
│                                               │   ┌── Dialog ───┐
│                                               │   │             │
│                                               │   │             │
│                                               │   │             │
│                                               │   │             │
│                                               │   │             │
│                                               │   │             │
│                                               │   │             │
└───────────────────────────────────────────────┘   │             │
                                                     └─────────────┘
┌─────────────────── Trace ─────────────────────────────────────────┐
│                                                                    │
│                                                                    │
└────────────────────────────────────────────────────────────────────┘
```

Use first letter of option or select with -> or <-

Figure 2-11.   A customized window arrangement

it will be hidden off to the right. You can see that information by changing the window's size or by moving the cursor around within the window. Windows can also overlap. The active window is the one that appears on top at any given moment.

As with the other Setup choices, you can keep your new configuration until you leave Turbo Prolog, or you can store it more permanently. Figure 2-11 shows a window arrangement that is sometimes useful. See the Load Configuration and Save Configuration choices in the following sections to learn how to customize your configuration.

Directories

Turbo Prolog needs to know where to find and put files. To save you the trouble of always typing the complete pathname, it stores a list of default disk drives and pathnames. The Directories menu (see Figure 2-12) lets you inspect or modify the current default settings. The directories are as follows:

- The PRO directory is used for all file handling in the Files Command submenu.

- The OBJ directory is used for .OBJ and .PRJ files, and the EXE directory is used for .EXE files. Both of these concern compilation to disk and will be described later.

- The TURBO directory tells where the program goes to find the PROLOG.EXE, PROLOG.ERR, PROLOG.HLP, PROLOG.SYS, and PROLOG.LIB files. These are the program's main, error message, help, system configuration, and library files.

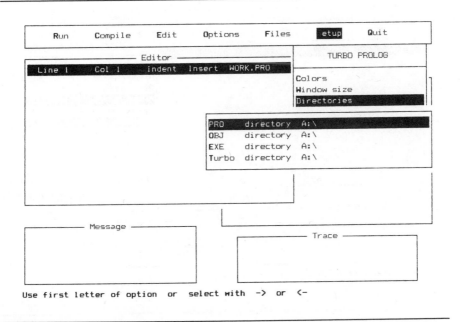

Figure 2-12.   Setup Directories menu

Miscellaneous Settings

These are the leftover settings (see Figure 2-13). Each time you press
either I or A, you'll *toggle* (turn off if it's on, turn on if it's off) the
IBM-CGA Adapter or the Auto Load message function. If the IBM-CGA
Adapter choice is on, special synchronization will be employed to generate a better color screen display. If the Auto Load message is turned on,
the error messages will be loaded into memory when you turn on Prolog.
Normally this choice is off, so each time an error occurs, the error
message has to be found and loaded from the disk file PROLOG.ERR.

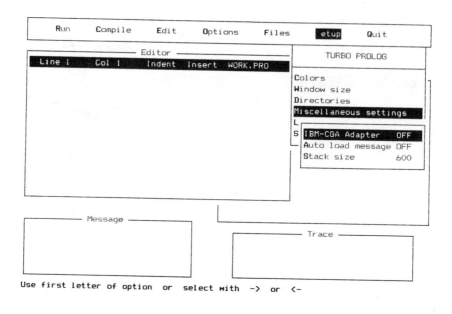

Figure 2-13.   Setup Miscellaneous Settings menu

If you press S, you can change the size of the *stack*, a software construct that is important for advanced programming tasks. The default size is 600 paragraphs of 16 bytes each. The stack can be as small as 600 paragraphs or as large as 4000 paragraphs.

Save Configuration

Once you have changed any aspect of the setup (using the Setup command submenu), you can save your new configuration by using the Save Configuration command. You'll be asked for a file name, and Turbo Prolog will save the new details in a file with a .SYS extension. The default file that is used when Turbo Prolog is started is PROLOG.SYS.

Load Configuration

If you have saved a customized configuration in a .SYS file as just described, you can change to that configuration by using the Load Configuration command. Just press L from the Setup command submenu and then give the name of the .SYS file you want to use. Your Turbo Prolog will be changed to that file's values. To switch back to the original, just load the PROLOG.SYS file.

3

The Editor

A Prolog program starts as a series of characters that are grouped into words, phrases, and other forms and stored in a file called the *source* file. Writing, erasing, or modifying the characters in that file is called *editing* the program. Most computers don't automatically know how to let you edit text. They need special "editor" software to tell them how to accept, display, move, and save characters.

An editor is basically a simple version of a word-processing program. It will let you enter, move, delete, and otherwise manipulate characters. Many early microcomputer language compilers did not include an editor. Those that did often had an editor with few functions and obscure commands.

The language designers assumed that if you had a lot of programming to do, you would use your own editor or word processor to create the source file. Once the source was complete, you would start the compiler, give it the name of your source file, and wait for the *object* file —the compiled, ready-to-run program —to appear.

Turbo Prolog has its own built-in editor that contains most of the word-processing functions you'll want for creating or working on a Turbo Prolog source file. To use that editor efficiently, you need to memorize a few key combinations that issue editing commands.

This chapter tells you how to use the Turbo Prolog Editor. If you have experience in using other programs with similar editing commands (WordStar, MultiMate, Turbo Pascal, or SideKick, for example), you'll feel right at home with the Turbo Prolog Editor. If you do, skip this chapter, but tear out and keep the command card. Also remember that the F1 function key will give you Help information.

Come back to this chapter later if you feel a little lost with the Editor. The Turbo Prolog Editor doesn't include all of the editing commands you find in other programs, but it does have the basics.

Getting Into the Editor

As mentioned previously, once you have Turbo Prolog running and have the main menu in front of you, just press the E key to get into the Editor.

The Editor window (shown in the upper-left part of the screen in Figure 3-1) will be highlighted, and the cursor will appear in that window to show you where your typing will take effect.

Getting Help

If the tables in this book aren't handy, you can press the F1 key (on the far left of the IBM PC keyboard) to get Help information about editing. Block functions, position, delete keys, and status will show you a list of relevant commands. Help information will show a large

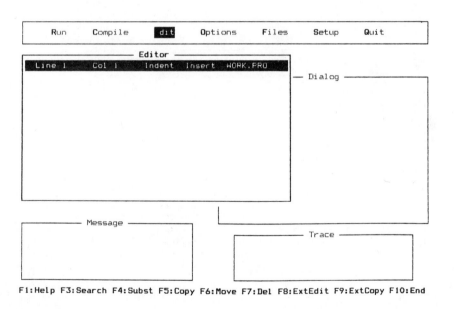

Figure 3-1.   The Editor window in the main screen

window of editing, color, standard predicates, and special predicates that you can scroll through with the arrow keys. External copy, aux edit, and quick edit launch you into those functions. Figure 3-2, the main menu for help information, shows an example of the Editing help.

Preparing to Enter Text

If there is already some text in the window, erase it before going any further. There are a number of ways to do this, but one of the fastest (especially when dealing with a large amount of text) is to leave the Editor and use one of the options in the Files submenu.

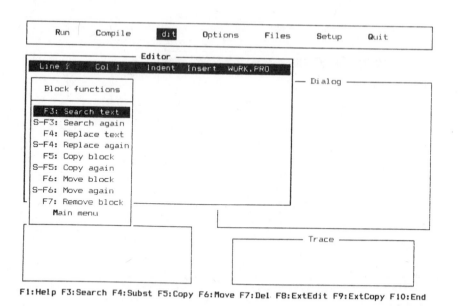

Figure 3-2.   Editing help main menu

Getting Out of the Editor

As a general rule in Turbo Prolog, when you want to get out of a window and back to the main menu, press the ESC key. That applies also to leaving the Editor.

Press the ESC key. That will take you back to the main menu. Then press the F key, which will show you the Files submenu. Press the Z key to select the Zap File in Editor option (see Figure 3-3). You'll be asked if you really want to do that. You do, so press the Y key for "yes." You now have a clean Editor window. Tap the ESC key (to make sure you're in the main menu), and press the E key to get back into the Editor.

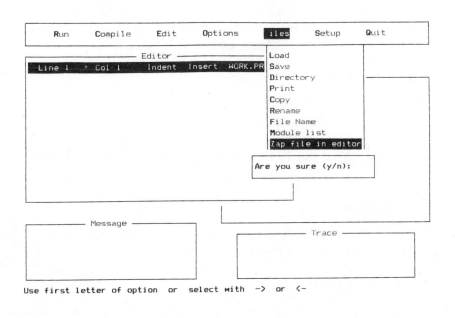

Figure 3-3.   Files submenu with Zap File in Editor option

Fundamentals

Entering, deleting, saving, and loading text are the absolute fundamentals of editing.

Entering Text

Begin by typing the following:

```
Jackie Robinson
```

Type it just as you would on a typewriter, using the SHIFT keys to get capital letters. Don't bother to press the RETURN key yet. If you already did, hit the BACKSPACE key once (that's the left-pointing arrow key above the RETURN key). The cursor will move as you type letters, ending up right after the "n." This is the simplest way to add text to your file. You can also add text in several other ways: copying blocks, importing text from other programs, or loading text from the disk. Don't press any other keys yet.

Deleting Text

There are two single keys that delete one character at a time: the BACKSPACE key and the DEL (delete) key. They operate in different ways.

BACKSPACE Key

Press this key to delete the character just to the left of the cursor. Try it when the cursor is at the end of

```
Jackie Robinson
```

and you'll see

```
Jackie Robinso
```

as a result. Besides erasing a character, the cursor moved backward, resting just after the "o." Press BACKSPACE a few times, then type the missing part of the name back in.

DEL Key

With the full name back in place, press the left arrow key (on the numeric key pad) three times. The cursor will be under the "S." Try pressing the DEL key (at the bottom of the numeric keypad). You'll see

```
Jackie Robinson
```

change to

```
Jackie Robinon
```

The DEL key erases the character above the cursor. This difference between the functions of the BACKSPACE key and the DEL key is employed in many IBM PC computer programs. Try it a few times to get a feel for it.

Saving

While you edit program text, it is constantly saved in the computer's RAM memory chips. However, you should periodically save it to the disk. Unless you have an uninterruptable power supply of some kind, you could lose all of your work the instant there is a power drop or surge to your computer. This can come in many forms, from a car running into a power pole to a child turning off the power switch on your computer. Saving is so quick, it pays to do it every five minutes when you're making a lot of changes or every fifteen when you're a little slower.

To save the file that's in the Editor window, you need to use the Save option in the Files command submenu. If you're in the Editor, press ESC to return to the main menu. Then press S for the Save option. You'll be asked for a file name. The name should be just like DOS file names: one to eight letters with an optional extension of a period, and from one to three letters. Precede your file name with a disk-drive designation that will put it on your Sample Programs disk. If you answer

```
b: temp
```

to the file-name question, your file will be stored as TEMP.PRO (the .PRO is automatically added by Turbo Prolog) on the B drive.

Loading Text From the Disk

If you want to come back tomorrow to work on the file you made today, you'll need to know how to load it back into the Editor window from the disk. Because you still have a file in the Editor, first erase everything in the Editor. Use the Zap File in Editor command in the Files submenu as described previously in the section of this chapter called "Getting Out of the Editor."

Once you have done that, you should be back in the main menu. (Press the ESC key if you want to make sure.) Press the F key for the Files submenu, and press the L key for the Load command. Type the name of the file you want to get, as in the following:

```
b: temp
```

Then press RETURN. Your file will appear in the Editor window. Press ESC to return to the main menu, and then press E for the Editor. Now you're back in the Editor window, ready to make some changes.

Cursor Movement

No matter what is in your Editor window, use the Zap File in Editor command from the Files submenu to erase it. Then get back into the Editor as just described. Type

```
domains
```

and press the RETURN key. It will return your cursor to the beginning of the next line. Then type the following lines:

```
predicates
gola
clauses
```

Now that you have this strange text in your Editor (as shown in Figure 3-4), you need to correct the spelling of "gola" to "goal." There are better ways to do this than to delete all the characters back to the mistake. You can move the cursor directly to the problem and make the correction there.

There are several cursor-movement commands. These break into the following two groups with many of the same functions: numeric keypad commands, and control-key commands or function keys.

The numeric keypad at the right of the keyboard includes a number of cursor-movement commands that are described right on the keys. The arrows (up, down, right, and left on the 8, 2, 6, and 4 keys) move the cursor one character at a time. Give them a try. The PGUP and PGDN keys move the cursor over an entire page of text, scrolling it if necessary (you don't have enough text in the window to try this yet). HOME and END move the cursor to the beginning of a line or to the end of a line.

As with many software programs, cursor movement during editing in Turbo Prolog can be accomplished through the use of command keys. Command keys are either function keys that are programmed to accomplish specific commands, or are control-key sequences that invoke specific commands. After mastering the use of the control-key sequences, some users may find it easier to use the single function key corre-

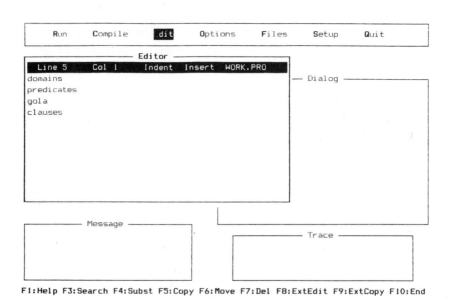

```
    Run      Compile    dit     Options    Files    Setup    Quit

                        Editor
    Line 5     Col 1        Indent  Insert  WORK.PRO
  domains                                                    Dialog
  predicates
  gola
  clauses




                      Message
                                                      Trace



F1:Help F3:Search F4:Subst F5:Copy F6:Move F7:Del F8:ExtEdit F9:ExtCopy F10:End
```

Figure 3-4.　Text in Editor

sponding to a specific command. To issue control-key commands, you need to hold the CTRL (Control) key down (it is just to the left of the A key) and some other key down at the same time. Table 3-1 lists the control-key commands.

For cursor movement, there is a "diamond" shape of control key commands. CTRL-S moves the cursor one character to the left, and CTRL-D moves it to the right. CTRL-E moves the cursor up a line, and CTRL-X moves it down. These four commands behave exactly the same as the four arrow-key commands in the numeric keypad. Use the control-key commands to move to the "l" of "gola" in the text you have already entered. Delete the "l," move the cursor beyond the "a," and add an "l." Now you have the correctly spelled outline of a Turbo Prolog program. Save this file under the name "Outline" on the B drive.

Table 3-1.   Control-Key Editing Commands

Help

Help information	F1 (always)

Delete Keys

Delete character under the cursor	DEL or CTRL-G
Delete character to the left of the cursor	BACKSPACE
Delete the cursor's word to the right	CTRL-T
Delete the cursor's line	CTRL-Y or CTRL-BACKSPACE

Cursor Movement

Up one line	Up arrow or CTRL-E
Down one line	Down arrow or CTRL-X
Left one character	Left arrow or CTRL-S
Right one character	Right arrow or CTRL-D
Left one word	CTRL-Left arrow or CTRL-A
Right one word	CTRL-Right arrow or CTRL-F
To beginning of the cursor line	HOME or CTRL-Q-S
To end of the cursor line	END or CTRL-Q-D
Up one page	PGUP or CTRL-R
Down one page	PGDN or CTRL-C
To beginning of marked block	CTRL-Q-B
To end of marked block	CTRL-Q-K
To beginning (top) of file	CTRL-PGUP
To end of file	CTRL-PGDN
Go to a certain line number	F2, type the line number, and press F2 again
Display the cursor's line number	SHIFT-F2 (version 1.0 only)
Turn on automatic indenting	CTRL-Q-I (second press turns it off again)

Block Functions

Mark beginning of block	CTRL-K-B (or special function key)
Mark end of block	CTRL-K-K (or special function key)
Hide block markings	CTRL-K-H (second use redisplays markings)
Delete marked block	CTRL-K-Y or F7
Move marked block to the cursor	CTRL-K-V or F6
Copy marked block to the cursor	CTRL-K-C or F5
Repeat copy of marked block	SHIFT-F5

Table 3-1.   Control-Key Editing Commands (*continued*)

Block Functions	
Read block from disk to the cursor	CTRL-K-R or F9
Write marked block to disk	CTRL-K-W
Text Entry	
Enter the Editor window	E
Enter the Auxiliary Editor window	F8
Leave Editor or Auxiliary Editor (end editing)	F10 or ESC
Toggle between Insert and Overwrite modes	CTRL-V or INS
Search and Replace	
Search for (also called ~Find") a given string	F3 or CTRL-Q-F
Repeat most recent search	SHIFT-F3 or CTRL-L
Search for and then replace a given string	F4 or CTRL-Q-A
Repeat most recent search and replace	SHIFT-F4 or CTRL-L

PGUP and PGDN also have their control-key equivalents. CTRL-R moves the cursor up a page, and CTRL-C moves it down. Sometimes it is necessary to add yet another keystroke to a control-key command. Press CTRL and Q at the same time, and then press one of the previously mentioned keys to get a "quick" combined command (one that does what a number of the individual commands might do). You don't have to continue to hold the CTRL key down while pressing the final key. For example, press CTRL-Q and then S to move to the beginning of a line or CTRL-Q and then D to get to the end. These commands parallel HOME and END. CTRL-Q-R moves to the top of the file —the first character in the Editor window. CTRL-Q-C moves to the end of the file. You can also get to these locations by using CTRL-PGUP and CTRL-PGDN.

Finally, you can move the cursor a word at a time instead of a character at a time by using CTRL-F (one word to the right) and CTRL-A (one word to the left). Combining the CTRL key with the left and right arrows of the numeric keypad has the same effects.

Moving to a Given Line

The lines of a Turbo Prolog source file are numbered in order from top to bottom. In releases of Turbo Prolog other than version 1.0, the cursor's current location is identified by the Line/Col specifier on the Editor window status line. To find out which line the cursor is on in version 1.0, you can press the SHIFT key and the F2 function key at the same time. To move the cursor to a particular line, press F2. Then type the number of the line you want to reach and press F2 again.

Insert Mode and Overwrite Mode

The Editor begins with Insert mode on. This means that if you place the cursor on top of characters on the screen and start to type, the new characters will insert themselves into the old text without erasing that text. You can turn Insert mode off —also known as putting the Editor in Overwrite mode —by pressing the INS (Insert) key (next to the DEL key) or by pressing CTRL-V. When the Editor is in Overwrite mode, anything you type will obliterate what was previously beneath the cursor.

To see the effects of Insert and Overwrite modes, look at Figures 3-5 and 3-6. In Figure 3-5, the Editor was in Insert mode when the cursor was positioned at the beginning of the word "predicates" and "phillip" was typed. In Figure 3-6, the Editor was in Overwrite mode when the same thing was done.

Character Deletion

Use of the BACKSPACE and DEL keys and their different ways of liquidating a letter have been discussed previously. You can also delete the character directly underneath the cursor, even if it is a blank space, by pressing CTRL-G.

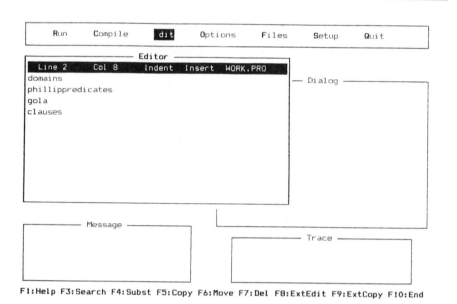

Figure 3-5.   Editor in Insert mode

Word and Line Deletion

Pressing CTRL-Y or CTRL-BACKSPACE will delete the entire line the cursor is on. If you only want to trim part of a line, try CTRL-Q-Y to delete all text to the right (from the cursor to the end of the line).

Advanced Commands

You've now moved from editing characters to editing lines. You can also make the computer do the work of editing whole blocks of text and

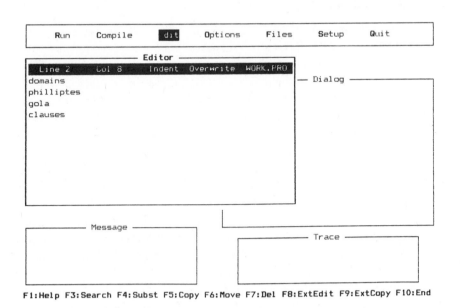

Figure 3-6. Editor in Overwrite mode

searching for chosen pieces of text. These operations are a lot easier to do than you might think, and they are the major reason computerized word processing is better than typewriting or pen-and-paper word processing.

Block Operations

You perform block operations by identifying a block and then telling the Editor what to do with it. Type or load the Outline file described earlier in this chapter (it is shown in Figure 3-4).

Marking the Block

Move the cursor to the "g" in "goals." To mark the beginning of the block, press CTRL-K-B. (The CTRL-K combination is used for many block commands.) Then move the cursor to the letter "s" in "clauses." Mark the end of the block by pressing CTRL-K-K. You'll see the marked block change in intensity on the screen. (If you don't, adjust the contrast and brightness of your screen until you do.) Once the block is identified or marked, you can move it, copy it, or delete it.

To move it, move the cursor to the place in the Editor window where you now want the block to start —perhaps at the "d" of "domains." Then press CTRL-K-V or the F6 function key (see below). The block will disappear from its old position and reappear in the new.

To copy the block, move the cursor back to its original position (after the "s" of "predicates") and press CTRL-K-C or the F5 function key (see below). You'll see a second version of the block appear at that point. Deleting the block is just as easy. Use CTRL-K-Y or F7 at any time to delete a marked block.

If you want, you can use the special function keys both for marking blocks and for manipulating them. For instance, to move a block, you can move the cursor to the block's beginning and press F6, and then move the cursor to the end and press F6. Finally, move the cursor to the block's new position and press F6 a third time. This also works with the F5 key (for copying) and F7 key (for deleting).

While a block is marked and highlighted, you can use CTRL-Q-B to move to the beginning of the block or CTRL-Q-K to move to the end of the block.

CTRL-K-H will toggle the marked block between highlighting and no highlighting; that is, it will change a highlighted block to unhighlighted and an unhighlighted block to highlighted. A highlighted marked block can be copied, moved, or deleted. An unhighlighted marked block cannot. The commands for moving to the end of a block and moving to the beginning of a block work on both highlighted and unhighlighted blocks.

Reading a Block From the Disk

This may seem like an obscure operation, but it is very useful in programming. You may want to get a snippet of program code from another file into the file you are working on. Move the cursor to where you want to put the block. If you're not sure, you can just put the cursor at the end of the file. Press CTRL-K-R or F9. The Load option of the Files submenu will appear. Type the name of the file you want to get a block from. The file will appear in a window (as, for example, in Figure 3-7). Find the block you want by moving the cursor with Editor commands,

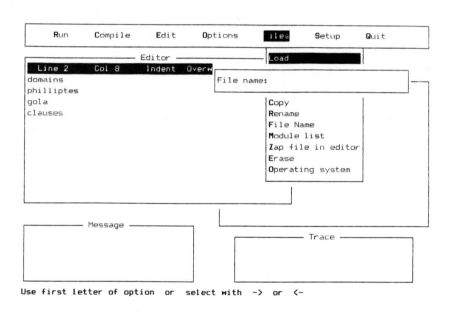

Figure 3-7. Loading a disk file into a program

and then mark the beginning and end of the block with CTRL-K-B (or F9) and CTRL-K-K (or F9).

Search and Replace Commands

The Editor contains several commands that let you find or replace a particular part of your file. A *string* is simply a series of characters in a row. Turbo Prolog can search any string you name that is up to 25 characters long and can replace the string. It can either jump the cursor to the string or replace the string with any other string of up to 25 characters.

Search

Press F3 or CTRL-Q-F. You'll then be asked for the string you want to find. Type the string, and then execute the command by pressing either F3 (if that's what you started the command with) or RETURN (if you used CTRL-Q-F). The cursor will appear at the first occurrence in the file of the chosen string. If you want to find the next occurrence of that string in the file, press SHIFT and F3 or CTRL-L.

Replace

To replace a string, press F4 or CTRL-Q-A. Then type the string you want to replace. Follow that with either the F4 key (if that's how you started the operation) or RETURN (if you used CTRL-Q-A to start). Then type the new string and follow it with F4 or RETURN (as done previously).

At this point, you'll be asked if you want a *local* or a *global* search and replace (see Figure 3-8). Local will replace only the first occurrence of the old string with the new string. Global will replace all occurrences in the file of the old string with the new string.

You'll then be asked if you want to verify each replacement. If you just want it to get done quickly, press N.

If you do, however, want to verify each occurrence, press Y. In this case, the computer will find an occurrence of the old string and then ask

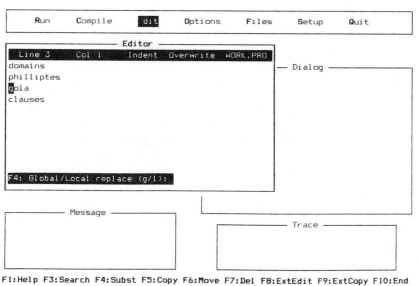

Figure 3-8. Global search and replace

you for a "yes" or "no" (Y/N) answer about replacing it. If you want this particular occurrence replaced, press Y. It will be replaced and the next occurrence of the old string will be found.

If you don't want this particular occurrence replaced, answer N, and the Editor will leave it alone and find the next occurrence. With a global search and replace, this will continue to the end of the file or until you press the ESC key. ESC will end the search and replace operations at any point.

To repeat a search and replace operation, press the SHIFT and F4 keys or CTRL-L.

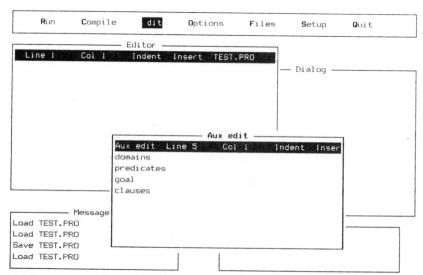

Figure 3-9. Example of Auxiliary Editor window

Auto Indent

You may notice while you practice editing a file that the cursor doesn't always return to the far left column of the Editor window. When the Auto Indent feature is turned on and you press the RETURN key at the end of a line, the cursor will return to the left only as far as the starting column of the line you just terminated. That's helpful to programmers, because many program text files are easier to read and better organized when they use indenting to identify subsections, much as outlines do.

To move to another column, just use your cursor-movement commands. To turn Auto Indent off, press CTRL-Q-I. Press those keys again when you want to turn it back on.

Auxiliary Editor

Turbo Prolog will even provide you with another editing window for those occasions where you want to modify some text before moving it into the main Editor. Press F8 to see this window (see Figure 3-9). You can use all of the same editing commands in this window.

The Auxiliary Editor window can even be sized, just as the other windows can. This is explained back in Chapter 2. Take a look at the Window Size choice of the Setup submenu. When you have finished work in the Auxiliary Editor window, press F10.

Ending an Edit

When you are done with a file, you can either press ESC to return to the main menu, or press F10. If you were editing the file because you tried to compile it and Turbo Prolog told you there was a syntax error to fix, F10 will not only exit the Editor, it will also automatically try to compile the newly edited program.

Every Turbo Prolog program is built around a few basic concepts. Part II explores these concepts, beginning with facts and rules. The section then moves on to topics such as backtracking, arithmetic, and structures (functors, lists, and strings). By the time you complete this section, you'll be writing powerful Turbo Prolog programs of your own.

4

Facts: Objects and Relationships

If you feel comfortable with Turbo Prolog's windows, menus, and Editor, you're ready for the language itself. This chapter will tackle the first step in using Prolog: understanding clauses about objects and relationships.

Don't believe the myth that Prolog is good only for artificial intelligence (AI) applications like natural languages and expert systems. You can do virtually anything with Prolog that you could do with any other programming language, including games, accounting, graphics, and simulation. It isn't always the most practical or efficient language for some applications, but it can handle them. And just because you learn Prolog doesn't mean you're learning AI. Prolog is a popular language for many AI tasks and applications, but natural-language processing and expert systems, for example, could be built in BASIC or even COBOL. Prolog isn't a magic key. It just makes some of those programming jobs easier and quicker.

You probably shouldn't skip this chapter. If you already know about Prolog objects, relationships, facts, predicates, arguments, and goals, you could skim this chapter and zero in on the sections entitled "Syntax," "Predicates," and "Domains." Turbo Prolog syntax is close to the Prolog version of Clocksin and Mellish, and it includes a number of controls that are similar to those in Turbo Pascal.

Procedural Versus Declarative

Most of the languages that have been used on microcomputers — BASIC, Pascal, Modula-2 — have been *procedural*. Such languages let the programmer tell the computer what to do, step by step, procedure by procedure, to reach a conclusion or perform a function.

Prolog is not procedural. It is *declarative*. If you haven't used a declarative language before, learning Prolog is going to take more adjustment than just learning another procedural language. But the effort will definitely be worth it, because a declarative language does a lot of programming work for you. While a procedural language demands that you enter both the recipe and the ingredients, a declarative language asks only for the ingredients and the goal. You declare the situation to work with, and declare where you want to go. The language itself — the compiler or interpreter — does most of the work of deciding how to reach the goal.

For instance, if you are a BASIC programmer who wants to know some Pascal, you soon notice many constructs that are very similar from language to language. You recognize assignment statements, IF-THEN choices, FOR-NEXT loops, and the like. But if you're moving from BASIC to Prolog, you have to take a bigger step. You won't recognize many of the text structures. A Prolog program may look just like a database of facts — lots of parentheses on unrelated lines without rhyme or reason. But don't worry. You'll find it as easy to read as BASIC after just a little practice. Furthermore, as you get more advanced, you'll discover some practical commands that are quite similar to advanced statements in Pascal or other procedural languages. And you'll be amazed at how much you can accomplish with just a few lines of code.

Objects and Relationships

Prolog at its simplest deals with objects and the relationships between them. You may even hear it called an *object-oriented* language. An object isn't necessarily something tangible. It can be anything you can represent symbolically on the computer.

Prolog has been more popular in Europe than in the United States for some years. It was invented in France and has been widely used from Hungary to England. The European connection might be the reason that members of a royal family are frequently used as objects in Prolog texts. Here are some examples of objects:

```
charles
philip
diana
elizabeth
```

Here are some relationships that are useful when considering those objects:

```
king
queen
prince
princess
mother
father
son
```

You may have noticed that none of these words are capitalized. That's not just a slip; they are *supposed* to start with a lowercase letter. Beginning a word with an uppercase letter has a particular meaning in Prolog that will be explained later when variables are discussed. For now, stick to lowercase typing.

If you're not a royalist, here's another set of objects and relationships. The objects are

```
cow
bat
iguana
redwood
fern
ibm pc
apple macintosh
```

and the relationships are

```
animal
mineral
vegetable
mammal
reptile
computer
```

Now you're ready to write a few Prolog statements that employ these objects and relationships. But before you jump to the task, you should first consider syntax.

Syntax

The *syntax* of a programming language is the body of rules that governs what words are acceptable to use, what position those words must be

written in, where the punctuation goes, and so on. Even if you understand the theory of a language, you won't get anywhere if you don't stick
to its syntax.

Several types of syntax exist in Prolog. Different implementations
of the language from different software companies sometimes look very
different. Still, many of the constructs in the language will work the
same, even if they come in different clothing.

Turbo Prolog contains most of the features and the syntax of the
Prolog described in W. F. Clocksin and C. S. Mellish's popular book,
Programming in Prolog (New York: Springer-Verlag New York, Inc.,
1984). This is good reading if you're interested in learning more about
Prolog after you finish this book and the tutorial in the Borland Turbo
Prolog *Owner's Handbook*. Turbo Prolog loosely follows the Clocksin and
Mellish Prolog. The Clocksin and Mellish text used a particular style of
written Prolog, with a particular set of punctuations and spellings. That
style has since become an "unofficial" standard with many Prolog users.
Because the book is so admired and popular, the style it describes is as
close to a standard as is available.

Facts

The first way to combine an object and a relationship is to use them to
define a *fact*. Turbo Prolog's syntax wants you to write facts in the
following way:

```
relationship (object)
```

Note the object is inside the parentheses, and the relationship precedes
it. This "object" has that "relationship." When written in this form, the
the relationship is known as the *predicate* and the object is known as
the *argument*. You could grab some objects and relationships from the
previous two lists and make up the following facts:

```
mammal (bat)
prince (charles)
```

The second fact means that the object "Charles" has the "prince" relationship. The English translation is necessarily vague, because the logic of the Prolog fact doesn't specify whether "Charles was a prince," "Charles is a prince," or "Charles saw a prince."

As you use Prolog, you need to keep in mind what the relationships stand for —Prolog can't do that for you. Your programs will make sense only if you are consistent throughout a single program as to the meaning of a given relationship. It helps sometimes to use relationship words that more closely approximate what you mean. For instance, if you wanted to indicate the fact that Charles is a prince, you might use this relationship with him as an object:

```
is_a_prince (charles)
```

The underlines indicate to the computer and compiler that this is all one long word for a relationship.

The old computer acronym GIGO (garbage in, garbage out) definitely applies to Prolog. The compiler has no way of ascertaining if a fact is true or false in the real world. If you put the fact

```
king (diana)
```

into the program, Prolog will accept it and use it for future work. Whatever you tell Turbo Prolog is a fact, it will accept as a fact. You have to be responsible for verifying your facts to whatever level you need. There are cases where you might want to use blatantly false facts. If you are trying to decide what might happen in a certain situation, for example, you may want to use *what-if* facts that aren't necessarily proven, demonstrated, or even close to the present truth.

Entering the First Program Example

The following are some more facts from the second list of objects and relationships mentioned previously:

```
animal  ،cow)
animal  (bat)
animal  (iguana)
vegetable  (redwood)
vegetable  (fern)
computer  (ibm_pc)
computer  (apple_macintosh)
```

Again, the underline is used to make a single object out of several words.

These facts can make the foundation of a Prolog program. Before you enter them, though, there are two more things you need to know: how to make a comment and how to divide a Turbo Prolog program.

Comments

The Turbo Prolog compiler turns your source file into an object file — a program that can run directly. It converts each bit of text into machine-language code. But sometimes you'll want the compiler to ignore certain parts of the text. For instance, you might want to start the text of a program source file with the words

```
Silly Example Turbo Prolog Program
```

If you enter only those words, the compiler will be confused while trying to interpret them. Turn them into a *comment* by surrounding them with comment marks like the following:

```
/* Silly Example Turbo Prolog Program */
```

When a section of text is preceded and succeeded by the slash-asterisk marks, the compiler ignores it. This lets you add text to a program that will explain what it is, what it does, and how it does it.

Program Divisions

Most Turbo Prolog programs will be organized into four major sections:

- Clauses
- Predicates
- Domains
- Goal.

Although not all of these sections need to be present in all programs, you should be familiar with all of them.

Clauses

The facts that you build out of your objects and relationships are listed in the clauses section. Clauses will also hold rules and other constructs that will be discussed later.

Predicates

Predicates are the relationships. The term "predicate" is borrowed from formal logic, which is one of the initial seeds for Prolog. Whenever your program is going to use a particular predicate in the clauses, you need to formally declare it in the predicates section.

Domains

Turbo Prolog wants one more level of explanation before you call a program complete. You need to tell it about the arguments your predicates will use. To keep computer-memory use to a minimum and to make programs easier to debug, Turbo Prolog has a lot of the *type checking* with which Pascal programmers are familiar. It wants to know in advance what "type" of thing an argument can be.

Goal

This is the section that tells Turbo Prolog what you want to find out or what you want the computer to do with the information you've provided in the three other sections. Normally a program will have at least the predicates and clauses sections, but it is possible to have a program that is only a goal section. The goal section is one place where Turbo Prolog differs from Clocksin and Mellish's Prolog. Clocksin and Mellish keep the goal outside of the program. Because Prolog can be used interactively, it is common to run a program and then wait for it to ask you for a goal. You type the goal into a terminal and then wait to see what Prolog gives you back.

Turbo Prolog can also work that way, but it provides a goal section to let you run programs noninteractively. You can build the goal right into the original code so that as soon as you run the program it can be working toward the desired solution.

The First Program Example

Run Turbo Prolog, get into the Editor, and type this first line:

```
/* UTP Example 1 -- Animal, Vegetable, or Computer */
```

Then press RETURN. The screen may scroll while you type the first line, but it will return to the initial position when you press RETURN. Figure 4-1 shows what you should see.

Then type the words

```
domains
```

```
predicates
```

```
goal
```

```
clauses
```

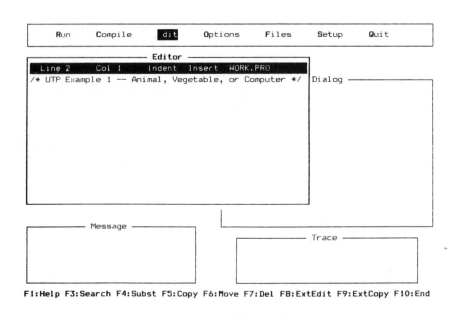

Figure 4-1.   Example of acceptable comment line in Editor window

while pressing RETURN twice between each two words. Figure 4-2 shows the result. You have the skeleton for a Turbo Prolog program.

Move the cursor to the line after the word "clauses" and press the TAB key. Then enter the facts as shown in Figure 4-3, ending each individual fact with a period and a return (press RETURN). The period tells the compiler that this clause is done and that it should prepare for another clause or the end of the file. Pressing RETURN will move the cursor to the next line, and if Auto Indent is on, you'll see the cursor stop at the same horizontal position as the beginning of the previous line. If Auto Indent doesn't seem to be turned on, press CTRL-Q-I to get it.

Now that you have some clauses, you need to tell Turbo Prolog about the predicates (relationships) you're using in the clauses. Move the

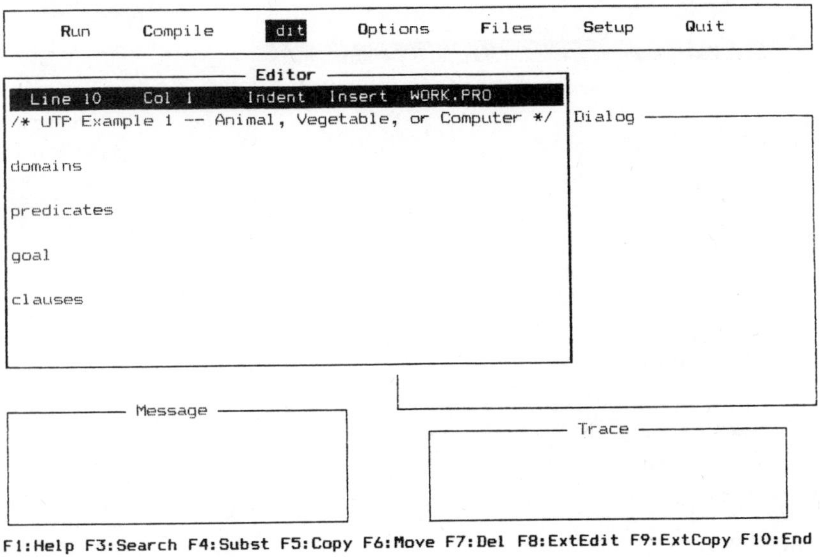

```
 ┌──────────────────────────────────────────────────────────────┐
 │  Run      Compile     dit    Options    Files    Setup   Quit  │
 └──────────────────────────────────────────────────────────────┘
 ┌──────────────────── Editor ─────────────────────┐
 │ Line 10   Col 1      Indent  Insert   WORK.PRO   │
 │ /* UTP Example 1 -- Animal, Vegetable, or Computer */ │ Dialog ────────────
 │                                                  │
 │ domains                                          │
 │                                                  │
 │ predicates                                       │
 │                                                  │
 │ goal                                             │
 │                                                  │
 │ clauses                                          │
 │                                                  │
 │                                                  │
 └──────────────────────────────────────────────────┘
 ┌─────────── Message ────────────┐   ┌──────── Trace ────────┐
 │                                 │   │                       │
 │                                 │   │                       │
 └─────────────────────────────────┘   └───────────────────────┘
 F1:Help F3:Search F4:Subst F5:Copy F6:Move F7:Del F8:ExtEdit F9:ExtCopy F10:End
```

Figure 4-2.   Skeleton of Turbo Prolog program

cursor to the line just after the word "predicates" and press the TAB key. Then type

```
animal (thing)
vegetable (thing)
computer (thing)
```

on three lines as shown here. The predicate declarations don't need to end with a period as the clauses do. Your Turbo Prolog screen should now look like the one in Figure 4-4.

Your predicate declarations have informed Turbo Prolog that the predicates animal, vegetable, and computer all concern "things." Not

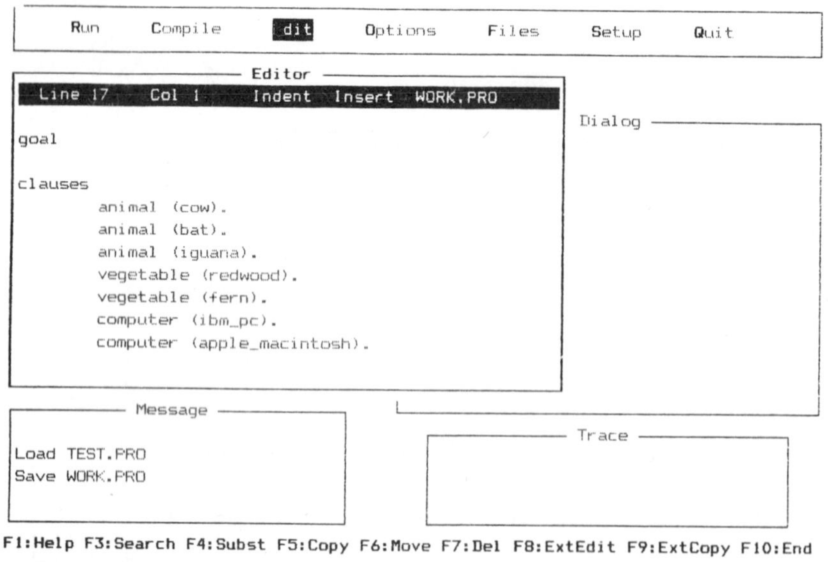

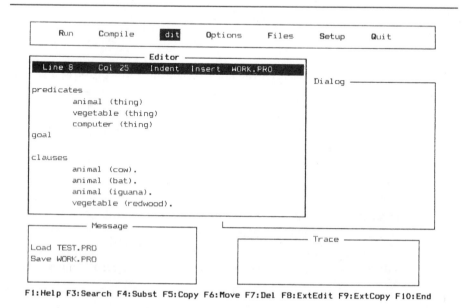

Figure 4-3.   Facts entered in as clauses with periods at end

Figure 4-4.   Predicate declarations (without periods)

surprisingly, the compiler now wants to know what kind of "things." That's what the domains section is for.

Move the cursor to the line just after the word "domains," press the TAB key, and type the line

```
thing = symbol
```

with a space after "thing" and another space after the equal sign. Now you're done typing.

Save What You've Got

Before going any further, protect yourself against power loss or the attack of a small, keyboard-loving child by saving the source file you're working on. Press ESC to get to the main menu and then F to get the Files submenu. Choose S for Save, and type the name of the file. Use "utpex1" for "Using Turbo Prolog Example 1." This will save the file to the A drive (if that is your preselected disk drive). You'll see a message like

```
Save utpex1.PRO
```

in the Message window confirming the action.

Compiling the First Program Example

Now you're ready to compile the program. Press ESC enough times to return to the main menu. (If you just saved the file, you'll already be in the main menu and pressing ESC won't do anything.) Press C for Compile. You'll see an error notice at the bottom of the Editor window as shown in Figure 4-5.

Syntax Checking

Because the goal section did not have anything in it, the compiler thought it was another predicate declaration in the predicates section. The compiler even put the cursor right on the problem it found: the word "goal." This built-in syntax checking is an enormous help during programming and debugging.

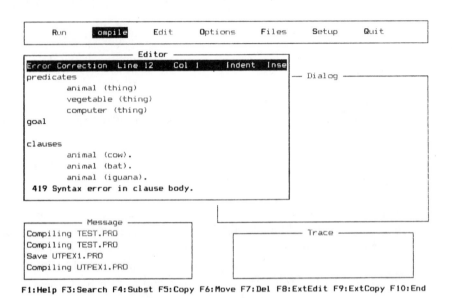

Figure 4-5.   Error message for problem encountered during compile

Delete the "goal" line and press the F10 key. That will automatically recompile the new, fixed source file. In some programs you may then find another error and have to return again to editing, but in this case you should see the message

```
Compiling utpex1.PRO
```

in the Message window without any more error messages. This means that you have a compiled program. The use of F10 after a syntax-editing error lets you combine the ESC and Compile (pressing C) functions in a single keystroke.

Running the First Program

Now the program is compiled into memory, waiting to do something. Press the R key to run the program from the main menu. You'll see the Dialog window come to life, as shown in Figure 4-6. It will be asking for a goal. The program is now running. Remember, because Prolog is a logical, declarative language, you just have to enter a logical goal, not a long-winded description of how to get there.

Goals and Questions

Although the goals you set for your Prolog programs may eventually be as complex as deciding on medical treatment or showing a graphics

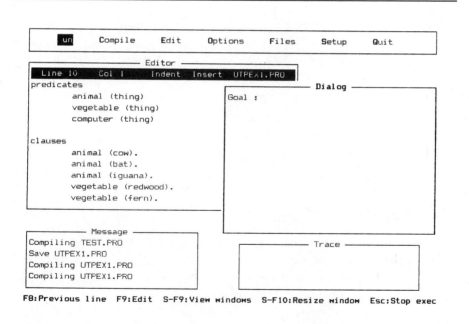

Figure 4-6.   Goal prompt in Dialog window

simulation of an aircraft in flight, the goals for this first example have to be considerably less exalted. There just isn't enough information in the clauses section for Prolog to squeeze much out of the program.

Later programs in this book will have internal goals. This one deals only with external goals —goals that you enter in the Dialog window. That window is now active and will let you type in information by using many of the same Editing commands that the Editor window uses.

Checking Facts

The least complex goal just checks a fact. If you enter a fact in the Dialog window, Turbo Prolog will take it as a question and will tell you if that fact is in its list —the clauses section. For this example program, type

```
animal (bat)
```

and press RETURN. You have asked, "Is a bat an animal?" or more precisely in the logic, "Does the bat object have the animal relationship?" You'll immediately see the answer —the word "True" appears, as shown in Figure 4-7. The program will still be running and will then ask for another goal. Try the goal

```
computer (ibm_pc)
```

and you'll see the answer: "True."

Stopping the Program

If you want to stop the program and leave the Dialog window, just press ESC. That will get you back to the main menu. You'll be working more with the program, so if you stopped it just now, run it again with an R from the main menu. Try this goal next:

```
vegetable (ibm_pc)
```

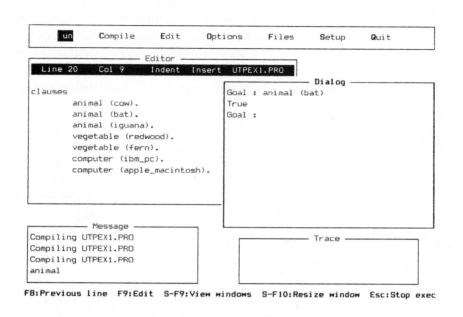

Figure 4-7. Turbo Prolog response to simple external goal

You'll see that Prolog returns "False."

Neither "True" nor "False" means that anything is verifiably true or false in the outside world. They just mean that Turbo Prolog was able to search through its clauses and come up with information that produced those results. If Turbo Prolog's information is wrong, its answers will be wrong.

Search for Information

Prolog searches through the clauses from top to bottom and from left to right. In the cases of "animal (bat)" and "computer (ibm _pc)," it found facts that exactly matched the goal. In the case of the goal "vegetable (ibm __pc)," it searched all through the database and couldn't find any exact match. Therefore, as far as this program is concerned, there is no way to know if an ibm __pc is a vegetable. It could be, logically. Just because an object has one relationship —as in computer (ibm __pc) —doesn't restrict it to only that relationship.

Variables

There is another way to ask questions. If you know the relationship but not the objects, you can use *variables*. Any object word that begins with a capital letter is considered a variable. After the capital, you can have any number of letters (upper- or lowercase), along with digits and under-

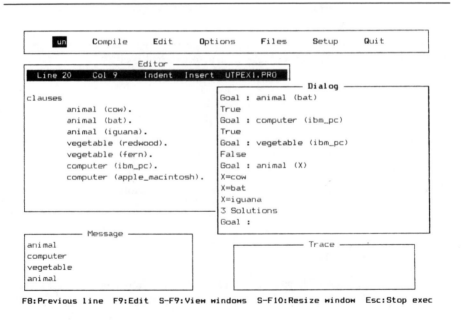

Figure 4-8.   Turbo Prolog response to variable query about animal

characters. The quickest way to see what a variable can do is to ask a question of the program. Try

```
animal (X)
```

as a goal. You'll soon see the display shown in Figure 4-8.

Turbo Prolog takes the goal with the variable and compares it to the clauses. First it checks to see if the predicate is the same as in the first clause. If it is, then it tests to see if the goal and the predicate have the same number of arguments. If either of these things isn't true, Turbo Prolog gives up on the first clause and moves on to test the goal against the second clause. If both do come true —same predicate and same number of arguments —Prolog then tests to see if the arguments are the same.

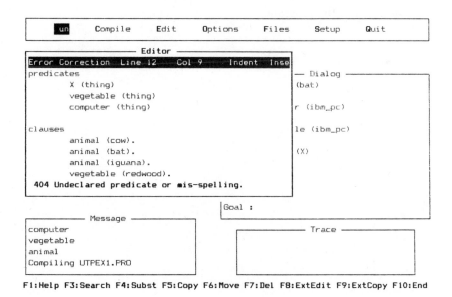

Figure 4-9.   Error caused by using variable as predicate

In this case, the goal argument is a variable, and it can stand for anything. So the compiler *instantiates* it to the value in the clause; in other words, the compiler assumes for a time that it has the value of the argument in the clause. In the language of Turbo Prolog, this is called *binding* a value to a variable. Now the goal and the clause are in exact agreement, and Turbo Prolog can report to you in the Dialog window that it has found an instance of the fact you asked about. It tells you the instance, along with the value it temporarily set the variable equal to, and then goes back to the clauses.

Because you used a variable, Prolog will look for all clauses that might fit the goal or make the goal true. It will release the "X" from the first value and will move on to the next lower (or farther to the right) clause. It will inspect this clause just as it did the first clause. Eventually, Prolog will serve up all cases that allow the goal to be true. The current example will yield three instances of the goal being true.

Keep in mind that if you try to use a variable for a predicate (such as a predicate "X (thing)") you'll get an error, as shown in the Editor window in Figure 4-9. Turbo Prolog expects predicates to be used and declared in the program.

5

Rules and Backtracking

Turbo Prolog has much more to offer than just the elementary facts and variables described in Chapter 4. This chapter will introduce facts with multiple arguments, compound goals, blank variables, rules, backtracking, and tracing. By the time you finish this chapter, you'll see that these concepts are simpler than you might have thought.

If you're an old Prolog hand and know about rules, backtracking, and compound goals, you can skim most of this chapter to see how Turbo Prolog implements such things. But you should take a look at the "Tracing" section because you'll want to know how to use Turbo Prolog's built-in Trace window.

Terms

Terms are the basic building blocks of Prolog programs. A term can be a constant, a variable, or a structure. In the previous chapter you worked mainly with constants, such as

```
bat
cow
ibm_pc
apple_macintosh
```

You also worked briefly with variables, depending only on the ever-popular "X." A constant represents a specific object or relationship. A variable (which always begins with a capital letter) stands for an object whose name you don't yet know in the setting of the program. We'll look at structures later in the book.

Arity: Facts With Multiple Arguments

The *arity* of a predicate is the number of arguments that predicate has. Chapter 4 employed only predicates with a single argument, or an arity of one. But you will find that most Prolog programs depend heavily on predicates with much greater arities. For example, you might want to use the predicate

```
shark (leg, human)
```

to describe the relationship (predicate) between the two objects (arguments) "leg" and "human." This could be translated as "Sharks eat the legs off of humans." But remember that the meaning is what you define it to be. This same predicate could mean "Legs are the parts of humans that attract sharks." You can write comments in your program to record what you intended a predicate to mean, but the comment will only help the next reader of the program to understand your meaning. It won't help the compiler understand your intention.

You might want to use a predicate with a sizable arity to describe your computer system. For instance,

```
computer (ibm_pc,_512K,_2_floppy,_DOS_2,_2serial,_1parallel,
_Hercules,_Princeton)
```

could handle most of the basic, descriptive characteristics of your system. You can even have a predicate with no arguments, but that's a case that will be addressed later. (Notice in the above example that most entries are lowercase letters. Uppercase letters will be treated as variables unless they are preceded by an underline character. Numbers should be avoided or preceded by an underline as well.)

Goals With Multiple Arguments

After making a short program of single-argument predicates in Chapter 4, you interrogated that program with single-argument goals. Programs that employ predicates with greater arities can also work with more complex goals. The following are a few clauses for a simple example:

```
watches (bill,bob)
watches (john,jane)
watches (fred,felicia)
watches (mitch,bill)
```

```
watches (brenda,greg)
watches (bob,bob)
watches (fred,greg)
watches (bill,phillippe)
```

Get into the Editor window and type the lines you see in Figure 5-1. This will set up the title comment line, the main divisions, and major clauses for this program. Remember to put periods at the ends of the facts in the clauses section. Facts don't have to have periods when standing all alone, but the Clauses section needs to have them to separate one fact from the next. The goal section has been left out because you will use external goals with this program.

The predicate "watches" will mean that the object in the first

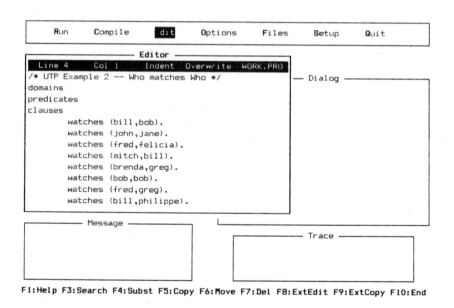

Figure 5-1.   Initial divisions and clauses in sample program

position watches the object in the second position. In other words,

```
watches (bill,bob)
```

means "Bill watches Bob," not "Bob watches Bill."

Now you can add some quick predicate and domain declarations, as shown in Figure 5-2. These follow the same pattern used in Chapter 4. All of the arguments are of the same type and they can be in the same domain ("symbol" is the best domain to use for names of things or people). Remember that "person" is just our term for them. The word "symbol" always means a certain thing when used in Turbo Prolog's

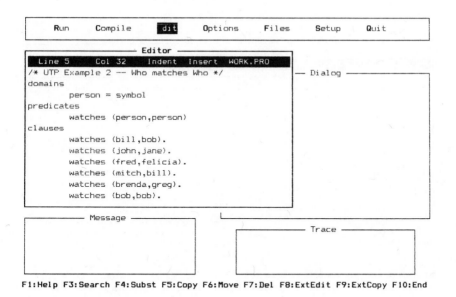

Figure 5-2.   Predicate and domain declarations

domains section. You should delete the "goal" line, too. It can make trouble when no goal is listed.

Now save your work as "utpex 2" (use ESC to get out of the Editor, F to get the Files menu, and S to save; type the disk drive and file name, press RETURN, and you're done). You may notice in the Message window that the file is actually saved as "utpex 2.PRO." You don't have to add the .PRO extension — Turbo Prolog does that for you if you don't supply a file-name extension.

Now compile and run the program by pressing C and then R. You'll see the word "Goal" appear in the Dialog window. Now you're ready to experiment with more complex goals.

Figure 5-3.   Goal with multiple arguments

Let's begin with something simple. Type

```
watches (fred,greg)
```

and press RETURN. Turbo Prolog will search from top to bottom through the list of facts to find one that matches the goal you presented it. First it tries to match the predicate "watches." The very first fact uses that predicate. Then Turbo checks to see if the fact has the same number of arguments as the goal (two). They all do, so the match is still a possibility. Then it tries to match the first argument of the predicate with the first argument of the goal, but does not find a match.

At this point Turbo passes on to the next fact and tries to match to it, going through the whole process described previously. Eventually, it will find the exact same fact, and it will respond as shown in Figure 5-3.

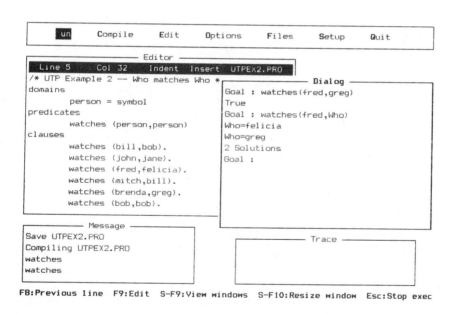

Figure 5-4.   Goal with multiple arguments and a variable: part 1

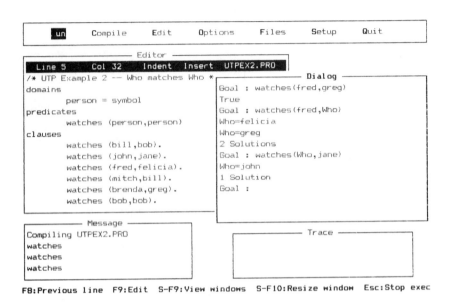

Figure 5-5.   Goal with multiple arguments and a variable: part 2

Now try using a variable in the multiple-argument goal. Try the goal

```
watches (fred,Who)
```

to see what happens (check Figure 5-4). You might try pressing the F8 key to type this particular goal. The F8 key repeats the previous goal line and leaves you with only the duty of changing "greg" to "Who." "Who" is a variable because it begins with a capital letter.

It just happens that Fred watches two different people, so you get two solutions in your answer. You could have used a variable in the other "person" position, as shown in Figure 5-5. No rule prevents an object from appearing in both positions. You might have defined the predicate so that wouldn't make sense, but it would still be syntactically legal in Turbo Prolog.

Now try using two variables in a single goal. The goal

```
watches (Who,Who2)
```

will produce the display shown in Figure 5-6. In effect, this is a list of all of the facts in the clauses database. If the program also included predicates other than "watches," this could be a useful operation for seeing how many "watches" facts are in the program.

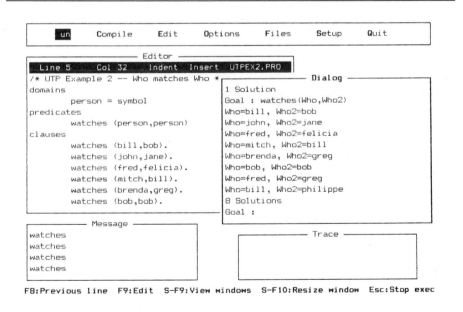

Figure 5-6. Goal with two variables

Anonymous or Blank Variable

Another type of variable that is handy in some situations is the *anonymous* variable. Other Prologs sometimes call this the "blank" variable. It is written just as an underline character. The anonymous variable is used in the same places that standard variables are used, but it never gets instantiated with any particular value.

Here's an example of a goal that uses the anonymous variable. Suppose you had the utpex2 program, and you wanted to know if Brenda watched anyone. You could pose the goal

```
watches (brenda,_)
```

and you would learn that it is "True": Brenda does watch someone (see Figure 5-7). But because you used the blank variable, you aren't told

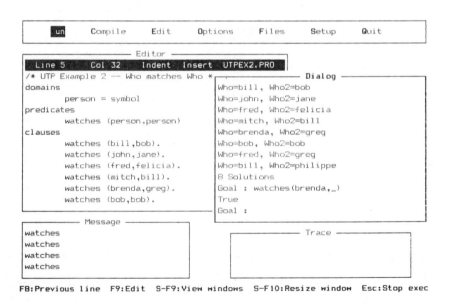

Figure 5-7.   Goal with anonymous variable

whom she watches. Turbo Prolog just searched for a fact that had the "watches" predicate, two arguments ("brenda" as the first argument and anything at all as the second argument). It didn't need to know more, so it didn't bother to ask and didn't relay any names to you.

If you try the goal

```
watches (_,_)
```

you'll know that someone watches someone (see Figure 5-8); if you try

```
watches (fred,_)
```

you'll see just the answer "True," meaning that "fred" watches someone or there is someone that "fred" watches.

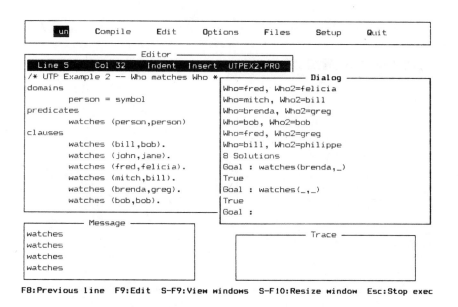

Figure 5-8. Goal with two anonymous variables

The anonymous variable can also be used in facts. If you add the line

```
watches (_,brenda)
```

to the clauses section, you'll be saying that "Everyone watches Brenda" is a fact or that "We don't care who is watching Brenda." Don't actually add that to the program, though, as it will just confuse what is described later.

Compound Goals

Goals can be even more complex. For example, goals can also deal with multiple facts.

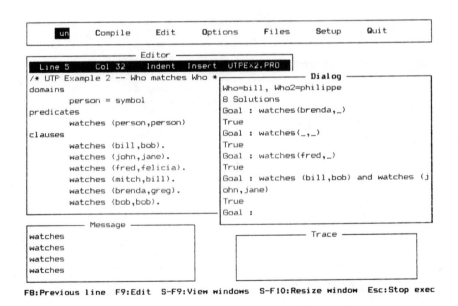

Figure 5-9. Compound goal

The AND Operator

If you pose the goal

```
watches (bill,bob) and watches (john,jane)
```

you'll be asking, "Is it true by the clauses that Bill watches Bob AND John watches Jane?" This compound goal will be judged true only if both of the individual goals are true. Try it (Figure 5-9).

You don't need to press the RETURN key to type a goal this long. The words in the Dialog window will automatically wrap to the next line.

Turbo Prolog initially tries to match the first subgoal. Once that is accomplished, it remembers that the first subgoal is satisfied and tries to match the second subgoal.

Now try

```
watches (bill,bob) and watches (greg,brenda)
```

The result will be "False," because both individual goals need to be true to make the compound goal true, and the

```
watches (greg,brenda)
```

goal isn't true. It cannot be matched by the facts in the clauses section. The fact

```
watches (brenda,greg)
```

isn't the same, because the values are in different positions.

Because many other implementations of Prolog use a comma to mean AND, Turbo Prolog also offers that option. So the compound goal above could be written as

```
watches (bill,bob),watches (greg,brenda)
```

The OR and Other Operators

You can also build compound goals, called *conjunctions* with other "glue" words. The compound goal that is made of two goals joined by the

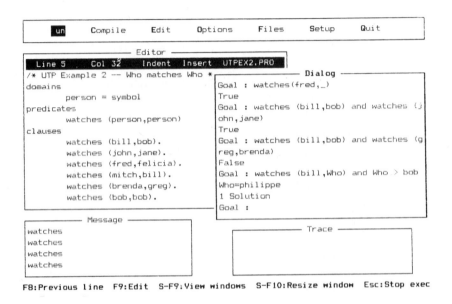

Figure 5-10.   Compound goals using > operator

word "or" will be true if either of the individual goals is true. (Just as a comma can be substituted for AND, a semicolon can take the place of OR.) The other individual goal can be true or false, and it won't affect the truth of the compound goal. The use of AND and OR operators is fundamental to many areas of computer science.

There are also several other operators that you can put into compound goals, including the greater-than and less-than signs. You aren't limited to using these with numbers. A "symbol" can be compared to another "symbol," letter by letter, with the letters that occur closer to "a" in the alphabet considered lesser than those that occur closer to "z."

To see how this works, try the following goal as Figure 5-10 illustrates:

```
watches (bill,Who) and Who > bob
```

You'll get the answer

```
philippe
```

because there is someone whom "bill" watches whose name comes alphabetically after "bob."

The NOT operator is discussed later in this chapter.

Rules

Facts aren't the only inhabitors of the clauses section. You can also enter *rules* into your database. A typical rule says that something is true (a goal will succeed) if some other things are true. Rules take Prolog beyond the status of just a searchable dictionary or database into the realm of a logical, thinking machine.

Let's add a few rules to the utpex2 example program. Type in the line

```
happy (greg) if watches (brenda,greg)
```

and the line

```
nervous (Who) if watches (bill,Who)
```

at the end of the facts previously listed (See Figure 5-11). Be sure to put periods at the ends of the rules.

Now you have to add some new predicate declarations before you try to compile the expanded program. Try the declarations shown in Figure 5-12. You don't need new domains, because no new arguments were used. All of the predicates deal with "person."

Compile and run the new program. Now, to try a few goals, type

```
happy (greg)
```

```
    Run       Compile     dit     Options    Files    Setup    Quit

                        Editor
   Line 20      Col 9      Indent    Insert   UTPEX2.PRO
clauses                                                      Dialog
        watches (bill,bob).
        watches (john,jane).
        watches (fred,felicia).
        watches (mitch,bill).
        watches (brenda,greg).
        watches (bob,bob).
        watches (fred,greg).
        watches (bill,philippe).
        happy (eric) if watches (brenda,eric).
        happy (greg) if watches (brenda,greg).
        nervous (Who) if watches (bill,Who).

            Message                             Trace

Load UTPEX2.PRO

F1:Help F3:Search F4:Subst F5:Copy F6:Move F7:Del F8:ExtEdit F9:ExtCopy F10:End
```

Figure 5-11.   Adding rules to a sample program

first. You should get the answer "True."

Turbo Prolog will attempt to satisfy (or match) the goal "happy (greg)." From top to bottom, it will search through the clauses looking for a predicate that matches the "happy" predicate. It finds that predicate near the bottom of the list. Then it checks if that predicate has the same arity —one. It does, so the process continues. Turbo Prolog finds the "if" and realizes that this is a rule, not a fact.

To make the left side of a rule "True" so that it can be used to match a goal, the right side of the rule has to be true. Turbo Prolog marks its place and adopts "watches (brenda,greg)" to satisfy the new goal. Then it can come back and satisfy the original goal.

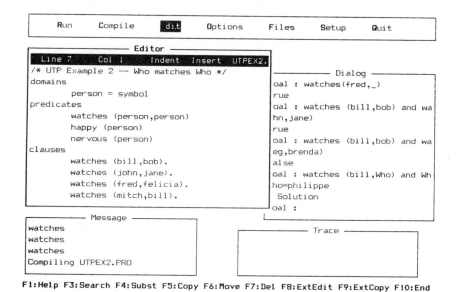

Figure 5-12.   Predicate declarations for rules

Backtracking

At this point, Turbo Prolog returns to the first clause and begins to search back through the list. This is called *backtracking* and is an important feature of Prolog. Whenever a subgoal needs to be satisfied, Prolog will backtrack through a database, always searching from top to bottom and left to right, to find a match. Backtracking can easily grow more complex when the rules and goals are more complex.

Searching through the facts, Turbo Prolog soon finds the "watches (brenda,greg)" fact. It matches the subgoal to that fact and returns to the rule "happy (greg) if watches (brenda,greg)," where it then knows that the left side of the rule, "happy (greg)," can be used to match the original goal, because the right side of the rule was "True."

Instantiation and Binding

If you try the goal

```
happy (Who)
```

you'll get the answer "greg" after much the same kind of search. The only difference is that the variable "Who" needs to be instantiated to "greg." Turbo Prolog will find the "happy" predicate, check the arity, instantiate the variable "Who" to the constant "greg", reset the goal to the right side of the rule, match that new goal, and return to the rule. It will then set the left side of the rule to "True," match the left side to the goal, report that the goal has succeeded, and print the "bound" value of the variable.

The word "binding" is used for setting a variable's value because the assignment is often very temporary. Unlike BASIC, where a LET statement will assign a variable a certain value until another statement changes that value, Prolog only binds values to variables as long as a goal is succeeding. If a goal is failing, even temporarily within the list of facts and rules, the single variable can be bound and unbound from a series of values. Each time a value is found that might work, the variable is bound to that value. When the value fails the next test, or rule, it is unbound so that some other may take its place.

For example, add the rule

```
happy (eric) if watches (brenda,eric)
```

to the database. Put it just above the rule

```
happy (greg) if watches (brenda,greg)
```

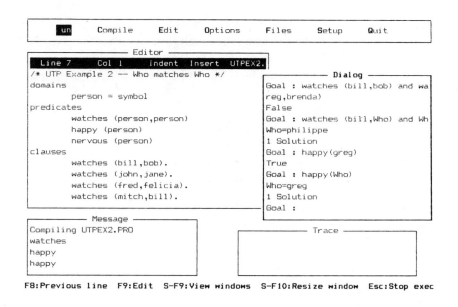

Figure 5-13. Backtracking and rules

as shown in Figure 5-13. (The order of the lines is important because Prolog searches from top to bottom.) Now try the goal

```
happy (Who)
```

to see who is cheerful and who isn't. You'll get the answer "Who=greg" in a second. But how did Turbo Prolog get this answer? The search pattern is a little more complicated this time, and instead of describing it in detail, we'll explore how you can follow the process.

Tracing

When you want to take a peek at the step-by-step progress of your program instead of just seeing the result, you can *trace* the progress of the program. Tracing makes the development environment stop the program after each step and tell what it has done, where it is, and what the variable values are.

One of Prolog's advantages as a programming language is its powerful tracing facility. Turbo Prolog has another advantage that many previous Prologs didn't have: retention of variable names. Other Prologs will sometimes convert your variable names (such as "Who" and "Whom") into the "A" and "B," "X" and "Y" type. Turbo sticks with

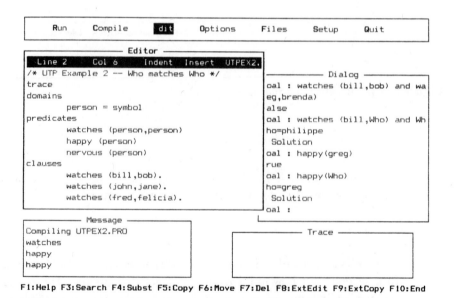

Figure 5-14.   The Trace statement

the variable names used in the program, making the tracing easier to follow.

There are a number of methods to trace the steps Turbo Prolog takes when it runs a program. Some methods require that you use special compile commands, but these won't be discussed until a later chapter. The Trace window allows easy tracing, which can help you understand backtracking and the success or failure of a goal.

Add the word

```
trace
```

to your program (utpex2) above the "domains" line (see Figure 5-14).

Figure 5-15.   Using the Trace window

This will tell the compiler right away, when you compile, that you want to run the program in Trace mode. Then compile and run the program.

Try the goal

```
happy (Who)
```

and watch what happens in the Trace window. You should see (as in Figure 5-15) this line:

```
CALL:   happy(_)
```

This means that the first step Prolog will take to satisfy the goal is to look for a "happy" predicate with any variable. Notice the anonymous variable as the argument. You should also notice that the cursor is on the "h" of "happy" in the Dialog window. That is where the action occurs at this point: defining the goal. You'll see the cursor move during the trace to show you where Turbo Prolog's logic is going.

Now press the F10 special function key to see the next step. F10 always performs this function when you are in Trace mode. The cursor will move to the first predicate that matches the CALL statement, which is the rule line

```
happy (eric) if watches (brenda,eric)
```

Press F10 again to see the next step. The cursor will move to the "w" of "watches" because Turbo Prolog has matched the left side of the rule to the original goal and now knows that it must satisfy the right side of the rule. In the Dialog window you'll see (as shown in Figure 5-16) the phrase

```
CALL:   watches ("brenda","eric")
```

The words will be broken up because the window is so small; Turbo Prolog wraps the words to the next line automatically. When you are doing a lot of tracing, you'll probably want to use the Setup submenu in the main menu to enlarge the Trace window.

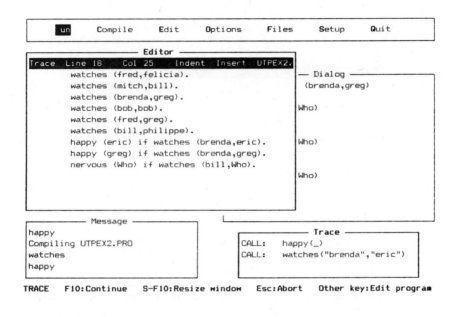

Figure 5-16.   Setting a new, temporary goal

The "CALL" line is the new, temporary goal. Turbo Prolog will now try to satisfy it by searching through the database from top to bottom, left to right, to match it to a known fact or another rule that can possibly be satisfied.

Press F10 again. The cursor will return to the first fact in the database. Press again. You'll see the display shown in Figure 5-17 with the line

```
REDO:   watches("brenda","eric")
```

in the Trace window. Turbo Prolog tried to match the new goal against

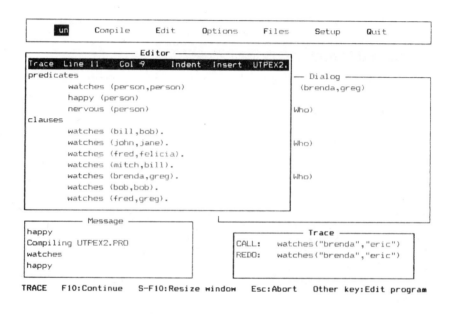

Figure 5-17. Trying to match the new goal in the trace

the first fact. Although the predicate and arity were correct, the values of the arguments in the goal differed from those in the fact. To match, the arguments must be exactly the same. Turbo Prolog knew it had to try again to match the new goal. It had to REDO the test against another fact or rule.

Press F10 several more times, and notice that the same thing happens. Turbo Prolog checks each line in order to see if it will match the goal; the cursor moves to the checked line, and the Trace window tells you what is happening.

Finally, when you press F10 you'll see the display shown in Figure 5-18. Backtracking has hit the "final stage." Turbo Prolog ran out of

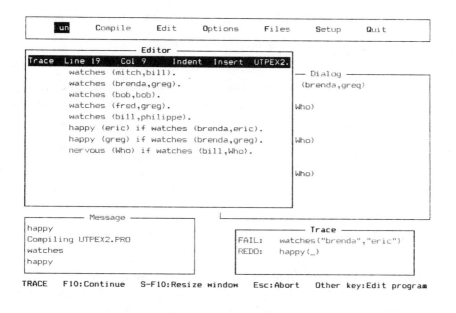

Figure 5-18.   Backtracking when the temporary goal fails

facts and rules that it could try to match to the new goal of

```
watches(brenda,eric)
```

It realized that the new goal had failed. At that point, it returned to the rule

```
happy(eric) if watches (brenda,eric)
```

and realized that the left side, "happy(eric)," had failed also, because the right side couldn't be satisfied. So the temporary goal of

```
watches(brenda,eric)
```

was released, and Turbo Prolog backtracked to the original goal of

```
happy (Who)
```

Turbo Prolog had marked that this goal had been tested against all the facts and rules above the just-failed rule, so it proceeded to the next fact or rule. It found

```
happy(greg) if watches(brenda,greg)
```

and began to match it against the goal. Press F10 repeatedly and watch the progress of this search. Turbo Prolog will take

```
watches(brenda,greg)
```

as a new goal in an attempt to satisfy the entire rule. It will search through the facts, trying to satisfy the new goal, and this time will find a fact that makes the new goal succeed. At that point (see Figure 5-19) you'll see

```
RETURN:   watches("brenda","greg")
```

in the Trace window. Turbo Prolog has found a fact that matches the temporary goal and is returning with that fact to the rule line that incorporates the temporary goal. With the right side of the rule satisfied, it will release the temporary goal, return to the left side of the rule, and instantiate the variable "Who" of the original goal to the value "greg." With the original goal satisfied, it will print out the result in the Dialog window, tell you how many solutions it found, and be ready for a new goal.

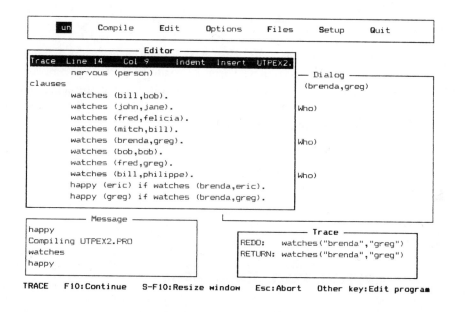

Figure 5-19.   Satisfying the temporary goal

The NOT Operator

Another operator you will find in many Prolog rules is NOT. Add to your program the rule

```
happy (fred) if not (watches (fred,felicia))
```

after the clause

```
happy (greg) if watches (brenda,greg)
```

as shown in Figure 5-20. The extra parentheses around the fact
"watches (fred,felicia)" help Turbo Prolog to know that this entire fact
has the "not" applied to it. Also, if you simply put this line at the end of
the clauses, you would get a 415 error, indicating that Turbo Prolog
wants all similar predicates grouped together.

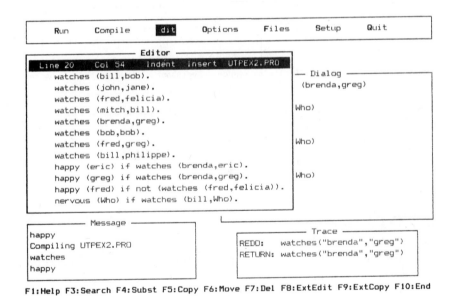

Figure 5-20.   Using the NOT operator in a rule

Delete the word "Trace" at the top of the program (you don't want to trace this time). Then compile and run the program, and try the following goal:

```
happy (fred)
```

You'll get the answer "False," because Fred can be happy only if he isn't watching Felicia. In other words, the left side of the rule, "happy (fred)," is only true if the left side, "watches (fred,felicia)," isn't true. But the left side is true. A fact shows it to be true, and Turbo Prolog will find that fact. Therefore, the right side of the fact will fail as a temporary goal; then the left side will fail as a possible match for the original goal; and because no other matches will be found for the goal, Turbo Prolog will report that the original goal fails or is "False."

The :- Symbol

Many Prolog programs, including Turbo Prolog, also allow the use of the symbol ":-" to mean "if." The following shows one of the rules you used before with the new symbol in place.

```
happy (eric) :- watches (brenda,eric)
```

6

Backtracking Control: Cut (!) And Fail

Turbo Prolog has a number of built-in predicates and commands that make it a general-purpose programming language instead of just an implementation of logic. This chapter takes a look at two of the most important program control functions that are available in many implementations of Prolog — "fail" and "cut" (!). Along the way you'll learn about the Example programs that are part of the Turbo Prolog package, the built-in procedural predicates for displaying information, and external versus internal goals.

If you have already loaded and taken a look at programs from the Borland Library/Example disk, you can skip that section in this chapter. Even if you are familiar with the workings and uses of the "fail" and "cut" (!) predicates, skim this section. Knowing what these commands are isn't enough. To create practical Prolog programs, you'll need to include these commands in the right places. You'll also learn the difference between internal and external goals and take a first glance at the built-in, procedural display predicates such as "write." These will be covered in more detail in a later chapter. Finally, you'll use recursion even in simple programs, not only in mathematical calculations. Recursion is fundamental to list processing and natural-language applications.

Borland's Example Programs

Turbo Prolog comes as two disks: the System/Program disk and the Library/Example disk. You've been using the System/Program disk so far in this book. That's the disk that holds the main compiler along with the error messages, Help information, and the like.

The Library/Example disk holds the natural-language geography demo, GeoBase, along with 64 Prolog examples that are referred to in the *Owner's Handbook*. You should use the example programs frequently while you learn Prolog: load them, read them, modify them, pose goals, trace the action, and sometimes save your new versions under a different name. Be sure to add comments to your modified source code so you know what you did and why.

The following discussion centers on how to load a program from the Library/Example disk. Use the standard arrangement —the Turbo Prolog System/Program disk in the A drive and the Library/Example disk in the B drive of a two-floppy PC.

From the main menu, press S for Setup and then D for Directories. The line

```
PRO     directory A:\
```

should be highlighted. Press RETURN, and then type

```
b:\
```

The "a: \" that was in the space will disappear when you start to enter the new default, working-file directory. Now your Load commands will automatically call upon the B drive unless otherwise instructed. Press RETURN once and ESC twice. This enters the new default directory into the active configuration and then returns you to the main menu. Remember that the active configuration will disappear for good when you quit Prolog unless you save it to a .SYS file (using the Save Configuration option of the Setup menu).

Press F for Files and then L for Load. Press RETURN without typing any particular file name. You'll see a directory of the files on the B drive that end with the .PRO extension. They are the example programs. One of them, EXAMPL1.PRO, will be highlighted. To load a highlighted file, you just press RETURN. You can move the highlighting around by using the arrow keys on the numeric keypad.

Press RETURN to load EXAMPL1.PRO. It will appear in the Editor window, as shown in Figure 6-1. Press the E key and you'll also be in the Editor window, ready to edit the code.

Backtracking Control

As discussed in Chapter 5, backtracking is an essential element of Prolog. When a program has been asked to satisfy a goal, it searches from

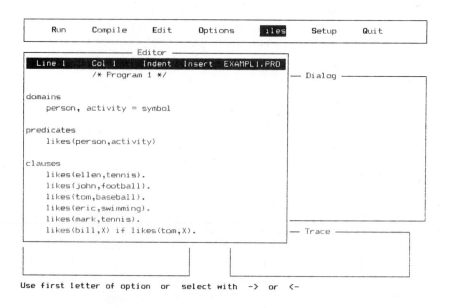

Figure 6-1. The EXAMPL1.PRO program loaded from the Library/Example disk

top to bottom and left to right through the clauses to match the goal. If it runs into a dead end, the program will back up just enough in the clauses to find another branch that can be searched.

This isn't always the best way for a program to proceed. Some programs spend too much time retrieving information that isn't needed on the way to finding material that you care about. These programs need the programmer's help in cutting down the huge search space. Computers are vulnerable to the "combinatorial explosion" that can result in Prolog from just a few levels of goals and subgoals. Atomic physics provides a good analogy for what can happen.

An atomic bomb is based on the principle of a fission chain reaction: a single neutron splits an atom and yields two neutrons, which split two atoms and yield four neutrons, which split four atoms and yield eight neutrons, which split eight atoms, and so on. Such a chain escalates geometrically. Your computer program can also become a bomb because of geometric or logarithmic increases in the search area. If each goal leads to two subgoals and each subgoal leads to two more subgoals, and so on, the number of goals to satisfy can quickly multiply to impractical levels.

Such a chain reaction can quickly overwhelm a computer and lead to huge increases in searching time. Imagine the number of matching attempts Prolog must make if a goal contains numerous clauses, all of which must be tested against every line in a large database. Then multiply the time this would take, because the search will probably encounter many rules and, therefore, subgoals that must themselves be matched against the entire database. Pretty soon you'll just be tapping your fingers on the table while Prolog searches and searches.

As the programmer, you can help. First, you can write the clauses in an order that will make for the most efficient searches. Some simple examples of that will be presented in this book, but you should know that a thorough understanding of how to organize clauses for greatest efficiency is an art, not a science. Second, because as a programmer you're more intelligent than your computer, you can tell Prolog when to skip part of a search that isn't necessary. You just insert a few special commands into the program. These can direct the logic and save computing time.

Cut (!)

This command (or special predicate) is called "cut" but is written in programs simply as an exclamation mark. The "cut" command behaves essentially as a built-in predicate with no arguments. You'll see it in a lot of programs; it is enormously helpful in cutting the search tree down to a manageable size. "Tree" terminology is widely used in computer science. When a search pattern grows from a single goal to subgoals and sub-subgoals, the metaphor of a main root producing branches and smaller branches is a natural one.

Prolog uses a *depth-first* search of a tree. It proceeds from the main goal to the first subgoal, then to the first sub-subgoal beneath that, and so on, until it either confirms the bottom level of subgoal or is sure that the subgoal fails. It then moves back up one level of subgoal (backtracking) and attempts to match the next subgoal at the same level. If the first series of subgoals is part of a larger goal that is a dead end, Prolog won't know that until it has worked through every subgoal.

To understand this type of search another way, think of a typical family tree. To simplify the analogy, imagine that your family consists only of female children, and that everyone has two girls. A depth-first search that began with one of your great-grandmothers would go first to the level of her two children, one of them your grandmother. Prolog would first deal with her. Then, before continuing with her sister, it would proceed one level "deeper" into the tree and work on one of her two children —your mother. Again, before moving on to your mother's sister, Prolog would proceed another level deeper to your generation. If yours is the last level or generation available (that is, if there weren't any branches beyond you), Prolog would then move from you to your sibling. At that point, having exhausted the deepest part of the tree on your sub-branch, Prolog would backtrack to your mother's generation and proceed with her sister. Remember again that Prolog would move back down to the offspring of your aunt and work through them before returning to your aunt and then to your grandmother.

But what if you know that the only useful answers will come from your mother and her children? If you don't want any of the information that could come from a search through your mother's or grandmother's siblings, why let Prolog waste its time there? You can stop that waste with "cut."

The ! ("cut") command prevents backtracking, acting like a one-way valve. The search can come through it from the leftmost clause but cannot retreat back through it from the right. When ! is encountered, it freezes the bound variables from a particular goal or subgoal search at their present values. That means it can work within a single rule or even between rules. If further clauses searched by the goal cause it to fail, Prolog cannot back up to the point before the ! within the goal search and look for other values for those variables —even if those other values might allow the goal to succeed.

If you write a rule with multiple clauses like

```
A if B and C and ! and D
```

the ! stops Prolog from finding multiple values for "B" and "C." Let's examine how that works.

In pursuit of a goal, Prolog moves down through the clauses section until it comes to the head ("A") of this rule. To satisfy "A," it must first satisfy the right side of the rule. First Prolog takes up "B" and tries to find a match for it. If Prolog cannot find a match, the entire rule fails (this is an "and" rule, in which all of the clauses on the right must succeed). If it can find a match for "B," it binds the variables of "B" to those of that match and then moves on to "C." There may be other possibilities in the clauses (such as other facts and rules) that could satisfy "B." That doesn't matter, because Prolog only wants one satisfaction —one set of bound variables —right now.

After settling on "C," Turbo Prolog looks for a match for it. Again, if it can't find a match, it will fail the entire rule, including "A." If it does find a match, it will then bind the variables in "C" to the matching value and move on to the "!" clause. Both the variables in "B" and the variables in "C" are now bound to the first values found that would satisfy the "B" and "C" clauses.

The "!" clause automatically succeeds. It doesn't have any arguments to consider, and it doesn't have to be matched against anything. It is automatically true. But it does have one other effect: the bound variables in "B" and "C" are now trapped in their current state. You'll see shortly what this does.

Turbo Prolog proceeds to "D." It will now search through all the possibilities for "D," trying to find something in the database that will match "D." If it does, the rule will succeed, because all the clauses that came before ("B," "C," and "!") have succeeded. If it does not find a solution to "D," it will fail the entire rule, because the "!" keeps it from

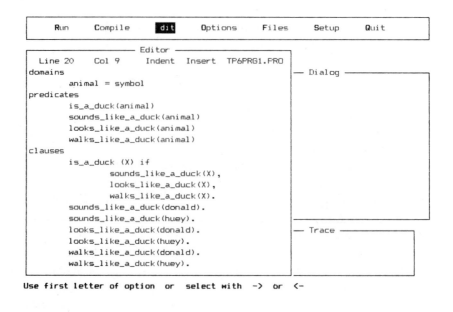

```
┌──────────────────────────────────────────────────────────────┐
│  Run      Compile    ▐dit▌    Options    Files    Setup    Quit │
└──────────────────────────────────────────────────────────────┘
┌──────────────── Editor ──────────────────┐
│  Line 20    Col 9    Indent  Insert  TP6PRG1.PRO │    ── Dialog ──────────────
│ domains                                    │
│        animal = symbol                     │
│ predicates                                 │
│        is_a_duck(animal)                   │
│        sounds_like_a_duck(animal)          │
│        looks_like_a_duck(animal)           │
│        walks_like_a_duck(animal)           │
│ clauses                                    │
│        is_a_duck (X) if                    │
│               sounds_like_a_duck(X),       │
│               looks_like_a_duck(X),        │
│               walks_like_a_duck(X).        │
│        sounds_like_a_duck(donald).         │    ── Trace ───────────────
│        sounds_like_a_duck(huey).           │
│        looks_like_a_duck(donald).          │
│        looks_like_a_duck(huey).            │
│        walks_like_a_duck(donald).          │
│        walks_like_a_duck(huey).            │
└────────────────────────────────────────────┘
Use first letter of option  or  select with  ->  or  <-
```

Figure 6-2.   An enlarged Editor window and sample program with an indented rule

backtracking to find other values of "B" and "C."

Remember that with normal backtracking, Turbo Prolog could look for the next value of "C" and then return to find a working value of "D." It might find such a "D" value once the "C" value was different. But the "!" does not allow that possibility. This rule must stop with the first solution it finds for "B" and "C."

Take a look at Figure 6-2. You might notice two things that are different in this figure from earlier figures. The Editor window has been enlarged using the Setup menu so that you can see the entire program. Also, the rule "is ‿a ‿duck" uses indenting to show the subgoals on its right side.

This program will let you know what "is __a __duck" is when you use the goal

```
is_a_duck (animal)
```

by searching through its database to satisfy the compound conditions of the "is __a __duck" rule. However, if you add "cut" (!) to it, as shown in Figure 6-3, you'll only get the first duck name. The rule won't be able to backtrack to the first subgoal ("sounds __like __a __duck") after going through the "cut." In this case, the position of "cut" doesn't make much difference. You could have put it after any of the subgoals of the

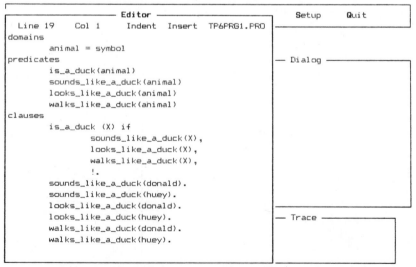

Figure 6-3.   Adding a "cut" (!) to a program

"is _a _duck" rule and you would still discover only the name of a single fowl. If you put it before all of the subgoals (as shown in Figure 6-4), you'll get both duck names, because Turbo Prolog can freely backtrack within the three "sounds _like _a _duck," "looks _like _a _duck," "walks _like _a _duck" clauses. It can find an answer ("donald") for the first, and then confirm it is also true for the second and third, and then report the name to you in the Dialog window. Because it is at the end of the rule, Turbo Prolog will then back up and do the same with the other name. Since it doesn't have to backtrack through the "cut," both solutions are all right.

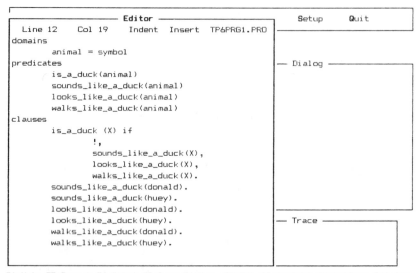

```
 ———————————— Editor ————————————        Setup    Quit
   Line 12    Col 19    Indent   Insert   TP6PRG1.PRO
 domains
         animal = symbol
 predicates                                   — Dialog ————
         is_a_duck(animal)
         sounds_like_a_duck(animal)
         looks_like_a_duck(animal)
         walks_like_a_duck(animal)
 clauses
         is_a_duck (X) if
                 !,
                 sounds_like_a_duck(X),
                 looks_like_a_duck(X),
                 walks_like_a_duck(X).
         sounds_like_a_duck(donald).
         sounds_like_a_duck(huey).
         looks_like_a_duck(donald).
         looks_like_a_duck(huey).                — Trace ————
         walks_like_a_duck(donald).
         walks_like_a_duck(huey).

 F1:Help F3:Search F4:Subst F5:Copy F6:Move F7:Del F8:ExtEdit F9:ExtCopy F10:End
```

Figure 6-4.   Backtracking clauses by using a "cut"

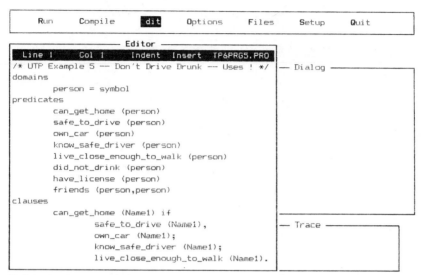

```
   Run      Compile    dit    Options    Files    Setup    Quit

                        Editor
 Line 1     Col 1       Indent   Insert   TP6PRG5.PRO
/* UTP Example 5 -- Don't Drive Drunk -- Uses ! */          -- Dialog
domains
        person = symbol
predicates
        can_get_home (person)
        safe_to_drive (person)
        own_car (person)
        know_safe_driver (person)
        live_close_enough_to_walk (person)
        did_not_drink (person)
        have_license (person)
        friends (person,person)
clauses
        can_get_home (Name1) if
                safe_to_drive (Name1),              -- Trace
                own_car (Name1);
                know_safe_driver (Name1);
                live_close_enough_to_walk (Name1).

F1:Help F3:Search F4:Subst F5:Copy F6:Move F7:Del F8:ExtEdit F9:ExtCopy F10:End
```

Figure 6-5.   Sample program "Don't Drive Drunk" (Part 1)

Take a look at Figures 6-5 and 6-6. This Prolog program is "made to order" for a huge convention party that is breaking up. You want to know who can get home safely and who will need special arrangements. An on-line computer contains information about addresses, license numbers, and car registration, as well as lists of those people who are at the convention and those of them who are friends. As people come to the front door, you administer a blood-alcohol test to see if they have been drinking. Then you feed their names and blood-alcohol results into the computer running this Turbo Prolog program, and (ignoring all the problems that would occur in actually getting the fictional database

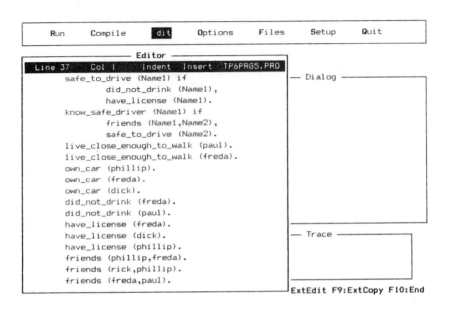

```
┌─────────────────────────────────────────────────────────────────────────┐
│   Run     Compile    │ dit │   Options    Files    Setup    Quit          │
│                      └─────┘                                              │
├──────────── Editor ──────────────────┐                                    │
│ Line 37    Col 1    Indent  Insert  TP6PRG5.PRO                            │
│         safe_to_drive (Name1) if          ┌── Dialog ──────────────┐       │
│                 did_not_drink (Name1),    │                        │       │
│                 have_license (Name1).     │                        │       │
│         know_safe_driver (Name1) if       │                        │       │
│                 friends (Name1,Name2),    │                        │       │
│                 safe_to_drive (Name2).    │                        │       │
│         live_close_enough_to_walk (paul). │                        │       │
│         live_close_enough_to_walk (freda).│                        │       │
│         own_car (phillip).                │                        │       │
│         own_car (freda).                  │                        │       │
│         own_car (dick).                   │                        │       │
│         did_not_drink (freda).            │                        │       │
│         did_not_drink (paul).             │                        │       │
│         have_license (freda).             └────────────────────────┘       │
│         have_license (dick).              ┌── Trace ───────────────┐       │
│         have_license (phillip).           │                        │       │
│         friends (phillip,freda).          │                        │       │
│         friends (rick,phillip).           │                        │       │
│         friends (freda,paul).             │                        │       │
└───────────────────────────────────────┘  └────────────────────────┘       │
                                         ExtEdit F9:ExtCopy F10:End          │
```

Figure 6-6.   Sample program ''Don't Drive Drunk'' (Part 2)

information) you wait for an answer as to who can get home. Notice that the subgoals of the main rule

```
can_get_home (Name1) if
        safe_to_drive (Name1),
        own_car (Name1);
        know_safe_driver (Name1);
        live_close_enough_to_walk (Name1).
```

include several semicolons. This symbol can be used instead of the word ''or.'' Someone ''can _get _home'' if he is a safe driver and owns a car, or if he knows a safe driver, or if he lives close enough to walk.

Because the whole thing will not fit into the visible Editor window, it is displayed as two pieces. Try compiling and running this program.

If you pose a certain person's name as a goal, you'll get the type of result shown in Figure 6-7. You'll simply be told whether or not this person can get home without further help. If you use a variable (as shown in Figure 6-8), you can get a list of all the people who can leave. This is probably quicker than processing people one at a time.

But there's a fly in the ointment: "freda" shows up twice, because she has two different ways of going home. This isn't much of a problem with such a small sampling, but imagine if you were making a list from any similar sort of program and were using a large database. For example, if you were making a mailing list, you could spend a huge amount of excess money and even annoy some of the people you were targeting if their names turned up on your list many times.

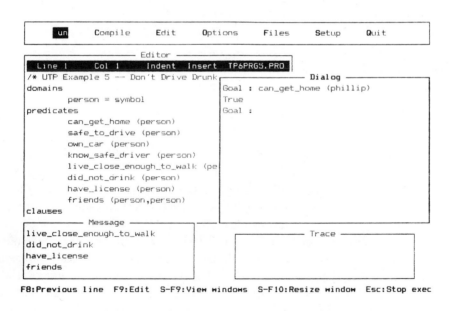

Figure 6-7. Typical results of "Don't Drive Drunk" program

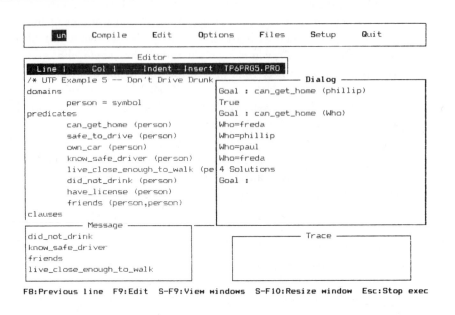

Figure 6-8.   Using a variable in the goal

The "cut" will come to your rescue. You don't want to backtrack through the subgoals of the "can _get _home" rule. See Figure 6-9 to see where "cut" could go, and then try the variable in the goal again as shown in Figure 6-10. Remember the shortcuts: you can use F10 to recompile and rerun after editing, and you can then use F8 to write the same goal as you had previously.

As mentioned earlier, "cut" keeps you from being overwhelmed with solutions, in terms of both the amount of output and the time spent achieving the goal. Again, note that the "cut" may seem like overkill when it is used in small programs like this one, which executes almost instantly and has small search patterns. But even small programs can get out of hand if you don't use "cut."

```
    Run       Compile      dit      Options      Files     Setup      Quit

                            Editor
    Line 19    Col 17    Indent  Insert  TP6PRG5.PRO
         live_close_enough_to_walk (person)              ── Dialog ──
         did_not_drink (person)                          _home (phillip)
         have_license (person)
         friends (person,person)                         _home (Who)
clauses
         can_get_home (Name1) if
                safe_to_drive (Name1),
                own_car (Name1);
                know_safe_driver (Name1);
                live_close_enough_to_walk (Name1),
                !.
         safe_to_drive (Name1) if
                did_not_drink (Name1),

 did_not_drink                              ── Trace ──
 know_safe_driver
 friends
 live_close_enough_to_walk

 F1:Help F3:Search F4:Subst F5:Copy F6:Move F7:Del F8:ExtEdit F9:ExtCopy F10:End
```

Figure 6-9.   Inserting a "cut" to backtrack variables (line 19, column 17)

For instance, if a program uses recursion (which you'll learn about in the next chapter), a single clause could keep it churning for a long time. Another example in which a "cut" would be appropriate is a short, deeply interrelated set of clauses that would print out a ream of answers when you wanted only one. This is the case in the conventioneers' program.

As a final note, you should know that Clocksin and Mellish advise that good programming style for readable programs will replace ! with "not" wherever possible. This creates slower programs that use more memory, but the programs will be much easier to read. The choice is up to you, of course, in each situation.

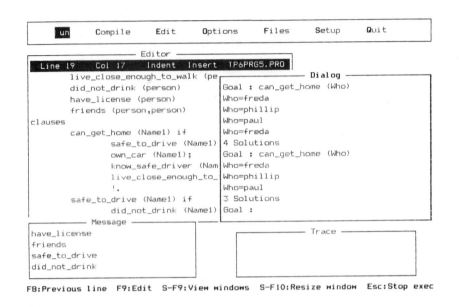

Figure 6-10.   The result of adding the "!"

Fail

Another built-in command to control backtracking, "fail," is a no-argument predicate that automatically fails and automatically forces backtracking. In a sense it is the opposite of "cut," which eliminates backtracking.

A New Type of Predicate

Pretend for now that Prolog has a built-in predicate that prints information on the screen (it does). Just as with any other predicate, Prolog tries to make this one succeed. But in this case, instead of looking elsewhere for matching material, Prolog knows that all it has to do to satisfy the predicate is to actually perform some function. Such predicates are quite "procedural" and prevent Turbo Prolog from being a strictly logical declarative programming language. They also make Prolog useful for everyday programming tasks.

Here's a peek at such a predicate: "write." In a rule, it might look like the following:

```
A if write ("Hello World")
```

When Turbo Prolog finds "A" in the clauses, it knows that it has to satisfy the right side of the rule to satisfy "A." The only action necessary for satisfying the right side is to write the phrase

```
Hello Earth
```

on the screen at the current cursor position. The predicate —write ("Hello Earth") —can then be assumed to be true, and in turn, "greetings" can be assumed to be true. See Figure 6-11 for an example of a program that uses this rule and predicate.

You'll notice that this program is very simple. The predicate declaration doesn't even have to deal with an argument. The clauses section contains only a single rule:

```
greetings if write("Hello Earth"),nl.
```

If you run this program and present it with "greetings" as a goal, Turbo Prolog will immediately go to this rule and try to make it succeed by finding a set of variable bindings that will satisfy the logic. As soon as it inspects the right side, Prolog sees that it can satisfy the first part of that side by printing the phrase

```
Hello Earth
```

in the Dialog box. The rest of the rule then needs to be satisfied, because the comma in

,nl.

indicates that this is a compound rule with an "and" in the middle. The second part of the rule, "nl," needs to be satisfied. The "nl" means "new line." To satisfy this built-in predicate, Prolog only has to move to the next line of the Dialog box before printing anything else. The period at the end indicates this is the end of the rule. Both parts of the right side have succeeded: write and newline. Therefore, the left side succeeds and the goal has been met. Prolog returns the answer "True."

This may seem like too small a program to work over very hard, but try the following three things:

- Take out the comma and the "nl" in the rule. Then compile and run the program again, and use "greetings" as a goal. You'll see

Figure 6-11.   Sample rule and predicate

that the "True" comment in the Dialog box is printed immediately after the "Hello Earth" phrase.

- Put the comma and "nl" back. Then put the word "trace" above the word "predicates." Then compile and run the program, using "greetings" as the goal again. Then use the F10 key to step through the program. You'll see Prolog work through each part of the rule.

- Finally, add a goal section to the program, as described in the following discussion.

Internal Versus External Goals

As mentioned before, there are two types of goals in Turbo Prolog: external and internal. Many Prologs get along with only external goals. So far in this book, you have been using external goals.

An *external goal* is one that you pose to the program in the Dialog window after the program has been edited and compiled and is running. You have seen external goals in action. Once the goal you type has been proven either true or false, the program will ask for another goal.

An *internal goal* has the same syntax as an external goal. The difference is that you enter it in the goal section of the program code. Then you complete editing, and compile and run the program. When the program has been run, it will automatically proceed to prove or disprove the goal and will report the answer to you. Then the program will end, and you won't be asked for another goal.

Add the two lines

```
goal
    greetings.
```

to the program you've been using just below the predicate declaration; then compile and run it. You have to press the space bar to end the program's run. You'll see the results in the Dialog window but won't see whether the goal is true or false.

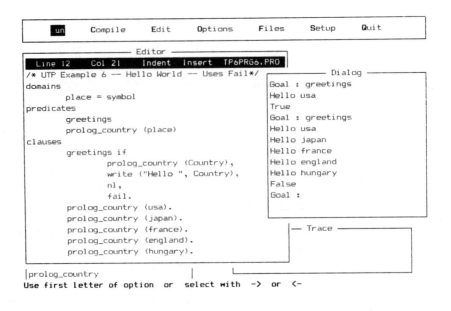

Figure 6-12. Program using a "fail" predicate

Back to Fail

Having the ability to type "greetings" into the onboard communications computer doesn't satisfy you. You want to send the world a series of messages, and you don't want to write a long series of these rules. Instead, you can use a single rule that includes the "fail" predicate and is then followed by the necessary data in facts.

The program in Figure 6-12 contains countries within its clauses. If you run this program without the "fail," you'll see that only the first country is greeted. Figure 6-12 shows the program and the results with the "fail" predicate at the end of the main rule. This predicate forces Turbo Prolog to backtrack to the beginning of the goal and to start over searching for matches. Each time Prolog finds one, it resatisfies the first subgoal by binding the variable to the country name; satisfies the second subgoal by printing "Hello" and the country's name; and then fails on the "fail" predicate, which is why it says "False" in the end. Fail forces backtracking as surely as cut eliminates it.

7

Domains, Arithmetic, And Recursion

Prolog wasn't originally designed to be good for arithmetic problems, but its clumsiness didn't last long. People who become proficient in a computer language usually want to use it for more and more types of tasks. Arithmetic facilities were soon added to Prolog, and the Turbo Prolog compiler has a full complement.

The discussion of arithmetic in this chapter is introduced by a more specific discussion of the domains section of a Turbo Prolog program. This part of the code usually protects you from the mistake of confusing argument types. It also helps many programs run faster, because such declarations often let the compiler more accurately pin down what sort of data it is dealing with and how much memory space it must reserve for that data.

Recursion is a staple of computer programming that lets you define some situations in simple terms that refer to themselves. It can seem confusing until you see it in action, but don't ignore it. It is fundamental to both arithmetic and list processing.

If you are used to type checking in a language such as Turbo Pascal, you can skim the "Domains" section of this chapter. You should probably read the arithmetic discussions, even if you know computer math quite well. The meaning of Prolog's logical arithmetic operators is sometimes not as obvious as it looks. But once you catch on to the style of arithmetic in Prolog, you should be able to finish the section in a hurry. The section entitled "Recursion" will again be redundant for advanced computer scientists, but its use in Prolog is definitely something you don't want to miss. Chapter 8 will provide an in-depth discussion of recursion.

Type Checking: Domain
And Predicate Declarations

The Turbo Prolog compiler uses *type checking* to improve the debugging of programs and to reduce the memory space requirements of those programs. Computer programs operate on a variety of types of data:

characters, symbols, integers, real numbers, and other types of structured information. Many operations are limited in the types of data they can work on. If the wrong type of data is used, a meaningless answer may result. Unfortunately, these errors are sometimes subtle and can therefore make debugging a program difficult.

If the types of data to be used are specified so that the language knows, each time it runs into a datum, whether that datum is real or integer, symbol or character, the compiler can scrutinize the source code to see if you are presenting an inappropriate type of data to an operation or predicate. If you are, you'll quickly receive an error message.

Turbo Prolog gets your help in type checking by asking for two declarations about the program's situation: it asks for predicates and domains. These sections are headed by the keywords "predicates" and "domains" in the Turbo Prolog program.

Predicates

In the predicates section of a Turbo Prolog program, you tell the compiler what predicates you're going to use (other than built-in predicates) and then specify the number and names of the arguments. You don't have to do this for built-in predicates, as Turbo Prolog already knows about them. Another kind of predicate declaration is *global*. If you want to have a declaration apply to more than one module, you should put it in a section headed by the keywords "global predicates." (See Chapter 12 for more details on global predicates.)

A typical predicate declaration might look like this:

```
predicatename (argument1,argument2)
```

However, predicates don't have to have any arguments. You could also use just

```
predicatename
```

in the declarations. Finally, you can have multiple predicate declarations, where the same predicate is defined more than once, each time with different argument domains, as in

```
predicatename (argument1,argument2)
predicatename (argument3,argument4,argument5)
```

or

```
has_toes (person,number)
has_toes (animal,number)
```

In this case, you'll be able to use the predicate in both ways. The different arguments also don't have to be of the same domain type.

Domains

Once Turbo Prolog knows which arguments go with which predicates, it needs to know what domain — what type of data — the arguments will be working with. The same arguments might be used with several predicates. For example, you might see the following:

```
has_toes (person,number)
has_fingers (person,number)
```

The compiler doesn't need a different domain declaration for each occurrence of "person" or "number," but it will want to know what those data will represent. This is done in the domains section, which is the first section in a Turbo Prolog program, preceded only by compiler directives and comments.

(If you want a domain declaration to apply to more than one program module, you put it in the global domains section, headed by those keywords as described in Chapter 12.)

Table 7-1 shows the standard domain types. You can also define your own types (which would be nonstandard, of course). The types are declared in the following four different formats. Remember that the words "argument1," "argument2," and so on, are just generic terms. A

Table 7-1.   Standard Domain Types

Symbol

There are two types of symbols: (1) A group of consecutive characters —letters, numbers, and underlines (by themselves, not underlines directly beneath a letter or number) —that begins with a lowercase character.

Examples

fred
freds__car
the__thing__in__the__cave

(2) A group of consecutive characters (letters and numbers) that begins and ends with double quotation marks ("). This type is useful if you wish to begin the symbol with an uppercase character or if you wish to include spaces between the characters within the symbol.

Symbols and strings look similar, and many objects can be used in either domain, but Turbo Prolog interprets them quite differently. Symbols take up more memory than strings but make matches more quickly when a program is run.

Examples

"fred"
"freds car that I drove into a tree."

String

Any group of consecutive characters (letters and numbers) that begins and ends with double quotation marks ("). This is the same as the second type of symbol described above. Remember, however, that symbols and strings are not treated the same by Turbo Prolog.

Examples

"fred"
"fred is a *&#%$&@*+"
"When in the course of human events it becomes necessary"

Table 7-1. Standard Domain Types (*continued*)

Integer

Any whole number from (and including) −32,768 to 32,767. The limit is imposed because the integers are stored as 16-bit values. Fifteen of the bits represent the number, and the sixteenth bit represents the sign of the number.

Examples

9
−200
21444

Real

Any real number in the range +/− 1E−307 to +/− 1E+308. The format includes these options: sign, number, decimal point, fraction, E (to indicate an exponent), sign for the exponent, exponent. Real numbers can range from very simple to very complex.

Examples

3
−3.1415926525E−218

(Both of these are reals, but it would be better in many cases to make the first one an integer instead of a real. The integer would take up less memory.)

Char

Any single character from the standard ASCII list, positioned between two single quotation marks (').

Examples

't'
'X'
'&'

File

To declare a file domain, you must declare the symbolic file names of the files you will use. You can only have a single file-domain declaration in a program, but that declaration

Table 7-1.   Standard Domain Types (*continued*)

may contain several symbolic file names. All symbolic file names must begin with a lowercase letter. There are two types of files.

(1) Predefined files. These are the files that are always available in Turbo Prolog. You don't have to declare these; in fact, you must not. Prolog knows they are there.

Examples

printer
keyboard
screen
com1

Note that "printer" refers to the parallel port and "com1" refers to the serial port. These examples are your only choices for file-domain declarations.

(2) User-defined files. These are files that you name. Any Turbo Prolog name that isn't reserved can be used.

Examples

thisfile
thatfile
the__other__file
employee__records__1986

---

real program would have argument words that you would choose.

- **Simple** This isn't the official name —these declarations are the normal ones that you'll find in almost every program. They use an equivalency of the form

```
argument1 = domain
```

  with the domain chosen from the standard list —integer, char, real, string, or symbol. An example that you've seen several times in this book is

```
person = symbol
```

If you have a number of these declarations in a row, you can shorten your typing work by using commas in between the arguments that have the same domain type. Instead of

```
argument1 = domain
argument2 = domain
argument3 = domain
```

you can write the single line

```
argument1, argument2, argument3 = domain.
```

In practical terms, instead of

```
price = integer
height = integer
position = integer
```

you could use

```
price, height, position = integer
```

- **List** This is used for list structures (which will be discussed later). Lists are made of multiple objects together in one piece of data. A declaration such as

```
thislist = things*
```

means that the individual objects in the list "thislist" (which is a single datum, even though it is a structure made up of smaller data) are each within the domain of "things." The asterisk is read as "list," so "things*" is read as "thingslist." The domain with the asterisk can be either a standard domain (see Table 7-1) or a user-defined domain.

- **Compound** Again, you haven't been introduced to compound objects yet, so gloss over this until the next chapter. Compound objects look like relationships within relationships. Here's an example:

```
predicate (argument1,predicate2 (argument3,argument4))
```

A practical example could be

```
person (first_name,last_name,dates(birth,start_employment))
```

The "predicate2" (or "dates") is called a *functor*. To declare a compound object, you declare the functor and then declare the domains of that functor's own arguments. The right side of such a declaration can also have several parts, each a declaration for a unique functor that can work in the original predicate.

- **File** This declaration is used when a program needs to refer to files by symbolic names. Only a single file declaration is permitted. That declaration uses an equivalency, with semicolons, to detail the files to be used:

```
file = thisfile ; thatfile ; othrfile
```

The best way to understand the predicate and domain declarations after this introduction is to look at example programs and to write (and debug) a few simple examples of your own. Also, list and file declarations will be discussed in more detail in the chapters devoted to lists and files.

Arithmetic

Turbo Prolog allows you to use numerous mathematical operations to work with both integers (between $-32,768$ and $32,767$) and real numbers (from $+/- 1E -307$ to $+/- 1E308$). The real numbers can have a sign, a mantissa, a decimal point, a fractional part, another sign, the "E" character (to set off the exponent), and an exponent. The sign, the fractional part with a decimal point, and the exponent are optional. Integers will be converted automatically to real numbers if the arithmetic operation requires it.

Turbo Prolog manipulates numbers with logical predicates. Not only do the arithmetic and mathematical predicates offer the normal possibilities for the success or failure of a goal, but the arguments of those predicates can be evaluated, using the predicates, to come up with a mathematical result. To make you feel at home, Turbo Prolog even offers you the ability to represent the standard arithmetic predicates as *infix* operators (operators that appear in between constants or variables). It also provides you with a generous list of logarithmic, trigonometric, and bit-oriented operations that can be used with standard predicate forms.

Operator Position

In general mathematics, an operation symbol doesn't have to be written in between the constants or variables, even though that is the way most of us learn to do it. The infix form

$$y * 4$$

may seem natural, but it isn't the only way this operation could be written. The signs $+$ and $-$ before a value just indicate whether it is positive or negative. They are unary operators and therefore don't have to be between two terms. It could also take the form

$$* y \ 4$$

which is called *prefix* notation. A common prefix operator is the minus sign as it is used to signify a negative number. Another possibility is to write an operation in *postfix* notation, as in the following:

$$y \ 4 \ *$$

The factorial symbol (!) is a common postfix mathematical operator. Unfortunately, it uses the same symbol (the exclamation mark) as the "cut" predicate in Prolog. Turbo Prolog doesn't include the factorial function as a built-in arithmetic ability, so you don't need to worry about confusing the two symbols.

Prolog could represent this multiplication as a relationship (*) between the two objects (the variable y and the constant 4). Here's how it would look:

```
*  (Y,4)
```

Either in this form or in the infix form, the operation doesn't mean that the values are actually being combined in the symbolized way. The operation just shows the relationship between the objects. When Turbo Prolog checks the predicate against the goal, the relationship will be evaluated.

Equality

The *equality* predicate is vital to working with arithmetic in Turbo Prolog. The equals sign (=) is used to indicate that the predicate succeeds if the objects on either side of the equality can be made to match. Instead of saying that the two things are equal, the predicate says that Prolog can try to make the two things equal by looking for the correct instantiated values. The operator is making a logical check; it is not assigning a value.

There are also inequalities that can be written as infix operators in Turbo Prolog. These relational operators are listed in Table 7-2. All of the relational operators work the same way, as you'll see in later examples.

Table 7-2.   Standard Relational Operators

Symbol	Meaning
<	Less than
>	Greater than
=	Equal to
<=	Less than or equal to
>=	Greater than or equal to
<> or ><	Not equal to

Table 7-3.   Standard Arithmetic Operators (Infix)

Symbol	Operation	Priority[1]	Operand 1 Domain	Operand 2 Domain	Result Domain
+	Addition	1	integer	integer	integer
			integer	real	real
			real	integer	real
			real	real	real
−	Subtraction	1	integer	integer	integer
			integer	real	real
			real	integer	real
			real	real	real
*	Multiplication	2	integer	integer	integer
			integer	real	real
			real	integer	real
			real	real	real
/	Division	2	integer	integer	real
			integer	real	real
			real	integer	real
			real	real	real
mod	Modulo division (result is the remainder of the division of operands 1 and 2)	3	integer	integer	integer
div	Div division (result is the quotient of the division of operands 1 and 2)	3	integer	integer	integer
+	Positive (unary)	4	integer		integer
			real		real
−	Negative (unary)[2]	4	integer		integer
			real		real

[1]"Priority" refers to the order in which operations are executed. Higher-priority operations are performed before lower-priority operations. Operations within parentheses are performed before those outside parentheses, and operations are performed from left to right within an expression. Both the "mod" and "div" operators have priority 3.

[2]"Unary" refers to the use of the symbol as a specification of the sign of a single value.

Arithmetic Operators

Table 7-3 lists the basic arithmetic functions in Turbo Prolog. It also shows what form of data the results will be in. As long as you remember that these are evaluated differently in Prolog than in a procedural language or in standard arithmetic, you can use the operators in the same sorts of expressions as you would in those other circumstances.

Table 7-3 also shows the order of precedence for the arithmetic operators. If a clause uses several operators, they are evaluated in the order shown in this table.

Addition and Subtraction

Take a look at the program shown in Figure 7-1. This demonstrates the use of the addition operator. The only clause is the "do __it" clause. It is

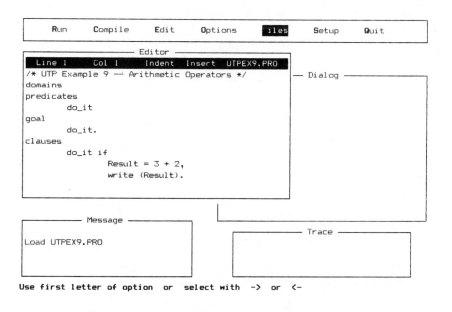

Figure 7-1. Use of the addition operator

also the only predicate that isn't built-in and is therefore the only predicate that needs a declaration. Also, the "do __it" predicate doesn't have any arguments, so it doesn't need any domain declarations.

The "do __it" rule can only succeed if the variable "Result" is instantiated to the value 5 *and* if that value is then written in the Dialog window. Because "do __it" is also the goal, that sequence is exactly what Prolog follows in its urge to satisfy the goal. The phrase "Press the SPACE bar" that appears in the running result (see Figure 7-2) is there because an internal goal was used.

Now take a look at Figure 7-3. The subtraction operator has been added to the rule. If you run this program, you'll get the result shown in the Dialog window of Figure 7-3. Why is the product of this program

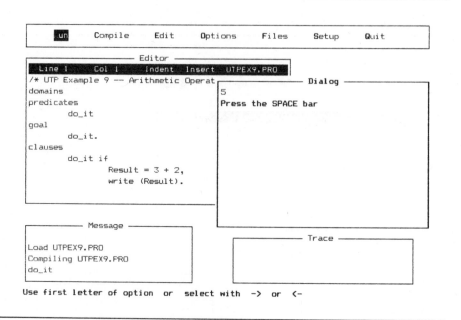

Figure 7-2.   The phrase "Press the SPACE bar" as a result of an internal goal

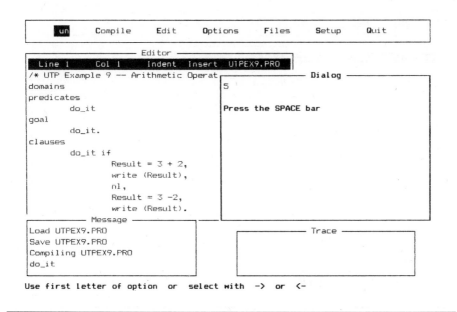

Figure 7-3.   Use of the subtraction operator

exactly the same as the product of the last program? Why wasn't the result of the subtraction written? Because this isn't BASIC or Pascal, and the equals sign doesn't work as an assignment statement that can give new values to variables.

Add the word "trace" to the top of the program (insert it on a new line just above "domains") and then recompile and run the program. Use the F10 key to step through the program's logic. Watch the steps in the Trace window. The seven major steps of the trace are shown in Figure 7-4. Here are the steps and an explanation of what has happened in each:

```
CALL:   goal()
```

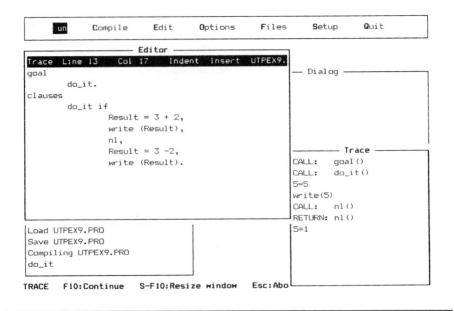

Figure 7-4. Major steps of the trace

Prolog has started by calling for the goal.

```
CALL:    do_it()
```

It then finds that the internal goal is the "do __it" predicate. Prolog finds a clause that matches that predicate and discovers that the clause is the beginning of a rule. It then moves to the right side of the rule and tries to satisfy the clauses there.

```
5=5
```

For the right-side clause, Prolog discovers an equality operator between a variable (on the left) and two constants (on the right). Prolog needs to find an instantiated value for the variable ("Result") before it can decide whether or not this clause succeeds. The equality operator along with the addition operator tells Prolog to use the arithmetic sum of the constants. It instantiates "Result" to that value, and then moves to the next clause. The commas between the clauses signify "and." They mean that all of the right-side clauses must be satisfied for the rule as a whole to be true.

```
write (5)
```

This clause asks Prolog to write the instantiated value of "Result." It does so. That is all that is necessary to satisfy the clause, so Prolog moves on. (Note that quotation marks are used in the text of this book to denote words as they appear on the screen. The quotation marks themselves should not be used unless indicated. For example, if the word "Result" had been enclosed in quotation marks within the parentheses, the write command would have written it as a word instead of writing its instantiated value.)

```
CALL:    nl () RETURN: nl ()
```

Be sure that you type "nl," which stands for "new line," with a lowercase l, not a 1. The "nl" predicate is built-in, and only needs the Dialog window cursor to move to a new line to be satisfied.

```
5=1
```

Finally, Prolog runs into a roadblock. It has been successfully satisfying each of the clauses on the right side of the "do __it" rule. It needs to satisfy that rule to satisfy the goal. But when it finds the expression

```
Result = 3 - 2
```

it isn't on the same ground as when it added 3 and 2 earlier. Instead of an equality with an unbound variable and several constants, this is an equality with a bound variable and several constants. Therefore, instead of evaluating the right side of the equality and binding the left-side variable to that value, Turbo Prolog merely checks to see if the two sides are actually equal. They have values that allow such a check.

Because the two sides aren't equal, the clause fails, the rule fails, and the goal fails. Turbo Prolog never gets to the final "write" predicate.

As you see, an uninstantiated variable can be used almost as if you were in a procedural language with assignment statements. This is true for both equalities and inequalities. The value of the instantiated and constant values will be bound to the free variable. This is called having them *share* the value. In a clause that doesn't have a free variable, however, Prolog will mathematically evaluate the expression and then deal with its truth or falsehood.

Figure 7-5 shows how this program could be rewritten to work.

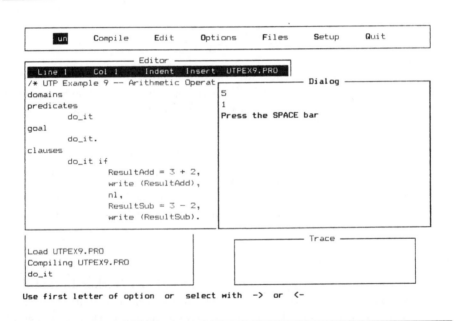

Figure 7-5. Rewritten program showing how Turbo Prolog will work

Multiplication and Division

Multiplication and division are performed with the standard infix symbols * and /. Two other division operators, "mod" and "div," can be written in infix form. The "mod" operator returns the remainder of a division; "div" returns the quotient. Don't uppercase them, or you'll turn them into variables instead of built-in operators. If "AnswerA" and "AnswerB" are unbound variables,

```
AnswerA = 9 div 4
```

will instantiate "AnswerA" to 2, and

```
AnswerB = 9 mod 4
```

will instantiate "AnswerB" to 1.

Mathematical Predicates

Table 7-4 lists a number of built-in mathematical predicates that you can use in Turbo Prolog. Each of these uses the standard Prolog format

```
relationship (object)
```

and will perform like the arithmetic functions previously described. Expressions with free variables will attempt to instantiate those variables, and expressions without free variables will be inspected for their success or failure.

The logarithmic and trigonometric operations are explained in Table 7-4. They work on a single argument and return the proper calculated value of that argument.

The bit-field operations work on three arguments. [Bit operations are primarily used to program ports and other hardware aspects of your PC. For more information on bit operations, see a book such as *An Introduction to Microcomputers: Volume 1*, 2d ed., by Adam Osborne (Berkeley, CA: Osborne/McGraw-Hill, 1980).] The operations, bitand,

Table 7-4.   Standard Mathematical Predicates

Miscellaneous

abs (x)	Binds x to absolute value of original x.
sqrt (x)	(Binds x to square root of original x.
random (x)	Binds x to "random" real number so that $0 <= x < 1$.

Logarithmic

log (x)	Binds x to base-10 logarithm of original x.
ln (x)	Binds x to base-e logarithm of original x.
exp (x)	Binds x to value of e raised to original x power.

Trigonometric (require x to be an angle value in radians)

cos (x)	Binds x to cosine of original x.
sin (x)	Binds x to sine of original x.
tan (x)	Binds x to tangent of original x.
arctan (x)	Binds x to arctangent of original x.

Bit-Logic

If x and y are bound to integer values when one of these predicates is called, the predicate will translate those integer values into signed, 16-bit binary values, perform the given operation on those values, translate the result back into an integer, and bind z to that integer. The bitnot predicate performs in the same fashion but only needs to deal with a single input value: x.

bitand (x,y,z)	Binds z to logical result of AND operation on x and y.
bitor (x,y,z)	Binds z to logical result of OR operation on x and y.
bitxor (x,y,x)	Binds z to logical result of XOR operation on x and y.
bitnot (x,z)	Binds z to logical result of NOT operation on x.

Bit-Shift

If x and n are bound to integer values, the bit-shift operation will translate the x value into a 16-bit, signed binary value, shift that value n spaces in the given direction, translate the result into an integer value, and bind y to that integer.

bitleft (x,n,y)	Binds y to result of shifting x left n positions.
bitright (x,n,y)	Binds y to result of shifting x right n positions.

bitor, bitnot, and bitxor will take the bound integer values of the first two arguments, translate them into 16-bit binary numbers, perform the appropriate binary operation, and bind the third argument (if it is a free variable) to that value. The other bit-field operations, bitleft and bitright, translate the bound integer value of the first argument into a 16-bit binary value, shift that binary value as many places as the second argument's value, and then bind the final, shifted value to the third argument.

Even with the bit-field operations, *the math isn't the same as in procedural languages*. The expression won't just get evaluated. If there is a free variable, the expression will be used to instantiate it. If there isn't a free variable, the expression will be evaluated to see if the arguments match —if they make mathematical sense together. If they do, the predicate succeeds. If they don't, the predicate fails.

While you're experimenting, remember that you can choose to leave any of the three arguments with a free variable. You don't have to work forward. You can work backward to see what the shift value would have been or what the first argument value before an AND operation would have been.

Arithmetic Summary

Do some calculating. If you run into trouble, trace what you're doing. You probably fell back into thinking procedurally instead of "Prologically." However, there is another common source of error: computer mathematics is sometimes less accurate than you might think. Turbo Prolog might calculate a difficult value to the extent of the computer's available accuracy, and still come up with 0.999999999 when you expected 1.00000000. Sometimes you'll need to watch for results that are nearly right but not exactly correct.

Recursion

Recursion is an important computer science concept. In Prolog, this topic could easily be discussed in Chapter 5 (because recursion sends control of the goal search back to itself) or in this chapter (because the factorial operation is the first sort of recursion people normally learn about in school). However, it is most useful with lists, so you'll examine it in detail in that chapter. In this chapter you will take a quick look at how Prolog recursion works and how you can figure a factorial value with it. You will look at the EXAMPL10.PRO program on the Library/Example disk.

Recursion is used to describe operations —not necessarily mathematical at all —that call themselves as part of a process. The factorial operation is recursive and is symbolized in general mathematics by an exclamation mark. The factorial looks like this:

$$Y!$$

This expression is evaluated as

$$Y! = Y * Y{-}1 * Y{-}2 * Y{-}3 \ldots * 1$$

The ellipsis ($\ldots$) signifies that there may be several numbers that you don't want to write out. Any factorialized number is equal to the number times itself and times every integer value less than itself down to 1. Don't repeat any integers on the way down, however. The series of $Y{-}1$, $Y{-}2$, and so on, is just there to show how this would work for large numbers.

To describe the factorial operation in a recursive way, you would write

$$Y! = Y * (Y{-}1)!$$

As you can see, for any number greater than 5 or 6, the recursive definition of a factorial is much shorter and easier to write. This definition says that "Y factorial is equal to Y times the factorial value of Y minus 1."

But how do you know what $(Y{-}1)!$ is equal to? You reuse —recursively call —the definition.

$$(Y{-}1)! = (Y{-}1) * ((Y{-}1){-}1)!$$

A recursive expression can get out of hand without a solid endpoint. The factorial operation stops when 1 is reached. Other recursive expressions need to have similar limits imposed. The computer uses a *stack* —a logical creation of its own in memory —to save the values and variables mentioned on the search for the recursive endpoint. If the definition asks for too many levels of recursion, the stack could overflow: the data could be lost and the recursive value would come back in error. You can increase the size of the stack by going into the Miscellaneous Settings submenu of the Setup menu. (This isn't something you need to know how to do until you're an advanced programmer.)

Figure 7-6.   The EXAMPL10.PRO program on the Library/Example disk

Eventually, the recursive expression reaches the limit. It can then find an endpoint value that will work back through the many levels of parentheses to the final result. Remember, this factorial operation is not being shown in Prolog syntax. The parentheses do not contain relationships and objects; this is regular mathematics.

In Prolog, a recursive predicate definition marks the temporary CALL and RETURN points along the way and then, after grabbing an endpoint value for instantiation, works back up the chain to the beginning. This can be very powerful when you are working with long lists that need to be inspected, pulled apart, and put back together. You can even define recursive objects.

Turbo Prolog doesn't offer a factorial facility as a built-in operator. Figure 7-6 shows Example Program 10 (EXAMPL10.PRO) on the Library/Example disk. The program demonstrates how to build a recursive definition of the factorial.

8

Structures: Functors, Lists, And Strings

In most applications, you'll want to employ more complex data types than you've used up to this point. The ability to build data structures is fundamental to any sort of practical computing. Turbo Prolog not only allows more complex arguments, but it also has a number of built-in powers for manipulating lists of data. It even has built-in predicates that operate on strings as though they were lists.

So far in this book, you have dealt only with simple objects. Even if a predicate had an arity greater than one, each of its arguments was shallow, with no deeper structure. But in the last chapter's discussion of domain declarations, you learned that other, more complex structures were possible. If you're an experienced Prolog programmer, you know about complex objects and lists. However, pay some attention to the part of this chapter entitled "domain declarations." If you are not an experienced Prolog programmer, spend more time on this chapter than you've spent on the others. You can't have too clear an understanding of list manipulation. Use the Trace facility to follow the programs.

Functors

You know by now that a relationship and its objects are often written in Turbo Prolog as

```
relationship (object,object)
```

with the relationship preceding the objects and the objects surrounded by parentheses. You also know that this can be expressed as

```
predicate (argument,argument)
```

This is the only structure you've used so far. However, it won't always do. Even if you don't use lists (discussed later in this chapter), you can simplify the representation of knowledge by using more complex objects in your clauses.

For instance, a list of bills to be paid could be written as a series of facts:

```
paid (phillip,food)
paid (phillip,phone)
paid (phillip,rent)
paid (phillip,store)
```

Compound objects let you add more detail to the clauses. The following is an example using the information just presented:

```
paid (phillip, food  (good_earth,23.50))
paid (phillip, phone (pacbell,9999999,55.55))
paid (phillip, rent (landlords,1000))
paid (phillip, store (macys,250))
```

When an argument is itself a predicate, it is called a *functor*. The arguments of a functor are called *components*. Therefore, the structure of the clause just shown with compound objects looks like this:

```
predicate (argument), functor (component,component))
```

You wouldn't want to do this indefinitely, because too many levels of parentheses could make the program too difficult to read. Used in moderation, however, compound objects can make a program easier to organize. Also, even the components of the compound object can themselves be compound objects.

Predicate and Domain Declarations
For Compound Objects

One problem you may have with compound objects in Turbo Prolog is properly declaring the predicates and domains. Figure 8-1 shows a program for the bill-paying facts shown in the last section, along with the proper declarations.

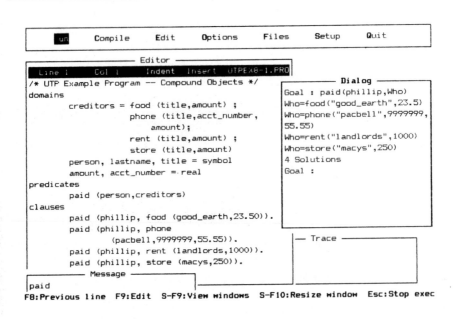

Figure 8-1. Bill-paying program with proper declarations

Figure 8-2 shows what happens if you set some external goals for the same program: it returns the entire functors with their components. In Figure 8-1, the use of the variable in the second position returned a list of all of the bills paid (along with their details). In Figure 8-2, the use of a variable in the first position accompanied by a constant ("phone") in the second position brought back an answer as to who had paid for the phone. The second goal needed the three blank variables. If it didn't have those, the goal functor "phone" wouldn't have matched the clauses functor "phone" (which had three arguments).

By carefully choosing the language of the functors and components, you can get useful answers from such a structure. You need to

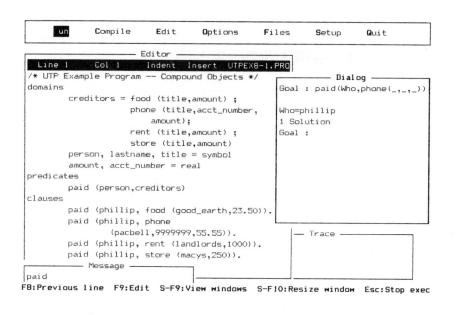

Figure 8-2.   External goals set for bill-paying program

declare each functor and the domains for all of that functor's components. Each functor must be unique, but the right side of a domain
declaration may have several alternatives separated by semicolons.

Lists

A list is just another form of a compound object, but it is an important
data structure. A list looks like a collection of terms —in this case,
elements —separated by commas and placed inside square brackets. Here

is a list of integers:

```
[1,2,3,5,8,13]
```

Here is another list of numbers:

```
[2,8,3.9E4,18,-200]
```

This is a list of symbols:

```
[igneous,metamorphic,sedimentary]
```

The following is a list of the same symbols represented as strings (which will be explained in the next section):

```
["igneous","metamorphic","sedimentary"]
```

Finally, this list containing nothing at all is called the *empty* list:

```
[]
```

Domain Declarations

As mentioned in the previous chapter, domain declarations for lists are not very different from declarations for other types of objects. The declaration, in a general form, looks like this:

```
domains
        thingslist = things*
        things = objects
```

The asterisk indicates that there are zero or more elements in the list. The first line of the declaration means that every object in the list "things-list" belongs to the type "things." All of the objects in any list must be of a single type, but because you can define the types to be as complex as you wish, that restriction won't be too confining. The second line defines "things" in terms of the standard domain declarations. Your declaration could be simpler if you used one of the standard types in the first line. For instance,

```
domains
      numberslist = integer*
```

declares that all the objects in "numberslist" are integers. You don't need a second line.

List Manipulation

Prolog works on a list by dividing the list into a *head* and a *tail*. The head of a list is the first member on the left. The tail is the rest of the list. The list

```
[list]
```

has the structural division written with a vertical bar between the head and the tail, as shown here:

```
[head | tail]
```

Because a list is just another type of object, it must be enclosed in parentheses when used in a clause, as shown here:

```
predicate ([list])
```

Here is another example:

```
predicate ([head|tail])
```

Again, because a list is an object, it can be used as you have used other objects. For instance, you can have several objects for a single predicate:

```
predicate ([list1],[list2],[list3])
```

Head and Tail Matching

The only other process you need to understand at present is how Prolog finds the head and tail. After that, you can use lists in the same situations in which you would use other objects. The processes of backtracking, instantiation, and so on work just the same with lists as they do with other objects.

Take a look at the program in Figure 8-3. This is a short program that uses a list. (Notice that the members of the list may be continued on consecutive lines if commas are present. This makes the program easier

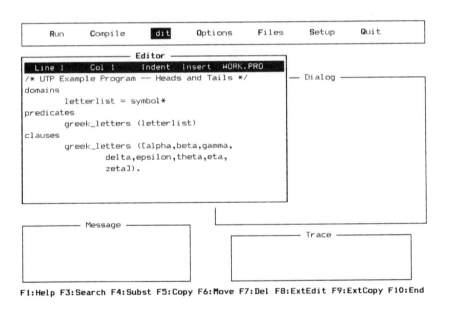

Figure 8-3.   Short program using a list

to read in a given window size.) If you use the goal shown in Figure 8-4

```
greek_letters ([Head:Tail])
```

where the words "Head" and "Tail" are used as variables, Prolog will tell
you what the head and tail of the list are. You could have used any other
variable names, such as X and Y.

    If you use the Trace window, you can see what happened as this goal
was pursued. Add the word "trace" above the word "domains" in the
program. Then recompile, run the program, pose the goal again, and use
the F10 key to step through the action. Figure 8-5 shows a large Trace
window containing notices about the steps you'll see.

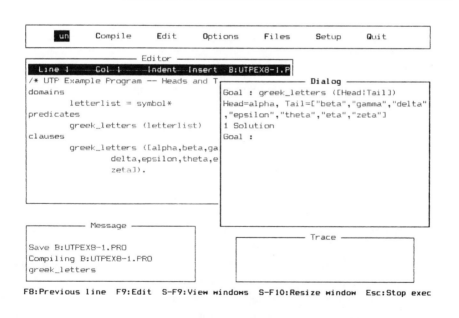

Figure 8-4. Using a goal with head and tail

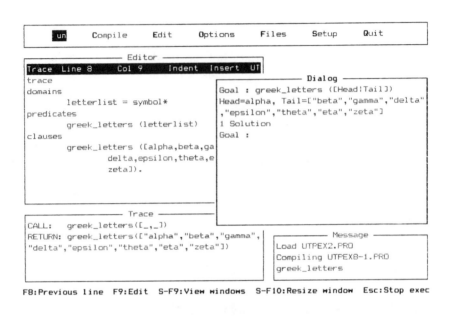

Figure 8-5.   Tracing the program

There are only three steps. The system looks for a clause that will match the goal. In this case, the predicate has to match, the number of arguments has to be the same, and the arguments themselves must directly match, or be made to match through legal instantiations. The only clause matches the "greek_letters" predicate. This predicate also has only one argument, and it therefore matches the second requirement. Finally, the actual list of the clause can be instantiated to the unbound variables of the goal to make a complete match. The system calls for the clause, returns the clause with the instantiated values, and then splits the list into a head and a tail.

Take the word "trace" out of the program, recompile and run, and use this goal:

```
greek_letters ([A,B!C])
```

Figure 8-6 shows the result. This goal splits the list into three parts: A and B are the first two elements of the list, and C is the tail (the rest of the list). Again, the tail is itself a list. It is always a list, even when there are no members left and it is an empty list. Try the goal

```
greek_letters ([A,B,C,D,E,F,G,H!I])
```

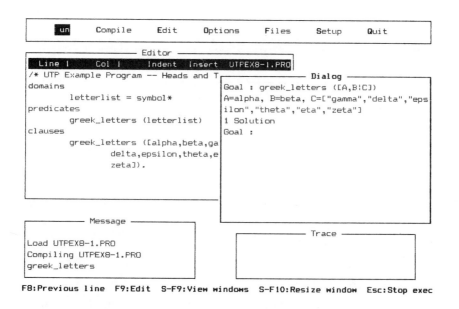

Figure 8-6. Goal split into three parts

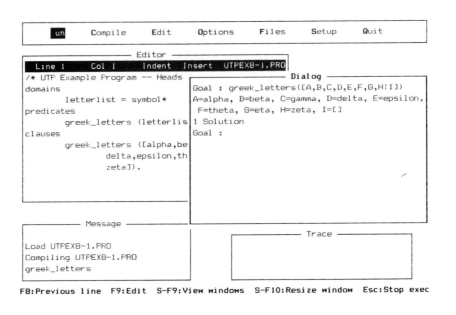

Figure 8-7.   Matching the letter "I" to the tail

to demonstrate that point (see Figure 8-7). This division takes longer than any program you have used so far. (If you want to know why, put the Trace command back in and see all the steps Prolog had to go through to get to the result.) "I" is matched to the tail and is shown as an empty list:

```
I=[]
```

If the original list is empty, both the head and the tail are undefined. Figure 8-8 shows how this looks on the screen. Figure 8-9 shows what happens if the head of the goal list doesn't match the head of the clause list. There is no solution to the goal; as with any other goal, the arguments must match in order to satisfy the goal.

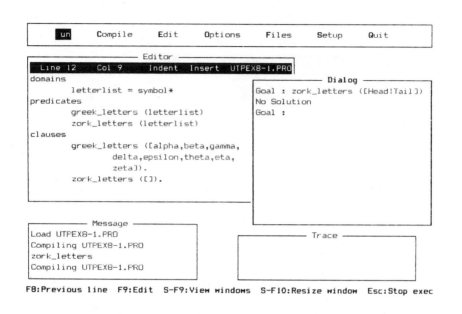

Figure 8-8. Empty list with head and tail undefined

Lists of Lists

You can make structures as complex as you want in Prolog. As previously demonstrated in this chapter, you can put compound objects within compound objects. You can also put lists within lists. The list

```
animals ([mammals,reptiles,birds,fish])
```

could be given more depth. Each element could be a list:

```
animals ([[monkey, buffalo, rat], [snake, iguana, crocodile],
[seagull, penguin], [bass, salmon]])
```

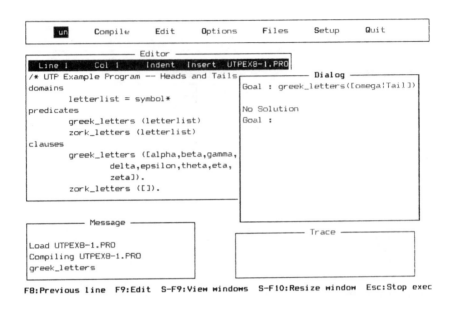

Figure 8-9.   Head of goal list not matching head of clause list

Also, each element could have a functor and a list as the functor's object, as in the following:

```
animals (mammals ([monkey, buffalo,rat]), reptiles ([snake,
iguana, crocodile]), birds ([seagull, penguin]), fish
([bass,salmon]))
```

Recursion

Many of the manipulations you'll want to perform on lists are easily written as recursive operations —operations that invoke themselves. A simple example is checking to see if a particular object is an element of a list. Suppose you have a geographical database that includes a list of these cities in Ohio and California:

```
cleveland
cincinnati
columbus
dayton
akron
zanesville
cupertino
santa_cruz
yreka
gualala
fresno
```

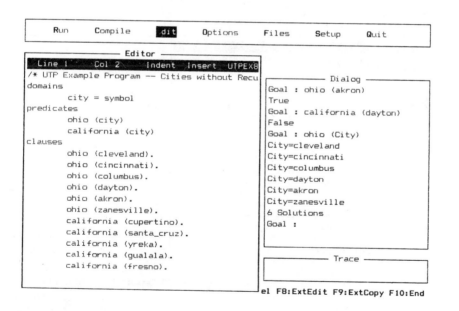

Figure 8-10.   Program listing facts about cities

To see if a particular city is in Ohio or in California, you could start by listing facts about the cities. See Figure 8-10 for a program that does just that. The program could be questioned by a goal such as

```
ohio (akron)
```

or the goal

```
california (dayton)
```

Lists and recursive member definitions will do the same thing in less space. The use of lists also lets you add more cities and states to the facts

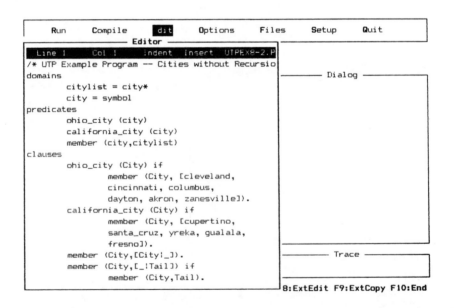

```
    Run      Compile     dit      Options    Files     Setup    Quit
                      Editor
   Line 1      Col 1     indent   insert   UTPEX8-2.P
 /* UTP Example Program -- Cities without Recursio
 domains                                                      Dialog
         citylist = city*
         city = symbol
 predicates
         ohio_city (city)
         california_city (city)
         member (city,citylist)
 clauses
         ohio_city (City) if
                 member (City, [cleveland,
                 cincinnati, columbus,
                 dayton, akron, zanesville]).
         california_city (City) if
                 member (City, [cupertino,
                 santa_cruz, yreka, gualala,
                 fresno]).
         member (City,[City!_]).                               Trace
         member (City,[_!Tail]) if
                 member (City,Tail).
                                              8:ExtEdit F9:ExtCopy F10:End
```

Figure 8-11. Lists replacing predicates

without having to make a tediously long list of all the predicates for each.

The program in Figure 8-11 shows how lists can replace the predicates in the previous program. This program is just as long as the previous program, but it is set up for a more general case and would therefore be shorter if more facts about cities were added.

The first two clauses are fairly straightforward. They define a city as being in a state if it is part of that state's city list. The next two clauses are the recursive heart of the operation. These two clauses tell Turbo Prolog how to determine if a city is an element of a city list by breaking that list down one step at a time.

Try this goal:

```
ohio_city (zanesville)
```

You'll get the result "True." Use the Trace command in the program to step through it and to see how the result was obtained. Figure 8-12 shows the effects in the Trace window. The first step is to call for the goal, as in the following:

```
CALL: ohio_city ("zanesville")
```

This immediately leads to the "ohio" rule in the clauses section. To satisfy this rule, Prolog moves over to the right side and takes up the subgoal:

```
CALL:  member ("zanesville", ["cleveland", "columbus",
"cincinnati", "dayton","akron","zanesville"])
```

To satisfy this goal —to know if "zanesville" is an element of the list —Prolog must move down to the "member" clauses.

The first "member" clause states that a city is a member of a city list if that city is the head of the list. In our case, it is not. The head of the list is "cleveland," and that cannot be matched to "zanesville."

The next "member" clause must be tried. It states that a city is a member of a list (or is an element in the list) if that city is an element of the tail of the list. Together with the previous clause, this makes sense. A

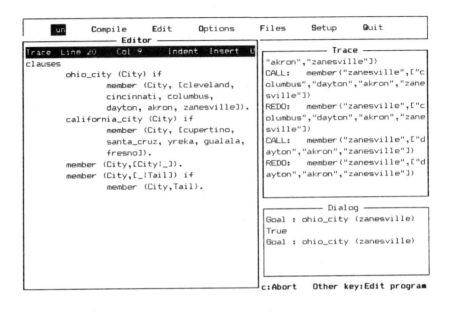

```
   un     Compile    Edit    Options    Files    Setup    Quit
              Editor
Trace  Line 20    Col 9    Indent  Insert  U        Trace
clauses                                         "akron","zanesville"])
      ohio_city (City) if                       CALL:   member("zanesville",["c
            member (City, [cleveland,            olumbus","dayton","akron","zane
            cincinnati, columbus,                sville"])
            dayton, akron, zanesville]).         REDO:   member("zanesville",["c
      california_city (City) if                  olumbus","dayton","akron","zane
            member (City), [cupertino,           sville"])
            santa_cruz, yreka, gualala,          CALL:   member("zanesville",["d
            fresno]).                            ayton","akron","zanesville"])
      member (City,[City!_]).                    REDO:   member("zanesville",["d
      member (City,[_!Tail]) if                  ayton","akron","zanesville"])
            member (City,Tail).

                                                           Dialog
                                                Goal : ohio_city (zanesville)
                                                True
                                                Goal : ohio_city (zanesville)


                                                c:Abort   Other key:Edit program
```

Figure 8-12.   Effects shown in Trace window

list is completely made up of its head and its tail; therefore, any element in the list will be in either the head or the tail.

The blank variables in each clause signify that you don't care about the other part of the list. If an element is the head of a list, you don't care what's in the tail. If the element is within the tail, you don't care what the head is, even though in the present case you have already checked the head for a match.

Turbo Prolog has stepped through several levels of goals to get to this point, but it must work through yet another subgoal. To fulfill the "member" subgoal, Turbo Prolog must satisfy the final clause: a rule that says a city is a member of a city list if it is an element of the tail of that list. Prolog determines if the city is an element of the tail by treating the tail as a new list (which, of course, it is) and dissecting it using the two "member" clauses.

This process is the recursion. As you press the F10 key to step through the trace of this program, the Trace window will show shorter and shorter lists. Each time Turbo Prolog comes to the final clause and realizes that it must determine if "zanesville" is a member of the new tail, it retreats to the first member clause, slices a new head from that clause, compares "zanesville" to the head, and then returns to the final "member" clause again if the heads don't match. This process appears as a series of CALL and REDO messages in the Trace window. At that point "zanesville" will be the head of the list and the "zanesville" goal will match with it.

Because Turbo Prolog went through a long series of recursive layers, it must back out again through those same definitions. That is, once it knows that "zanesville" matches the head of the list, "[zanesville]," it can back up one level and know that "zanesville" is a member of the "[akron,zanesville]" list. Then it can know that "zanesville," as a member of the tail at each stage, is also a member of the list composed of the tail and a head. Turbo Prolog will back up through these lists with RETURN statements, as in the following:

```
[zanesville]
[akron, zanesville]
[dayton, akron, zanesville]
[columbus, dayton, akron, zanesville]
[cincinnati, columbus, dayton, akron, zanesville]
[cleveland, cincinnati, columbus, dayton, akron, zanesville]
```

Then it will return to the "ohio" clause, with the affirmation that "zanesville" is in "ohio." The answer "True" will appear in the Dialog window, and the program will be ready for a new goal.

Use the Trace window to follow this sort of recursion until you understand how it works. At each stage, the stack in memory keeps track of how many levels of subgoals and returns have been made. This method of untangling lists is vital to all aspects of list manipulation. For instance, writing out all of the elements of a list could be accomplished with the two recursive clauses

```
write_list_elements ([]).
write_list_elements ([Head¦Tail]) if
    write (Head) and
    write (Tail).
```

The second clause would write the head of the full list and then make a new list of the tail. The first clause would then be examined to see if the new list was empty. If it was, the writing would be done. (This endpoint makes the routine stop and protects memory from a stack gone wild.) If the new list wasn't empty, the second clause would be called again recursively to cut a new head off the list, write the head, and make an even newer list of the now-shorter tail.

Appending

You can build many general-purpose predicates to work on lists. One that you'll find in almost any Prolog book is an "append" predicate. You can define

```
append (firstlist, secondlist, newlist)
```

to mean that the first list and the second list are combined in that order to produce a longer, new list. The second list is appended to the end of the first list. A recursive way to do this is to use the following two clauses:

```
append ([], B_List, B_List).
append ([Head¦Tail_old], B_List, [Head¦Tail_new]) if
    append (Tail_old, B_List, Tail_new).
```

Figure 8-13 shows these clauses in action. The same predicate can be used to join lists, as shown in the first goal. It can also be used to split a list, as shown in the second and third goals. It can either discover a particular solution or show all the solutions for splitting the list (as shown in Figure 8-14).

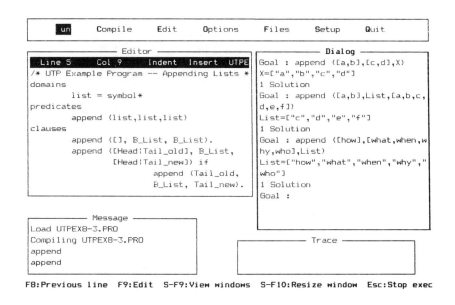

```
    un      Compile    Edit    Options    Files    Setup    Quit

 ─── Editor ───                              ─── Dialog ───
 Line 5    Col 9    Indent  Insert  UTPE     Goal : append ([a,b],[c,d],X)
 /* UTP Example Program -- Appending Lists * X=["a","b","c","d"]
 domains                                     1 Solution
        list = symbol*                       Goal : append ([a,b],List,[a,b,c,
 predicates                                  d,e,f])
        append (list,list,list)              List=["c","d","e","f"]
 clauses                                     1 Solution
        append ([], B_List, B_List).         Goal : append ([how],[what,when,w
        append ([Head:Tail_old], B_List,     hy,who],List)
             [Head:Tail_new]) if             List=["how","what","when","why","
                    append (Tail_old,        who"]
                    B_List, Tail_new).       1 Solution
                                             Goal :

 ─── Message ───
 Load UTPEX8-3.PRO
 Compiling UTPEX8-3.PRO                      ─── Trace ───
 append
 append

 F8:Previous line   F9:Edit   S-F9:View windows   S-F10:Resize window   Esc:Stop exec
```

Figure 8-13.   Recursive clauses

Strings as Lists

Turbo Prolog has several built-in predicates to handle *strings*. Strings are sequences of letters or characters. A string variable in Turbo Prolog may be bound to a string with a maximum of 64K characters. A string constant may consist of a maximum of 250 characters. The string data type is the one most often used to represent words and sentences. It is therefore very important for natural-language processing, one of Turbo Prolog's strengths. Two basic string predicates, "frontchar" and "frontstr," work on much the same principles as those previously explained for lists.

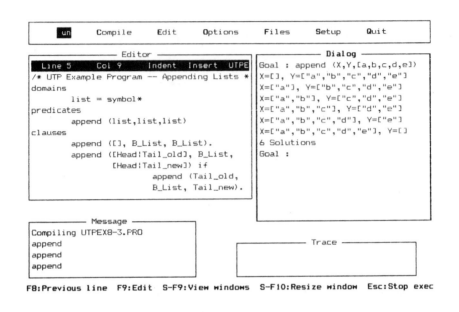

Figure 8-14.   Solutions to splitting the list

Built-in predicates are listed alphabetically in the "Reference Guide" section of the Turbo Prolog *Owner's Handbook*. In that section, each of the listings includes a selection of parenthetical comments such as "(o,o,o)," "(i,o)," or "(i)." The reason for this is that most predicates can work in several ways. The "i" stands for "instantiated." The "o" stands for "open," as in "unbound." Both refer to the arguments of the predicates.

For instance, the predicate

```
isname (StringParam)
```

only has the possibility "(i)." That means the argument must be instantiated when the predicate is reached in order for the predicate to succeed. If it isn't instantiated, Prolog won't look for something to instantiate —it will simply fail the predicate.

On the other hand, the predicate

```
right (Angle)
```

refers to the angle of the graphics turtle (discussed later in the book). This predicate has two alternatives: "(i)" or "(o)." The "Angle" can be instantiated or open. If it is instantiated when the predicate is reached, the turtle will be turned to that angle. If "Angle" is not instantiated when the predicate is reached, the opposite will happen —"Angle" will be instantiated to the actual, present angle of the turtle.

All of the predicates work in these ways. When "(o)" is available, the predicate can read from the situation into the variable to achieve success. When "(i)" is available, the argument must already have a value that can then be tested for success or written to the situation.

frontchar (String,FrontChar, RestString)

This predicate finds the front character of a string. The three arguments have the domain types string, char, and string, respectively.

frontstr (NumberOfChars,String1, StartStr,String2)

This is another "append" sort of predicate, except that this one is specialized. The four arguments have the domain types integer, string, string, and string, respectively. If you enter an integer for "NumberOf-Chars" and enter a "StartStr" (starting string), the predicate will return a "String1" of that many characters from the beginning of "StartStr" and a "String2" of the rest of the characters from "StartStr."

Up to now this book has discussed the basics of using Turbo Prolog. This section will introduce some of the program's unique features that will enable you to write more sophisticated and powerful programs. These advanced topics include windows, graphics, sound, and compiler features.

9

Writing, Reading, and Windows

This chapter is important because you probably don't want to create just short programs and see them work in the Dialog window. Although the heart of Prolog is the logical engine (which doesn't specify input and output niceties), you probably want more than "True" and "False" answers to the goals you pose. Add what you'll learn in this chapter to the file-handling, sound, and graphics information that you'll discover in the next chapters, and you can customize your interface as much as you want.

This and the succeeding chapters will run you through a heavy course of standard predicates. After the simple reading and writing predicates that will be described first, you'll quickly move into territory that is specific to Turbo Prolog and not to other Prologs. Up to this point in the book, most of what you have learned is germane to almost any Prolog. Only the syntax shows much difference.

However, the Turbo Prolog I/O predicates and special functions (such as windowing) are just not available or are handled by quite different predicates in other implementations of Prolog. Files, graphics, sound, and the like are different in Turbo Prolog than in other Prologs (as you will learn in later chapters). This is because such predicates are the procedural elements of Prolog and are not the direct descendants of pure logic. They are the elements least standardized in the field of logic programming.

The predicates are fairly straightforward, and you should be able to do much of your work with just a few reading, writing, and windowing predicates. You can come back later to learn the more specialized ones.

Two Ways to Work

Many of the standard predicates in Prolog work in two ways: they take bound argument values and assert these to the system; or they take free arguments and instantiate them to the current relevant values in the system. The "Reference Guide" of the Borland *Owner's Handbook* uses the specifiers "(o)" and "(i)" to indicate when a predicate can work with open (or previously free) and instantiated (or previously bound) variables. The state of the variable for the argument at the time the predicate is called is what counts. The words "free" and "bound" are used in the tables throughout this chapter. The two following standard predicates let you determine if a variable is free or bound.

free (Variable)

This predicate succeeds if the variable that it refers to is not instantiated to any value.

bound (Variable)

This predicate succeeds if the variable that it refers to is instantiated to some value.

findall

After specifying the predicate and variable name that you are interested in, you can use "findall" as the program runs to make a list of the values to which the variable successfully binds. This can be useful for tracing or for collecting correct answers to a particular logical exploration. Example Program 49 on the Library/Example disk uses "findall" to grab a series of numbers for averaging.

Simple I/O

Because Turbo Prolog has a built-in windowing system (and its Editor), you haven't needed to make your programs perform serious I/O operations like those required by other programming languages. All four windows — Editor, Trace, Message, and Dialog — have been busy displaying messages and results. In some Prologs, the only gesture toward friendliness is to show a question-mark prompt on the display. With these unfriendly computers, if you pose a goal that ends up being true, all you get is the question mark again. By such standards, Turbo Prolog is practically verbose.

However, the built-in windows are intended mainly as a development system. They are meant to get you to a working program, not necessarily to be part of that program. They shouldn't be seen as the only permanent home for a practical application you might develop. For that, you can build your own windows and read and write through them.

Writing

Old-fashioned (pre-Turbo) Prologs offered a printing command called "pp," which stands for "Pretty Print." That predicate helped the programmer put characters in the right places on the display. Turbo Prolog doesn't have a Pretty Print, but it does have several writing predicates, as shown in Table 9-1.

write

The first of the writing predicates is the general-use "write" predicate that you already know. The "write" predicate succeeds when it writes the arguments that follow it onto the screen at the current cursor position. Because "write" is defined as

```
write (e1,e2,e3,...,eN)
```

you can attach to it as many arguments as you would like. With a flow definition of "(i)," you can define each and any of the arguments as a constant (of a standard domain type) or an instantiated variable. (The

Table 9-1.   Standard Writing Predicates

---

write (e 1,e2,e3, . . .,eN)   (I*)

Writes any number of constants or instantiated variables in the active window of the active "writedevice." The asterisk means that it can work with an optional number of arguments.

nl

The "nl" predicate stands for *newline*. Causes the cursor to move to the next line of the active window or display. Any writing or reading done after "nl" will occur from the new cursor position. Technically, it writes a carriage return and a line feed to the active e "writedevice." This predicate has no arguments.

writedevice (SymbolicFileName)   symbol — (I) (O)

Lets you specify the active (current) "writedevice." It can work with any of three types of "SymbolicFileName" —one of the predefined symbolic files (screen or printer); a user-defined symbolic file name for an open file; or an unbound variable. If an unbound variable is used, the predicate will bind "SymbolicFileName" to the name of the current "writedevice." Values must be within the standard "symbol" domain.

writef (FormatString,Arg 1,Arg2,Arg3, . . .)   (I,I*)

Writes formatted output of any number of arguments. Arguments can be constants or bound variables. "FormatString" lets you tell Turbo Prolog the format to use to print the arguments. The asterisk means that it can work with an optional number of arguments, just like "write." These are the specifiers you can use within the form "%-m.p" to build "FormatString":

-   Forces left justification. The default (condition without "-") is right justification.

m   Specifies the minimum field width.

p   Specifies the precision of a floating-point number or the maximum number of characters to print from a string. Within this field you can add any of the three following letters for special conditions:

     f   Writes real numbers in fixed decimal notation (this is also the default)

     e   Writes real numbers in exponential notation

     g   Writes using the shortest format

display (String)   string — (I)

Must have an instantiated variable that is within the standard string domain. It writes the contents of "String" to the active window at the cursor position. Because you can then inspect the string using the Editor window's control-key commands, this predicate is also considered one of the special predicates that let you access the Editor from inside a program.

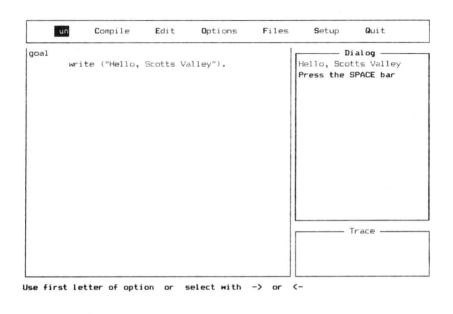

Figure 9-1.   Example of "write predicate"

flow patterns are contained in the "Reference Guide" section of the
Owner's Handbook.) If you try to use an uninstantiated variable, you'll
just get an error message. The predicate will write the constants and the
values of the variables to the currently active window of the currently
active "writedevice." Unfortunately, "write" won't work as a lone
predicate.

   Figure 9-1 shows an example of the "write" predicate in its most
primitive state. This program doesn't even have a clauses section.
(Remember that you don't have to declare a built-in predicate.) The
"write" predicate is merely written as an internal goal. It then performs

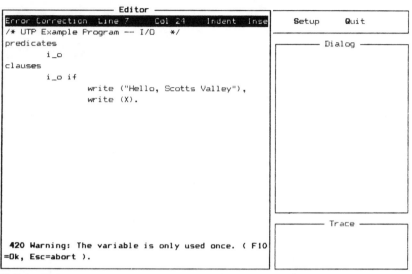

Figure 9-2.   Error message from uninstantiated variable

in the Dialog window. Figure 9-2 shows the error message you'll get if you use an uninstantiated variable. Figure 9-3 shows what happens if you use an instantiated variable.

nl

This built-in predicate —called *newline* —is similar to a "write" predicate without arguments. All it does is move the cursor to the next line. In technical terms, it writes a carriage return and a line feed to the current "writedevice" (the device you have defined as active for accepting

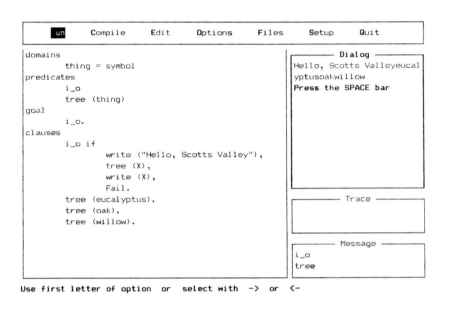

```
   un      Compile    Edit     Options    Files    Setup    Quit

domains                                          ┌──────── Dialog ────────┐
        thing = symbol                           │Hello, Scotts Valleyeucal│
predicates                                       │yptusoakwillow           │
        i_o                                      │Press the SPACE bar      │
        tree (thing)                             │                         │
goal                                             │                         │
        i_o.                                     │                         │
clauses                                          │                         │
        i_o if                                   │                         │
                write ("Hello, Scotts Valley"),  │                         │
                tree (X),                        │                         │
                write (X),                       │                         │
                Fail.                            │                         │
        tree (eucalyptus).                       ├──────── Trace ──────────┤
        tree (oak).                              │                         │
        tree (willow).                           │                         │
                                                 ├──────── Message ────────┤
                                                 │i_o                      │
                                                 │tree                     │
                                                 └─────────────────────────┘

Use first letter of option   or   select with   ->   or   <-
```

Figure 9-3.   Example of use of instantiated variable

"write" predicates). The default "writedevice" is the screen. It can help you improve the look of your output. Figure 9-4 shows the result when "nl" is added to the program shown in the previous figure.

Another way to get a newline is to write the string ("\n"). The backslash makes this a control character. Other control characters are shown in Table 9-2. If you want to print a single backslash mark itself (for example, in a DOS path specification), use two consecutive backslashes within the quotation marks. Figure 9-4 also shows examples of writing with the use of control characters.

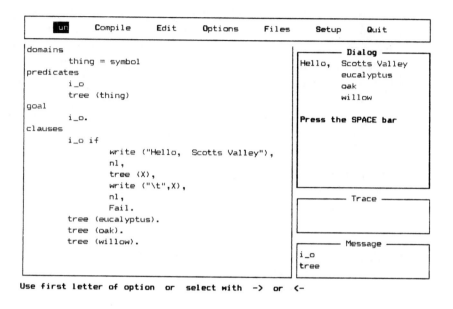

Figure 9-4. Addition of "nl" to program

Table 9-2. Control Characters for "write" Predicate*

\	Alone, indicates that the next character is a control character.
\n	The control character for a new line.
\t	The control character for a tab.
\b	The control character for a backspace.
\ \	The way to write a single backslash on the page.

*Other control characters depend on your system. For instance, if you want to send a control character that causes your printer to beep, you need to know what character the printer interprets as a beep. Then put that character after the backslash in a Turbo Prolog writing operation.

writedevice (SymbolicFileName)

The "writedevice" predicate lets you dictate what device (screen, printer, or other) the "write" predicate will send information to. This predicate can either work with a predefined symbolic file (screen or printer) or a file you name that is open. Table 9-3 lists the predefined devices for both this predicate and for "readdevice." Open files will be discussed later in the book.

Figure 9-5 shows what happens both when you change the "writedevice" predicate and when you use more arguments in the "write" predicate. The last two instantiated values for "tree" were sent to the printer instead of to the screen. You can trace this process to see the detail.

Figure 9-6 shows another use of the "writedevice" predicate. If the argument, "SymbolicFileName," is uninstantiated, the predicate will instantiate it to the current value. In this case, that value is "screen." Another "write" statement can tell you what that value is.

writef

If you want specially formatted writing, you can use the "writef" predicate. (Refer back to Table 9-1 to see how it works.) "FormatString"

Table 9-3. Standard (Predefined) Devices for "writedevice" and "readdevice" Predicates

Predefined Device	Output Device
printer	parallel port
screen	monitor
keyboard	keyboard
com1	serial port

Figure 9- 5. Changing "writedevice" and using more arguments in the "write" predicate

specifies how to print the arguments (of which there may be any number). The format specifiers

```
%-m.p
```

are used to punctuate "FormatString" in order to delineate which special instructions apply to which arguments. Figure 9-7 shows the "writef" predicate at work.

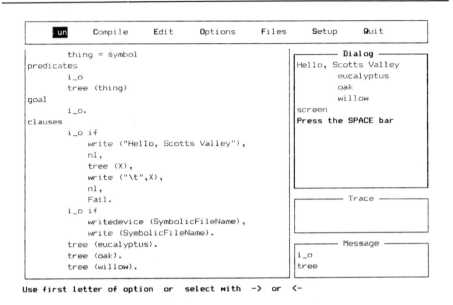

Figure 9-6.   Another use of the "writedevice" predicate

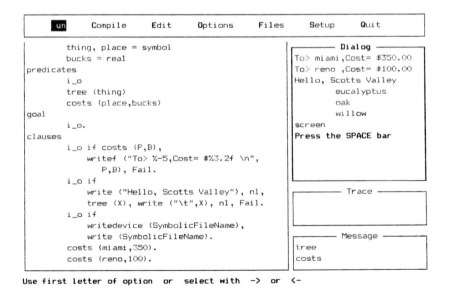

Figure 9-7.   The "writef" predicate

display

This predicate displays the string in the active window. You can then use the same cursor-key commands that work in the Editor window to inspect, but not modify, the string. See the "Editor Window Reprise" section at the end of this chapter for more about this predicate.

User-defined Writing Predicates

You can also build your own predicates to write things just the way you want them. This is generally true in Prolog, because you can use a rule to define what should logically be true in certain circumstances.

For instance, Example Program 20 on the Library/Example disk prints the elements of a list one at a time. Figure 9-8 shows this program. The "writelist" and "write5" predicates handle special writing tasks and

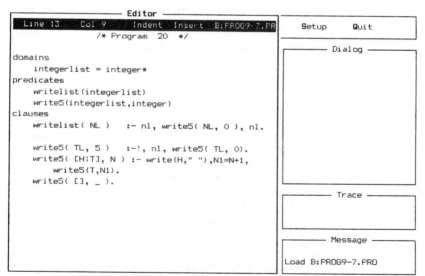

Figure 9-8.   Example Program 20 from Library/Example disk

are built from the "write" predicate itself and from other predicates.

Reading

Turbo Prolog can also read information from the keyboard or from a disk file. It can read anything from a single character to an entire line of characters. It cannot directly read compound objects or lists. Table 9-4 shows the standard reading predicates.

Table 9-4. Standard Reading Predicates

---

readint (IntegerVariable)   integer — (O)

Reads an integer. The variable must be free and the value it binds to must be within the standard "int" domain. Reads from the current input device until RETURN is pressed.

readreal (RealVariable)   real — (O)

Reads a real number. The variable must be free and the value it binds to must be within the standard "real" domain. Reads from the current input device until RETURN is pressed.

readchar (CharVariable)   char — (O)

Reads a character. The variable must be free and the value it binds to must be within the standard "char" domain. Reads a single character from the current cursor position. Unlike "readint" and "readreal," "readchar" doesn't wait until RETURN is pressed.

readln (String)   string — (O)

Reads a string. The variable must be free and the value it binds to must be within the standard "string" domain. Reads from the current input device until it encounters an ASCII carriage return.

readterm (Domain,Term)   (O,I)

Reads an object written by the "write" predicate. The "Term" variable will be bound to the object that is read if that object is within the domains section. This is useful in file manipulation, because it lets you bring in object information from outside the program.

readdevice (SymbolicFilename)   symbol — (I) (O)

Lets you specify the active (current) "readdevice" predicate. It can work with any of three types of "SymbolicFileName": the predefined symbolic files ("keyboard"); a user-defined symbolic file name for an open file; or an unbound variable. If an unbound variable is used, the predicate will bind "SymbolicFileName" to the name of the current "readdevice." Values must be within the standard "symbol" domain.

inkey (char-O)

Reads one character from the standard input device. If it cannot read such character, "inkey" fails.

---

readint (IntVariable)

Figure 9-9 shows the program presented in Figure 9-7, but with added lines. These lines show how "readint" will read a single integer value from the current "read" device, which is the keyboard in this case. The "readint" predicate doesn't know that you have offered an integer until you have pressed the RETURN key (Figure 9-10).

readreal (RealVariable)

This predicate works almost the same way as "readint," only it works with real numbers instead of integers. If you offer anything other than a real number, it will fail.

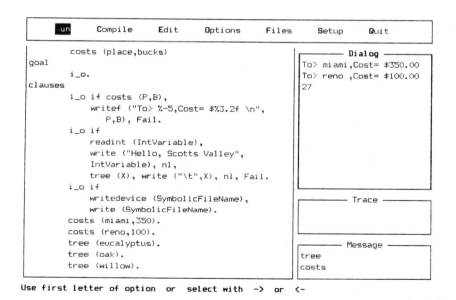

Figure 9-9.   Use of "readint" to read a single integer value from current "read" device

```
    un       Compile      Edit      Options      Files      Setup      Quit

           costs (place,bucks)                  ┌──── Dialog ────
goal                                            │To> miami,Cost= $350.00
           i_o.                                 │To> reno ,Cost= $100.00
clauses                                         │27
           i_o if costs (P,B),                  │Hello, Scotts Valley27
               writef ("To> %-5,Cost= $%3.2f \n",│          eucalyptus
                   P,B), Fail.                  │          oak
           i_o if                               │          willow
               readint (IntVariable),          │screen
               write ("Hello, Scotts Valley",   │Press the SPACE bar
               IntVariable), nl,                │
               tree (X), write ("\t",X), nl, Fail.│
           i_o if                               └────────────
               writedevice (SymbolicFileName),  ┌──── Trace ────
               write (SymbolicFileName).        │
           costs (miami,350).                   │
           costs (reno,100).                    └────────────
           tree (eucalyptus).                   ┌──── Message ────
           tree (oak).                          │tree
           tree (willow).                       │costs

Use first letter of option  or  select with  -> or  <-
```

Figure 9-10.   Display after typing an integer value and before pressing RETURN

readchar (CharVariable)

This predicate also works in a similar fashion to that of "readint." However, because it only wants to read a single character, it doesn't wait for a carriage return (a RETURN keypress) to get the variable. As soon as it has a carriage return, it returns to the rest of the program. The value must be in the "char" domain. Figure 9-11 shows "readreal" and "readchar" predicates added to the same program.

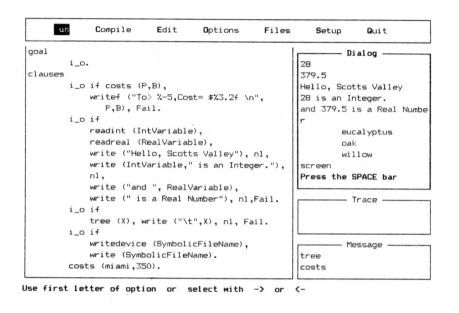

| un | Compile | Edit | Options | Files | Setup | Quit |

```
goal                                          ┌───── Dialog ─────┐
      i_o.                                     │28                │
clauses                                        │379.5             │
      i_o if costs (P,B),                      │Hello, Scotts Valley
          writef ("To> %-5,Cost= $%3.2f \n",  │28 is an Integer. │
             P,B), Fail.                       │and 379.5 is a Real Numbe│
      i_o if                                   │r                 │
          readint (IntVariable),               │        eucalyptus│
          readreal (RealVariable),             │        oak       │
          write ("Hello, Scotts Valley"), nl,  │        willow    │
          write (IntVariable," is an Integer."),│screen           │
          nl,                                   │Press the SPACE bar│
          write ("and ", RealVariable),        └──────────────────┘
          write (" is a Real Number"), nl,Fail.
      i_o if                                    ┌───── Trace ──────┐
          tree (X), write ("\t",X), nl, Fail.  │                  │
      i_o if                                    │                  │
          writedevice (SymbolicFileName),       └──────────────────┘
          write (SymbolicFileName).             ┌──── Message ─────┐
      costs (miami,350).                        │tree              │
                                                │costs             │
                                                └──────────────────┘
```

Use first letter of option   or   select with   ->   or   <-

Figure 9-11. Addition of "readreal" and "readchar" predicates

readln (StringVariable)

If you do want to read characters until a carriage return is encountered, the "readln" predicate allows you to do so. A string need not have only "char" domain types. Figure 9-12 shows how "readln" is used to read a line of text.

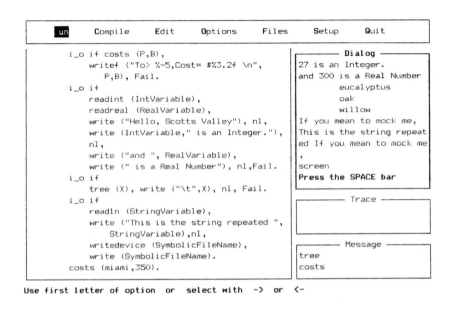

```
      un      Compile    Edit    Options    Files    Setup    Quit

      i_o if costs (P,B),                         ┌──────── Dialog ────────
          writef ("To> %-5,Cost= $%3.2f \n",      27 is an Integer.
              P,B), Fail.                          and 300 is a Real Number
      i_o if                                                  eucalyptus
          readint (IntVariable),                              oak
          readreal (RealVariable),                            willow
          write ("Hello, Scotts Valley"), nl,     If you mean to mock me,
          write (IntVariable," is an Integer."),   This is the string repeat
          nl,                                      ed If you mean to mock me
          write ("and ", RealVariable),            ,
          write (" is a Real Number"), nl,Fail.    screen
      i_o if                                       Press the SPACE bar
          tree (X), write ("\t",X), nl, Fail.
      i_o if                                       ┌──────── Trace ────────
          readln (StringVariable),
          write ("This is the string repeated ",
              StringVariable),nl,
          writedevice (SymbolicFileName),          ┌──────── Message ────────
          write (SymbolicFileName).                tree
      costs (miami,350).                           costs

Use first letter of option  or  select with  ->  or  <-
```

Figure 9-12. Using "readln" to read a line of text

readdevice (SymbolicFileName)

The "readdevice" predicate is quite similar to the "writedevice" predicate. It lets you dictate from what device (screen, printer, or another) other "read" predicates will receive information. This can be the predefined file name "keyboard" or a file you name that is open. (Table 9-3 lists the predefined devices.)

If the "SymbolicFileName" variable is uninstantiated, the "readdevice" predicate will bind it to the name of the current active "read" device. Because you haven't yet learned about file predicates, Figure 9-13 shows an example of binding the "readdevice" predicate's "SymbolicFileName" to the default name, and then writing that name.

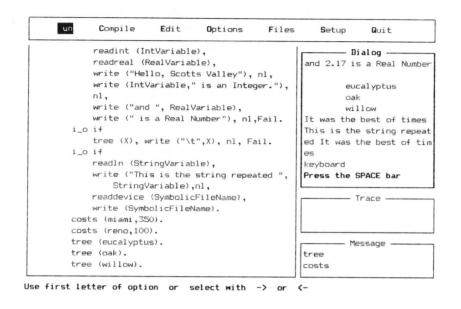

```
    un   Compile    Edit    Options    Files    Setup    Quit

          readint (IntVariable),                    ── Dialog ──
          readreal (RealVariable),           and 2.17 is a Real Number
          write ("Hello, Scotts Valley"), nl,
          write (IntVariable," is an Integer."),        eucalyptus
          nl,                                             oak
          write ("and ", RealVariable),                  willow
          write (" is a Real Number"), nl,Fail.   It was the best of times
      i_o if                                       This is the string repeat
          tree (X), write ("\t",X), nl, Fail.     ed It was the best of tim
      i_o if                                       es
          readln (StringVariable),                 keyboard
          write ("This is the string repeated ",  Press the SPACE bar
              StringVariable),nl,
          readdevice (SymbolicFileName),          ──── Trace ────
          write (SymbolicFileName).
      costs (miami,350).
      costs (reno,100).
      tree (eucalyptus).                          ── Message ──
      tree (oak).                                  tree
      tree (willow).                               costs

Use first letter of option  or  select with  ->  or  <-
```

Figure 9-13. Example of binding the "readdevice" predicate's "SymbolicFileName" to the default name

User-defined Reading Predicates

Just as with the writing predicates, you can create your own reading predicates: you can build rules by using the standard predicates. Experiment with both the writing and reading predicates to see what sort of specialized functions you can perform.

Windows and Cursor Position

Windows—portions of the screen that act as screens themselves — have become a standard part of microcomputer programs. Turbo Prolog depends heavily on its four built-in windows to make program development easier and more structured. But Turbo Prolog also contains predicates that let you make your own windows for program input and output. Even within a window, you can use the "cursor" predicate to start writing or reading at a particular place.

Table 9-5 lists the standard windowing predicates. These include instructions for controlling the color of the screen.

Table 9-5.   Standard Windowing Predicates

---

makewindow (WindowNo, ScrAtt, FrameAttr, Header, Row, Col, Height, Width) (int,int,int,string,int,int,int,int) (I, I, I, I, I, I, I, I)

Creates a cleared window. All variables must be bound.

WindowNo	Identifying number of the window. Each window has a different integer number.
ScrAtt	Determines the style of display for window. Tables 9-6 and 9-7 show attribute calculations.
FrameAttr	Determines the existence and style of display for frame around window. Tables 9-6 and 9-7 show attribute calculations. Attribute value of 0 means no frame.
Header	String written at top of window.
Row	Number (integer) of row. Rows counted from top of screen. If value beyond screen dimensions (25 rows), will get error message.
Col	Number (integer) of column. Columns counted from left side of screen. If value is beyond screen dimensions (80 columns), an error message will result.
Height	Number (integer) of rows in window. If sum of "Height" and "Row" would run the bottom of the window off the screen, an error message will result.
Width	Number (integer) of columns in window. If the sum of "Width" and "Col" would run the right side of the window off the screen, an error message will result.

Note: The "graphics" predicate can be used to change the number of columns and rows on the screen. The CGA and EGA modes go as high as 640×200 and 640×350, respectively.

window _attr (Attr)   integer — (I)

Will change attribute of active window to integer value of bound variable. Lets you change style of display or color of open window without retreating to "makewindow" predicate.

Table 9-5.   Standard Windowing Predicates (*continued*)

removewindow

Removes active window from screen. Has no arguments.

shiftwindow (WindowNo)   integer — (I) (O)

If variable is free, will bind it to window number of active window. If variable is bound, will make the "WindowNo" window the new active window. Lets you switch between multiple windows that can be on the screen. The "write" and "read" predicates only work on the active window.

clearwindow

Clears all characters out of the active window and replaces them with blank spaces of the background attribute.

cursor (Row, Column)   integer,integer — (I,I) (O,O)

Requires that either both variables be free or both be bound. If both are free, it will bind them to the integers representing the present row and column position of the cursor within the active window or on the screen. If both are bound, it will move the cursor to the point that they represent on the grid.

cursorform (Startline, Endline)   (integer,integer) — (I,I)

Within a single character display area, sets the X-Y cursor position. Each character occupies 14 scan lines of the screen. "Startline" and "Endline" must be bound to values between 1 and 14 (inclusive).

window _ str (ScreenString)   string — (I) (O)

If variable is bound, will write the value of "ScreenString" to the active window. It starts at the current cursor position, truncates each line that is too long (it doesn't word-wrap), and truncates lines that would be off the bottom of the window. If the variable is free, that variable will be instantiated to the string displayed in the active window. The variable will have as many lines as there are lines in the window, and each line will only be read as far as the last nonblank character.

makewindow

To create a window, you have only to use the "makewindow" predicate and fill in its arguments. All of the arguments must be instantiated at the time this predicate is called, and all except "FrameAttr" (which is a

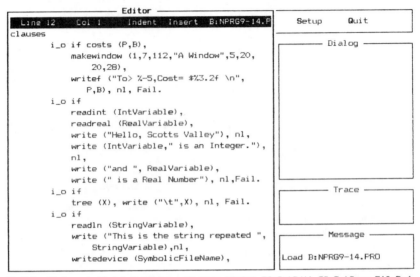

```
┌──────────────── Editor ────────────────┐  ┌─────────────────┐
│ Line 12   Col 1    Indent  Insert  B:NPRG9-14.P│ Setup    Quit   │
│clauses                                  │  └─────────────────┘
│       i_o if costs (P,B),               │  ┌───── Dialog ─────┐
│          makewindow (1,7,112,"A Window",5,20,│ │                 │
│             20,28),                     │  │                 │
│          writef ("To> %-5,Cost= $%3.2f \n",│ │                 │
│             P,B), nl, Fail.             │  │                 │
│       i_o if                            │  │                 │
│          readint (IntVariable),         │  │                 │
│          readreal (RealVariable),       │  │                 │
│          write ("Hello, Scotts Valley"), nl,│ │                 │
│          write (IntVariable," is an Integer."),│ │               │
│          nl,                            │  │                 │
│          write ("and ", RealVariable),  │  │                 │
│          write (" is a Real Number"), nl,Fail.│ └───────────────┘
│       i_o if                            │  ┌───── Trace ─────┐
│          tree (X), write ("\t",X), nl, Fail.│ │                 │
│       i_o if                            │  │                 │
│          readln (StringVariable),       │  └─────────────────┘
│          write ("This is the string repeated ",│ ┌──── Message ────┐
│             StringVariable),nl,         │  │                 │
│          writedevice (SymbolicFileName),│  │Load B:NPRG9-14.PRO│
└─────────────────────────────────────────┘  └─────────────────┘
 F1:Help F3:Search F4:Subst F5:Copy F6:Move F7:Del F8:ExtEdit F9:ExtCopy F10:End
```

Figure 9-14. Basic windowing predicate added to program

string) must be of the integer domain type. However, the values are constrained even more than that. Remember that the display shows 25 rows and 80 columns. If your position and size values would push a window beyond that territory, you'll just get an error message.

Figure 9-14 shows this basic windowing predicate added to the program built so far. Inspecting the following arguments shows us what sort of window it will be.

```
makewindow (1,7,112,"A Window",5,20,20,28)
```

WindowNo

The "1" for "WindowNo" simply specifies that this will be window number 1. Use the window number to identify the active window.

ScrAtt

The "7" value of "ScrAtt" (Screen Attribute) states that the main area of the window should be white characters on a black background if a monochrome display is being used. See Table 9-6 for a list of the values you can choose. To choose a monochrome display attribute, find the value for the major decision and adjust it by the possible minor-decision values. Table 9-7 shows the similar values for a color display. (The values in the original Borland manual were in error.) To calculate the attribute value you wish for a color display, choose a foreground color and a background color. Characters will be drawn in the foreground color. The sum of the values for the two colors is the final attribute.

Table 9-6. Monochrome Display Attributes

Major Decisions:

Style	Value	Foreground (Characters)	Background
Blank	0	Black	Black
Normal	7	White	Black
Inverse Video	112	Black	White

Minor Decisions:

1. Underline characters in foreground color: add 1.
2. Show white part of display in high-intensity: add 8.
3. Blink character: add 128.

Table 9-7. Color Display Attributes*

Color	Foreground	Background
By colors:		
Black	0	0
Gray	8	na
Blue	1	16
Light blue	9	na
Green	2	32
Light green	10	na
Cyan	3	48
Light cyan	11	na
Red	4	64
Pink	12	na
Magenta	5	80
Light magenta	13	na
Brown	6	96
Yellow	14	na
White	7	112
High white	15	na
By values:		
Black	0	0
Blue	1	16
Green	2	32
Cyan	3	48
Red	4	64
Magenta	5	80
Brown	6	96
White	7	112
Gray	8	na
Light blue	9	na
Light green	10	na
Light cyan	11	na
Pink	12	na
Light magenta	13	na
Yellow	14	na
High white	15	na

*The "na" designation means that this particular color is not available for the background ("high white" means high-intensity white).

FrameAttr

The "112" value for "FrameAttr" (Frame Attribute) dictates that an *inverse video* (black characters on a white background) shall surround the window. If you choose "0" for this attribute, you'll have more space to maneuver in the window, because the frame uses two rows and two columns —it is a single character wide all around the window.

Header

The header "A Window" is just a string shown at the top of the window as a title.

Row,Col

The next two arguments should be considered together. The "5,20" values for these two specify that the window should start at row 5, column 20.

Height,Width

These two arguments can also be considered as a pair. The values of "20,28" specify that the window should be 20 rows tall and 28 columns wide. Figure 9-15 shows the window this line creates. The "write" predicates that come after "makewindow" in this rule perform their duties in the window. They always apply to the active window.

window _attr

This predicate must have an instantiated argument. The value of that argument becomes the screen attribute of the currently active window.

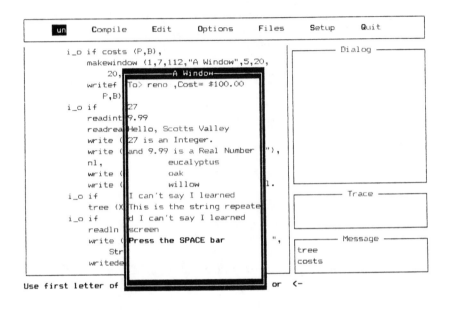

Figure 9-15.   Window created with height and width arguments

removewindow

If you want to delete an entire window from the screen, all you need to do is invoke the "removewindow" predicate. The active window will promptly disappear.

shiftwindow

This predicate lets you determine which window will be active. Without it, the most recently created window will be the active window. The cursor will return to its most recent position in that window. The only argument "shiftwindow" asks for is the number of the window to which you wish to shift. If you leave that argument unbound, the "shiftwindow" predicate will bind it to the number of the active window.

If you have created overlapping windows, the "more recently active" windows will appear to lie over the "less recently active" windows.

clearwindow

If you want to clear an entire window of characters, use this predicate. All that will be left is the background color.

cursor

All of the reading and writing predicates work from the current cursor position in the current window. Once a cursor position is set, Turbo Prolog will remember it even if you shift from window to window. However, you can also affect the position with this predicate. See how it was added to the program in Figure 9-16. To make it clearer, the window has been enlarged. Figure 9-17 shows the effect. Compare this to Figure 9-15.

Notice that although the cursor started at row 4, column 6 of the window (not of the entire display), the carriage return caused by pressing the RETURN key (which must be done to tell "readint" that the integer is complete) moved the cursor back to column 0 of the window. From then on, the cursor returned to that column.

You can also use this predicate to discover the row and column of the cursor. If "Row" and "Col" are unbound variables when this predicate is called, they will be instantiated to the present row and column values.

The "cursorform" predicate lets you have even finer control over the cursor's position.

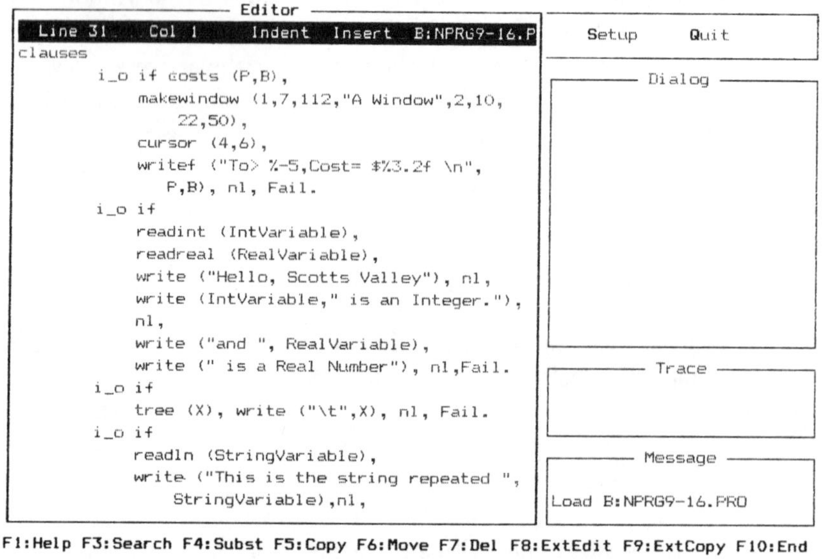

```
                      ─── Editor ───
  Line 31    Col 1      Indent  Insert   B:NPRG9-16.P      Setup    Quit
clauses
        i_o if costs (P,B),                                ─── Dialog ───
            makewindow (1,7,112,"A Window",2,10,
                22,50),
            cursor (4,6),
            writef ("To> %-5,Cost= $%3.2f \n",
                P,B), nl, Fail.
        i_o if
            readint (IntVariable),
            readreal (RealVariable),
            write ("Hello, Scotts Valley"), nl,
            write (IntVariable," is an Integer."),
            nl,
            write ("and ", RealVariable),
            write (" is a Real Number"), nl,Fail.     ─── Trace ───
        i_o if
            tree (X), write ("\t",X), nl, Fail.
        i_o if                                        ─── Message ───
            readln (StringVariable),
            write ("This is the string repeated ",   Load B:NPRG9-16.PRO
                StringVariable),nl,
```

F1:Help F3:Search F4:Subst F5:Copy F6:Move F7:Del F8:ExtEdit F9:ExtCopy F10:End

Figure 9-16.   Addition of "cursor" predicate to program

window__str

This is a difficult predicate to classify. It reads or writes, works with strings, and is window-oriented. If its argument is unbound, it instantiates that argument to the string displayed in the active window. It reads all of the lines in the window and ends each line after it comes to the last nonblank character. If its argument is already bound to a string value, "window__str" will write that string to the active window. It will truncate each line to fit the window (no string wrapping) and will truncate the entire string if it runs into the end of the window.

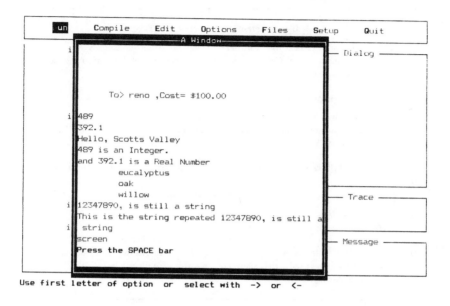

Figure 9-17. Effect of enlarging window

Editor Window Reprise

You know about using the Editor window as a development tool for programs. You can also enter the window directly from a Turbo Prolog program by using the two predicates described in this section and listed in Table 9-8. The "display" predicate that was previously described in the "write" predicates section is sometimes considered as one of these predicates because it lets you use the cursor keys to inspect the string it displays.

Table 9-8. Editor Window Predicates

---

display (String)   string — (I)

Must have an instantiated variable that is within the standard "string" domain. Writes contents of "String" to active window at the cursor position. You can then inspect the string using the Editor window's control-key commands.

edit (InputString,OutputString)   string,string — (I,O)

The "InputString" variable must be instantiated and the "OutputString" variable must be free. Lets you use the Editor window commands within the active window to edit "InputString." The result becomes "OutputString."

editmsg (InStr, OutStr, LeftHeader, RightHeader, Message, Position, HelpFileName, Code)
   string,string,string,string,string,string,integer,string,integer (I, O, I, I, I, I, I, O)

All variables except "OutStr" and "Code" must be instantiated. Activates Editor commands in the active window, inserts the two headers into the main header, and writes "Message" at bottom of window. The cursor is at "Position" in "InStr" which you can then edit. The result becomes "OutStr" and "Code" tells how editing was ended. A "0" code means the F10 key was used; a "1" code means the ESC key was used. "HelpFileName" specifies what file will be called if the F1 key is pressed to get help during the edit.

---

edit

This predicate writes a string to the active window and then lets you edit the string with the Editor window's commands. The edited string is then instantiated to the "OutputString" variable.

editmsg

The eight arguments of this predicate let you call the Editor, write a string to it, edit that string, insert two texts in the header, relocate the cursor, and display a message at the bottom of the window. The "editmsg" predicate also specifies which Help file to load when the F1 key is pressed. The value of the "Code" variable tells you how the editing was terminated. A value of 0 means the F10 key was used. A value of 1 means the ESC key was used.

Screen Handling: Characters And Fields

Several predicates allow you to work on each character position or field position within the full screen or within a window. (A field is a stretch of side-by-side character positions in a row. You define fields before using them —they are not predefined by the system.) These predicates are listed in Table 9-9. You can get work done more quickly by using the field predicates instead of the character predicates.

Table 9-9.   Screen-Handling Predicates

---

scr__char (Row,Col,Char)   integer,integer,char — (I, I, I) (I, I, O)

If all variables are bound, writes "Char" with current attribute at position specified by integer values of "Row" and "Col." Rows are counted from the top, and columns are counted from the left side. If "Row" and "Col" are bound and "Char" is free, "scr__char" will read the character that is at the position specified by "Row" and "Col."

scr__attr (Row,Col,Attr)   integer,integer,integer — (I, I, I) (I, I, O)

If all variables are bound, sets the attribute of the position specified by integer values of "Row" and "Col" to "Attr." Rows are counted from the top, and columns are counted from the left side. If "Row" and "Col" are bound and "Attr" is free, "scr__attr" will read the attribute that is at the position specified by "Row" and "Col."

field__str (Row, Col, Length, String)
integer,integer,integer,integer — (I, I, I, I) (I, I, I, O)

If all variables are bound, if the "Row" and "Col" values specify a value in the active window, and if a field "Length" long that fits in the window starts at the "Row,Col" position, then "String" will be written to that field. If "String" is longer than "Length," any characters beyond "Length" will be truncated. If all variables except "String" are bound, if the "Row" and "Col" values specify a value in the active window, and if a field "Length" long that fits in the window starts at the "Row,Col" position, then "String" in the field will be bound to "String."

field__attr (Row, Col, Length, Attr)
integer,integer,integer,integer — (I, I, I, I) (I, I, I, O)

If all variables are bound, if the "Row" and "Col" values specify a value in the active window, and if a field "Length" long that fits in the window starts at the "Row,Col" position, then all positions of the field are set to the attribute "Attr." If all variables except "Attr" are bound, if the "Row" and "Col" values specify a value in the active window, and if a field "Length" long that fits in the window starts at the "Row,Col" position, then the attribute of the first position (the one at "Row,Col") of that field will be bound to "Attr."

---

scr — char

This predicate uses a row number and a column number to specify the position of a single character. It can either write a character to that position or read a character from that position, depending on the binding of its "Character" variable.

scr — attr

The "scr__attr" (screen attribute) predicate deals with an attribute value of the character position specified by the row and column numbers. It can either specify or read the attribute there (see Tables 9- 6 and 9- 7 for what the attribute values signify).

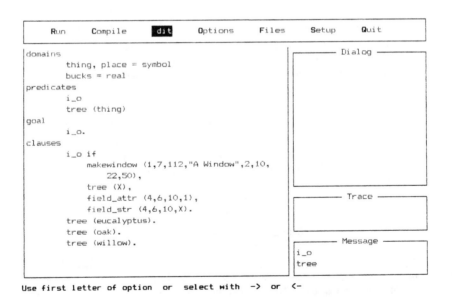

```
  Run      Compile    dit     Options    Files    Setup    Quit
┌─────────────────────────────────────────────┐┌─── Dialog ───┐
│domains                                        ││              │
│      thing, place = symbol                    ││              │
│      bucks = real                             ││              │
│predicates                                     ││              │
│      i_o                                      ││              │
│      tree (thing)                             ││              │
│goal                                           ││              │
│      i_o.                                     ││              │
│clauses                                        ││              │
│      i_o if                                   ││              │
│         makewindow (1,7,112,"A Window",2,10,  │└──────────────┘
│            22,50),                            │
│         tree (X),                             │┌─── Trace ────┐
│         field_attr (4,6,10,1),                ││              │
│         field_str (4,6,10,X).                 ││              │
│      tree (eucalyptus).                       ││              │
│      tree (oak).                              │┌── Message ───┐
│      tree (willow).                           ││i_o           │
│                                               ││tree          │
└─────────────────────────────────────────────┘└──────────────┘
Use first letter of option  or  select with  ->  or  <-
```

Figure 9- 18. Adding "field__str" and "field__attr" to program

field ___ str

Analogous to the "scr ___ char" predicate, "field ___ str" specifies a field (by choosing the row, column, and length in characters) and then either reads or writes a string for that field.

field ___ attr

This predicate allows you to set or read the attribute for an entire field at once. It too specifies the field through the row, column, and length arguments. When reading the attribute of a field, "field ___ attr" depends on the attribute of the first character position of that field. This specificity is necessary because a field may have its string written by a field predicate, and its attributes dictated a character at a time by the "scr ___ attr" predicate. Figures 9-18 and 9-19 demonstrate the action of both "field ___ str" and "field ___ attr."

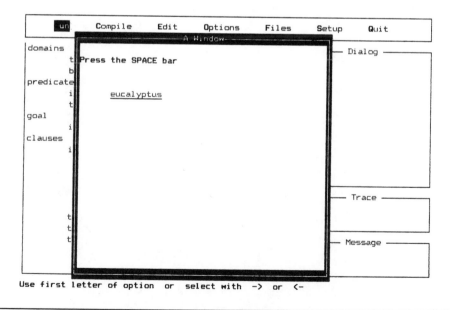

Figure 9-19.   Effect of "field ___ str" and "field ___ attr"

attribute

A more general-purpose predicate than the previous one, "attribute" lets you decide or read what the general screen attribute is.

10

Files

To write large, practical programs that use stored facts and rules, you need to be able to read and write disk files from inside an executing program. This type of I/O is no more complex than the screen reads and writes described in Chapter 9. But to do it, you need to learn a few more standard predicates. We won't spend too much time on "files" because once you have declared and opened a file, reading from it or writing to it works just the same as reading or writing screen information. Anything that you were going to send to the screen or printer can instead be sent to a disk.

This chapter describes three things: file predicates, direct use of DOS commands from inside Prolog, and conversion of data types. The file predicates let you read, write, and modify files on disk, and the DOS predicates let you go directly to memory or I/O ports. If you aren't ready to read and write files from your Prolog programs, skip this chapter. All you really need to know about files is that you must declare them before using them, you must open them before calling them, and you must close them to save any changes to them.

File Predicates

Files are logical entities in computer programming that are used to collect related data. The pieces of data can be from any other domain (character, real, integer, string, symbol, or user-defined), and the relation between them can be as simple as "these are all in one place" (the term "relation" is used in a general sense here, not in the specific "objects-relationships" sense introduced early in the book).

Every file has a name, as you know from having seen directories of disks. Disk operating systems use files (with specific types of file names) to organize the data on the disk. The Turbo Prolog documentation refers to these as "DosFileNames."

One interesting fact to remember is that Turbo Prolog treats disk files, the screen, the printer, the parallel port, the serial port, and the keyboard all as files. You can read from or write to any of those "files" or "devices." In fact, you can read or write to several of them in the same program. You use the same reading and writing predicates (the ones described in Chapter 9) to work with any device or file. You therefore don't have to learn anything more about reading and writing. All you have to learn is how to specify, open, and close files.

Specifying Files or Devices

The standard devices are listed in Table 10-1. These don't have to be declared and are always available for use. The default devices, or the ones that are specified automatically until the program dictates otherwise, are *keyboard* for input and *screen* for output. One thing to watch out for is that although the *printer* and *coml* devices are automatically declared, they are not automatically alive. That is, if you decide to write to the printer, but the printer (or whatever else should be attached to the parallel port) isn't connected or isn't turned on, Turbo Prolog will enter into a limbo state. Use the CTRL-BREAK key combination to try to break out of this condition. The same problem can arise if you try to use (read or write) the serial port, coml. If there is no serial card in your computer, you'll get a run-time error.

The predicates that let you redirect input and output are shown in Table 10-2. These are easily used and are available to specify or inspect

Table 10-1.   Standard Devices

Device	Comment
keyboard	(this is the input —or read device —default)
printer	parallel port
coml	serial port
screen	(this is the output —or write device —default)

Table 10-2. Device Specification Predicates

---

readdevice (SymbolicFileName)   symbol — (I) (O)

The default read device when Turbo Prolog starts is the keyboard. You can use this predicate in two ways: to change the current read device or to discover the name of the current read device. Any "read" predicates will act upon the current read device.

    If the "SymbolicFileName" variable is instantiated (or bound) to a standard device or to a user-defined file, the "readdevice" predicate will change the current read device to the value of "SymbolicFileName." You can do this as many times within a program as you wish, and you can change back to the original read device if you wish.

    If the "SymbolicFileName" variable is not bound —for a standard device or a user-defined file, the "readdevice" predicate will bind it to the value of the current read device.

writedevice (SymbolicFileName)   symbol — (I) (O)

The default write device when Turbo Prolog starts is the screen. You can use this predicate in two ways: to change the current write device, or to discover the name of the current write device. Any "write" predicates will act upon the current write device.

    If the "SymbolicFileName" variable is instantiated (or bound) to a standard device or to a user-defined file, the "writedevice" predicate will change the current write device to the value of "SymbolicFileName." You can do this as many times within a program as you wish, and you can change back to the original write device if you wish.

    If the "SymbolicFileName" variable is not bound to a standard device or a user-defined file, the "writedevice" predicate will bind it to the value of the current write device.

---

the current device. If the "SymbolicFileName" variable is bound, the current device will change to that variable's value. If the "Symbolic-FileName" variable is free, it will then be bound to the current value. The basic operation of these predicates was shown in Figure 9-13 in Chapter 9.

Declaring Files

You must declare the symbolic file names of the files you will use. These declarations belong in the domains section of the program. Table 10-3 gives the details on file declaration. Each program can have only one file-domain declaration, but the declaration may contain several sym-

Table 10-3.   File-Domain Declarations

SymbolicFileName

To declare a file domain, you must declare the symbolic file names of the files you will use. You can have only a single file-domain declaration in a program, but that declaration may contain several symbolic file names. Here is an example:

domains

    file = cloudnames ; remains ; employees __to __watch

All symbolic file names must begin with a lowercase letter.

Types of Files

There are two types of files:

- **Predefined files** These are the files that are always available in Turbo Prolog. You don't have to (in fact, you must not) declare these — Prolog knows they are there. Predefined (standard) files are listed in Table 10-1.

- **User-defined files** These are files that you name. Any Turbo Prolog name that isn't reserved (isn't a standard predicate or operator) can be used. Examples are

    thisfile
    thatfile
    the __other __file
    employee __records __ 1986

---

bolic file names. All symbolic file names begin with a lowercase letter. There are two types of files: predefined and user-defined.

Predefined Files

These are the standard devices — the files that are always available in Turbo Prolog and shouldn't be declared. They include printer, keyboard, screen, and com1.

User-Defined Files

These are disk files for which you can use any symbolic name you wish. However, you may use only a name that isn't the same as one of the reserved words in Turbo Prolog (the names of standard predicates and section delimiters).

Opening Files

A file must be opened before it can be worked with. Before you even try to open a file, you need to think of a symbolic name for it that you can declare in the file-domain declaration. There can be only one such declaration in each program, but the declaration can list several files. Several files can be open at once.

The predicates that open files also relate your symbolic name to an actual DOS file name. DOS names start with a letter and have up to eight letters before an optional period and three-letter extension.

Turbo Prolog will normally use the default directory path to find the drive and directory for a user-defined file. You can change this path by employing the "disk" predicate described later in this chapter in the section entitled "File-Handling Predicates."

Closing Files

When you are done with a file, you should close it to ensure that any modifications are saved. Otherwise, some or all of the modifications may just disappear.

File-Handling Predicates

Table 10-4 lists the file predicates. This section describes some of them and provides examples of their actions.

existfile, renamefile, deletefile

These are probably the most easily understood file predicates. The "existfile" predicate simply checks to see if there is a file with "DosFile-

Table 10-4.   File Predicates

___

FILE-HANDLING

existfile (DosFileName)   string — (I)

This predicate requires an instantiated (or bound) variable. It will check to see if a file with the name of the value of the variable is on the disk. (The "disk" predicate specifies the drive and path the predicate will check.) If it finds the correct file, it succeeds. Otherwise, it fails.

deletefile (DosFileName)   string — (I)

This predicate requires an instantiated (or bound) variable. It will delete the file that has the name of the value of the variable. (The "disk" predicate specifies which drive and path the predicate will search in order to find the file.) If it deletes the file or cannot find the file, it succeeds.

renamefile (OldDosFileName,NewDosFileName)   string,string — (I,I)

The predicate requires two instantiated variables. It will find the file with the name of the value of the first variable and will change its name to the value of the second variable. (The "disk" predicate specifies the drive and path the predicate will check.) It succeeds by renaming the file. If it cannot find the file to rename, it fails.

disk (DosPath)   string — (I) (O)

This predicate can work in either of two ways:

- With an instantiated (or bound) variable, it will set the active drive and path to the value of that variable.

- With an unbound variable, it will bind the variable to the value of the active drive and path.

OPENING A FILE

Note: Both variables must be bound for any of these predicates to succeed. The first variable is the symbolic name (the name you want to use within the Prolog program) of the file you want to open. The second variable is the name of the disk file (an official DOS name) that will respond to your symbolic file accesses. In other words, these predicates establish a direct relationship between the two names and refer to only a single file. Once the file is open, you can perform the relevant action upon it.

openwrite (SymbolicFileName,DosFileName)   file,string — (I,I)

Use this predicate to open a file for writing (sending information to the file). If there is already a file with the name "DosFileName," it will be deleted to be replaced by the new file created by this predicate.

openread (SymbolicFileName,DosFileName)   file,string — (I,I)

Use this predicate to open a file for reading (getting information from the file). You don't need to worry about closing a file you have only read from: there aren't any modifications to lose.

___

Table 10-4.   File Predicates (*continued*)

---

openappend (SymbolicFileName,DosFileName)   **file,string — (I,I)**

Use this predicate to open a file to which you want to add information.

openmodify (SymbolicFileName,DosFileName)   **file,string — (I,I)**

Use this predicate to open a file for writing and reading (sending information to and getting information from) the file.

POSITIONING WITHIN A FILE

filepos (SymbolicFileName,FilePosition,Mode)   **file,real,integer — (I,I,I) (I,O,I)**

There are two ways to use this predicate: to find the file position and to set the file position.

To find the file position, "Mode" must be instantiated (or bound) to 0 (see the list of modes that follows), "SymbolicFileName" must be instantiated (or bound), and "FilePosition" must be free. The predicate will bind "FilePosition" to the current position in the file where the next read or write operation will take place. This position moves forward after each read or write, or jumps to the position set by the second use of this predicate.

To set the file position, all three variables must be instantiated. "SymbolicFileName" tells what file to work upon, "FilePosition" gives a numeric value for the position, and the "Mode" tells Prolog how to interpret the "FilePosition" number. The number can count from the beginning of the file, from the current file position, or backward from the end of the file.

Mode	Where to count "FilePosition" from
0	Beginning of the file
1	Current position in the file
2	End of the file, moving backward

In each case, the first position is position 0, not position 1.

eof (SymbolicFileName)   **file — (I)**

Succeeds if the character at the current file position in file "SymbolicFileName" is ASCII 26 (also known as CTRL-Z). This code indicates the end of a file.

CLOSING THE FILE

closefile (SymbolicFileName)   **file — (I)**

Closes the file with the name "SymbolicFileName." If that file isn't open, this predicate succeeds anyway. Use this predicate to ensure that any files that are written to or modified are complete and won't lose any data.

Table 10-4.   File Predicates (*continued*)

OTHERS

filestr (DosFileName,StringVariable)   **string,string — (I,O)**

Finds the file specified by "DosFileName" and reads characters from it until a limit of 64K is reached or an end-of-file code (ASCII 26) is encountered. The characters are then assigned to the string "StringVariable."

Name." The "renamefile" predicate will change the file's name, and "deletefile" will erase the file. You may need to use the next predicate to ensure that these and other file predicates are searching in the right place.

disk (DosPath)

If "DosPath" is instantiated to a possible string value, that value will become the new default disk drive and path. If "DosPath" isn't instantiated, it will be bound to the current disk drive and path.

How the File-Handling Predicates Work

Figure 10-1 shows these four file predicates at work in a simple program. Before you run this program, you must save it on the A drive as the "filetest.pro" file. (You could save it on another drive if you changed the argument of the "disk" predicate correspondingly.)

Run the program. Pose the goal

```
file_play
```

Figure 10-1. Four file predicates at work

in the Dialog window. The result will be "True." Then run the program again. You'll see the display shown in Figure 10-2. What happened? Why did the program work once and then not again? Because it changed the status of the files on the disk —the very files it depends upon.

To use the Trace command to figure out what happened, first use the Files menu to again store the program as "filetest.pro" on the A drive. Then add the "trace" predicate just above the "domains" line. Run the program and pose the "file_play" goal. Start pressing the F10 key to step through the action.

You'll see Prolog call the goal and then move to the first and only clause. The first step in satisfying that rule is to call the first predicate on

Figure 10-2.   The result of running the "file—play" program a second time

the right side, the "disk" predicate. The disk-drive path will be set to "A:" and this predicate will succeed. You'll see it return; then the second predicate on the right, the "existfile" predicate, will be taken up. Because you just stored the "filetest.pro" file on that very drive, you know that this predicate will also succeed.

In turn, the "renamefile" predicate will be called and will change the name of the "filetest.pro" file to the "newname.pro" file. One predicate is checking on the next. The trace to this point is shown in Figure 10-3.

Then the second "existfile" predicate will test to see if "renamefile" did its job. It should have, and this predicate will succeed. Finally, the

Figure 10-3.   Result of the trace of "file—play"

"deletefile" predicate will make absolutely certain that the original "filetest.pro" file is erased from the disk. This isn't necessary, but it shows that the "deletefile" predicate can succeed even if it cannot erase a file because the file isn't present. This part of the trace is shown in Figure 10- 4. Finally, the original goal will have been met, and "True" will appear in the Dialog window.

If you try the same goal again at this point, you'll get a different result. Try it. Then start stepping through with the F10 key. The "disk" predicate will again succeed, but as soon as Turbo Prolog gets to the "existfile" predicate, it meets with failure and returns "False" in the

Figure 10-4.   Part of trace showing the function of "deletefile"

Dialog window (see Figure 10-5). There is no longer a file by the name of "filetest.pro" on the A drive.

File-Opening Predicates

If you want to work with a file in any way other than just checking for its existence or changing its name, you need to *open* that file. The file-opening predicates offer a variety of styles for opening, depending on

Figure 10-5. "False" result shown in Dialog window

what you want to do to a file. By offering that variety, Turbo Prolog lets you protect files from such corruptions as improper changes in their contents. For instance, in many cases you'll want someone to only be able to read a file and not to write to it. In this case you can open it just for reading and not for writing. In another instance you may want to capture data in the file but you may, at the same time, not want to lose the data already there. Turbo Prolog allows you to open the file for appending and not for writing or modifying in any other way.

openwrite

Before you read from a file, you want to write a file. You could just as well read from one of the files already on disk. The program in Figure 10-6

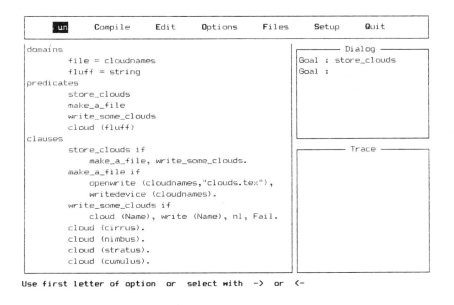

Figure 10-6.   Opening a file to write names of clouds to it

opens a file called "clouds.tex" and writes the names of some clouds to it. During the execution of the program, you'll be able to hear your floppy disk drive come to life while it opens the file.

After you have run the program and have used the external goal "store __ clouds" to make it do your bidding, press ESC to end the execution, choose the "O" option under the Files submenu, and use the command

```
type clouds.tex
```

to see the contents of the file you just created (as shown in Figure 10-7). The "False" at the end comes from the "Fail" in the "write__some__ clouds" predicate. Type the **exit** and press RETURN to return to Turbo Prolog. If you run the program again with a different set of cloud facts,

```
Type EXIT to return from DOS


The IBM Personal Computer DOS
Version 2.00 (C)Copyright IBM Corp 1981, 1982, 1983

A>type clouds.tex
cirrus
nimbus
stratus
cumulus
False

A>
```

Figure 10-7.   Contents of the "clouds.tex" file

you'll only find the *new* "clouds.tex" file when you check the disk. The old file with the same name is deleted automatically.

openread

To read the "clouds.tex" file back in, you can use the program shown in Figure 10-8. This program demonstrates both string and character reads, which are then rewritten to the Dialog window. Notice that the character read doesn't start again at the beginning of the file. It takes up after the carriage return that ended the string read.

filepos

If you want to specify what position in the file to read from, you can use this predicate. In fact, the count to the position can be made from the beginning of the file, the current position, or from the end of the file back toward the beginning.

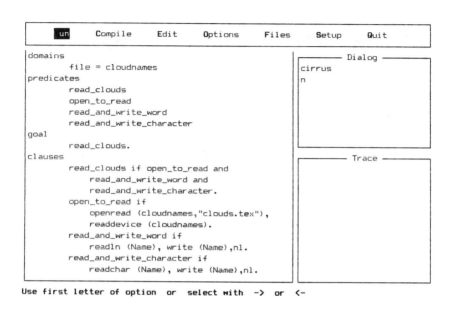

```
    un      Compile    Edit    Options    Files    Setup    Quit

domains                                         ──────── Dialog ────────
        file = cloudnames
predicates                                      cirrus
        read_clouds                             n
        open_to_read
        read_and_write_word
        read_and_write_character
goal
        read_clouds.
clauses                                         ──────── Trace ────────
        read_clouds if open_to_read and
            read_and_write_word and
            read_and_write_character.
        open_to_read if
            openread (cloudnames,"clouds.tex"),
            readdevice (cloudnames).
        read_and_write_word if
            readln (Name), write (Name),nl.
        read_and_write_character if
            readchar (Name), write (Name),nl.

Use first letter of option  or  select with  ->  or  <-
```

Figure 10-8. Reading the "clouds.tex" file back in

Example Program 44 on the Library/Example disk (shown in Figure 10-9) lets you interactively inspect a given position in any file. Figure 10-10 shows the previously developed file-reading program being read from a point that is not the beginning of the file. The "readln" predicate begins work at the second position (the second character) and stops work when it meets a carriage return. The "readchar" predicate skips two positions from the current position in the file (which was the first character of the second string) and begins work in the middle of that string.

The "filepos" predicate can also be used in reverse (with an uninstantiated "Number" variable) to discover, in relation to the beginning of the file (Mode 0), what the current position in the file is.

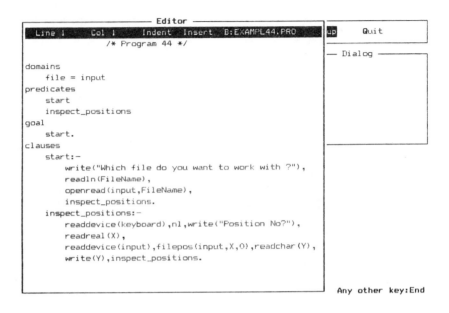

```
─────────────── Editor ───────────────
Line 1      Col 1      Indent  Insert  B:EXAMPL44.PRO
                /* Program 44 */

domains
    file = input
predicates
    start
    inspect_positions
goal
    start.
clauses
    start:-
        write("Which file do you want to work with ?"),
        readln(FileName),
        openread(input,FileName),
        inspect_positions.
    inspect_positions:-
        readdevice(keyboard),nl,write("Position No?"),
        readreal(X),
        readdevice(input),filepos(input,X,0),readchar(Y),
        write(Y),inspect_positions.
```

up   Quit

── Dialog ──

Any other key:End

Figure 10-9.   Example Program 44

eof

This simple predicate succeeds if the current file position is at the end of the file. (The code that indicates the end of a file is a decimal ASCII 26. Many systems produce this code when you press the CTRL-Z key combination.) The "eof" predicate is useful in that you can know when you have worked all the way through a file. Figure 10-10 shows this test added to the file-reading program developed earlier in the chapter. One of the easiest ways to use it is to enclose it within a "not" predicate and make it part of a series of "and" clauses in a rule. The clause will then succeed only if Turbo Prolog is not yet to the end of the file.

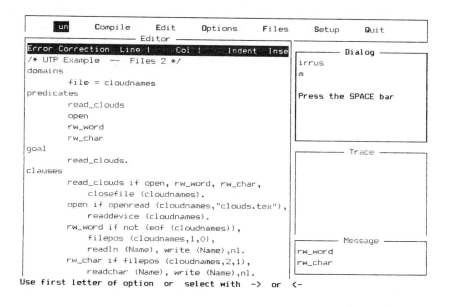

```
       un      Compile    Edit     Options    Files    Setup    Quit
                       Editor
Error Correction  Line 1     Col 1      Indent  Inse           Dialog
/* UTP Example  --  Files 2 */                         irrus
domains                                                m
        file = cloudnames
predicates                                             Press the SPACE bar
        read_clouds
        open
        rw_word
        rw_char
goal
        read_clouds.                                           Trace
clauses
        read_clouds if open, rw_word, rw_char,
            closefile (cloudnames).
        open if openread (cloudnames,"clouds.tex"),
            readdevice (cloudnames).
        rw_word if not (eof (cloudnames)),
            filepos (cloudnames,1,0),                          Message
            readln (Name), write (Name),nl.           rw_word
        rw_char if filepos (cloudnames,2,1),          rw_char
            readchar (Name), write (Name),nl.
Use first letter of option  or  select with  ->  or  <-
```

Figure 10-10.   Reading a file from a point other than the beginning

file ＿ str

This is both a "string" predicate and a file predicate.It reads characters from a file until it meets the ASCII "eof" (end-of-file) code.

openmodify

Use the "openmodify" predicate if you want to read from and write to the same file.

openappend

If you want to add information to the end of a file, you can open the file with this predicate. If "openappend" doesn't find the specified file, Turbo Prolog will give you an error message.

closefile

When you are done modifying a file, you should close it to ensure that all information went into it properly and that the information will be there the next time you want it. Without the "closefile" predicate, you are taking a chance that some information will be lost because the system doesn't know that the file is complete.

flush

When your program is writing information, it is writing to an internal buffer first. The "flush" predicate will make sure all of the contents of that buffer will be written to the "SymbolicFileName" variable. You probably won't use this often until you begin advanced programming.

DOS Predicates

Turbo Prolog lets you get directly at the disk operating system (DOS) capabilities. Within the Files menu are several options that let you direct, erase (delete), copy, rename, or print files on the disks without leaving Turbo Prolog.

In addition, an "Operating System" option lets you leave Turbo Prolog temporarily in order to perform more complex DOS operations. If you type O to choose this option, you'll find yourself back in the operating system with the disk-drive prompt on the screen. To return from DOS, you don't have to type the word "prolog" again to load Turbo Prolog—it's already in memory. All you have to do is type the word "exit" and press RETURN. If you do type the word "prolog," you'll probably get an error message telling you that there isn't enough room left in memory to load the program.

Turbo Prolog also lets you get at the DOS from inside programs. The predicates shown in Table 10-5 are the tools that give you this ability.

Table 10-5.   Standard DOS-Related Predicates

---

dir (Pathname,FileSpecString,DosFileName)   string,string,string — (I,I,O)

Forces the Turbo Prolog file directory window to open and to show the files in "Pathname" and in "FileSpecString" (both of which must be instantiated or bound). The program user can then employ the cursor keys to highlight a particular file, and press RETURN; the name of the file will be bound to "DosFileName."

date (Year,Month,Day)   integer,integer,integer — (I,I,I)(O,O,O)

There are two ways to use this predicate: to learn the date or to set the date. Both act upon the PC's internal clock, which always runs from the moment the computer is started and can be set by DOS commands outside of Turbo Prolog. Some systems have permanent clocks that continue to run even when the main power supply isn't kept on. The unenhanced PC does not have this benefit.

To learn the date, all three arguments must be uninstantiated. Each will then be bound to the current value, and the predicate will succeed.

To set the date, all three arguments must be instantiated, and their values will be sent to the clock.

time (Hours,Minutes,Seconds,Hundredths)
integer, integer, integer, integer — (I,I,I,I) (O,O,O,O)

There are two ways to use this predicate: to learn the time or to set the time. Both act upon the PC's internal clock, which always runs from the moment the computer is started and can be set by DOS commands outside of Turbo Prolog. Some systems have permanent clocks that continue to run even when the main power supply isn't kept on. The unenhanced PC does not have this benefit.

To learn the time, all four arguments must be uninstantiated. Each will then be bound to the current value, and the predicate will succeed.

To set the time, all four arguments must be instantiated, and their values will be sent to the clock.

Table 10-5.   Standard DOS-Related Predicates (*continued*)

---

beep

This predicate doesn't have any arguments. It beeps the computer's speaker.

bios (InterruptNo,RegsIn,RegsOut)   integer,regdom,regdom — (I,I,O)

This predicate requires two instantiated variables (the number of "Interrupt" and the register values to use for that interrupt) and will bind the third variable to the value of the registers after the interrupt. Registers are the internal storage areas of the microprocessor. The "regdom" domain is internally defined by Turbo Prolog and has places for integer values from all of the registers:

regdom = reg(AX,BX,CX,DX,SI,DI,DS,ES)

membyte (Segment,Offset,Byte)   integer,integer,integer — (I,I,I) (I,I,O)

If all three variables are bound, "membyte" will store the "Byte" value at the memory address calculated from "Segment" and "Offset." If only "Segment" and "Offset" are bound, "membyte" will bind "Byte" to the value found at that address.

memword (Segment,Offset,Word)   integer,integer,integer — (I,I,I) (I,I,O)

If all three variables are bound, "memword" will store the "Word" value at the memory address calculated from "Segment" and "Offset." If only "Segment" and "Offset" are bound, "memword" will bind "Word" to the value found at that address.

portbyte (PortNo,Value)   integer,integer — (I,I) (I,O)

If both "PortNo" and "Value" are bound, this predicate will send (or write) the integer "Value" to the numbered port. If "PortNo" is bound and "Value" isn't, "portbyte" will read a byte from the given port and bind it to "Value."

ptr_dword (StringVar,Segment,Offset)
string,integer,integer — (I,O,O) (O,I,I)

If the only bound variable of the three is "StringVar," this predicate will search memory and return the address of that string. The address comes in two parts: "Segment" and "Offset." If the variable is unbound and the address is bound, the predicate will go to that address and bind "StringVar" to whatever string it finds there. The ASCII values of the bytes found starting at that address, and running until 0 is encountered, will be translated into characters and become "StringVar."

storage (StackSize,HeapSize,TrailSize)   real,real,real — (O,O,O)

This predicate can read the current available sizes of the variables.

system (DosCommandString)   string — (I)

Sends the instantiated value of the variable to DOS for execution.

---

dir

The "dir" (directory) predicate doesn't go directly to DOS. Instead, it uses the Turbo Prolog file directory that you are familiar with from the Files menu. The file directory uses the DOS directory abilities. By specifying a path, a file-name extension (like .PRO), and a file name, you can see what files are on your disks.

date and time

The "date" and "time" predicates are the simplest in the DOS group. Each one works with the PC's clock and either instantiates the free variable to the value within the clock or imposes bound values onto the clock. All of the relevant variables must be instantiated or all must be free

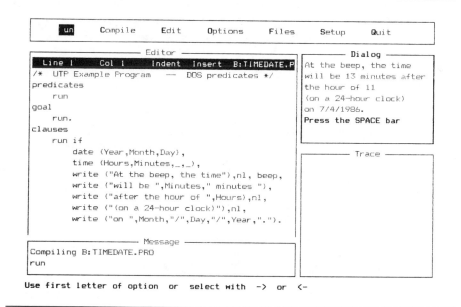

Figure 10-11.   The predicates "time," "date," and "beep" at work

before either of these predicates is called. Figure 10-11 shows how these and the predicate "beep" work.

beep

A predicate that competes mightily for the title of simplest predicate, "beep" just makes the computer's speaker squeak.

bios, membyte, memword, portbyte, ptr __dword, storage

You won't need these predicates unless you're interested in programming the computer at the assembly level. You can use "bios" to inspect or dictate the register values of the microprocessor at the heart of the PC. The "membyte," "memword," and "portbyte" predicates let you read or write data to and from memory or I/O ports. The "ptr __dword" predicate works with the segment and offset addresses of a string variable, while storage reads the sizes of the stack, the heap, and the trail.

system

The "system" predicate sends a string to DOS for execution. It is the general-purpose DOS command to use from inside Turbo Prolog programs. For example, if you had a program on the A drive called WORK. PRO and you wanted to copy it to the B drive, all you would have to do is add the clause

```
system ("copy a:work.pro b:")
```

to your program; the result would be achieved during the execution of the program. You could also use the clause

```
system (A)
```

if the variable "A" was instantiated by the time the "system" predicate was called.

Type Conversion

Sometimes the data you're working with isn't in the domain type you need. A number of predicates (shown in Table 10-6) will convert data from one type to another. Conversions between symbol/string types and integer/real types are automatic in the standard predicates.

char __int (CharParam,IntParam)

If both variables are bound, the char __ int predicate will succeed when the values are equivalent; that is, it succeeds when "IntParam" is the integer value that is the decimal ASCII code (see Appendix A for the character in "CharParam"). It works on "char" and "int" domains respectively. If one of the variables is unbound, that variable will be instantiated to the converted value of the bound variable.

Table 10-6.   Standard Type-Conversion Predicate

char__int
str__char
str__int
str__real
upper__lower

str_char (StringParam,CharParam)

If both variables are bound, "str_char" succeeds when the bound values are equivalent. This predicate works on "string" and "char" domains respectively. "StringParam" must be bound to a single character. If either variable is unbound, the other variable will be bound to its corresponding, converted value.

str_int (String,Length)

This predicate works on "string" and "int" domains. If both variables are bound, the predicate will succeed if "String" is "Length" characters long. If "Length" is unbound, it will be instantiated to the integer length of "String."

str_real (StringParam,RealParam)

If both variables are bound, the str_real predicate will succeed when the values are equivalent; that is, it succeeds when "RealParam" is the binary equivalent of the decimal integer value to which "StringParam" is bound. It works on "string" and "real" domains respectively. If one of the variables is unbound, that variable will be instantiated to the converted value of the bound variable.

upper_lower (StringIfUpperCase, StringInLowerCase)

This predicate works with two strings and is handy in natural-language processing. If both string variables are instantiated, the predicate will succeed when they represent two versions of the same string with only cases differentiating them. If one of the variables is unbound, it will be instantiated to the changed-case version of the other string.

11

Graphics And Sound

Graphics

Graphics has become a very popular element in many programming languages. Turbo Prolog has not one but *two* powerful methods for creating graphics from inside a program.

The first method is to use the dot and line predicates, which let you draw lines and dots in any of the colors the PC offers. The second method you can use is called *turtle graphics* because it lets you employ predicates that move an imaginary, line-laying "turtle" on the screen. If you have used Logo, you'll know all about turtle graphics.

If you don't want to use any graphics in your programs yet, you can skip this chapter. However, the chapter is short, and it may well be worth your while to know what the language offers. If you understand Logo, you can just skim the section on turtle graphics.

Dot and Line Graphics

The standard predicates that allow you to create dot and line graphics in Turbo Prolog are listed in Table 11-1. Two of the four predicates listed ("graphics" and "text") only serve to set the graphics stage or to clear it. You have to make do with a single dot-creating predicate and a single line-creating predicate.

Building Custom Rules   A general rule that you should keep in mind about Turbo Prolog, and about most programming languages, is that you don't need to have a command for every occasion. In fact, a language can be slow and extremely difficult to learn if it is loaded with specialized commands that may be of use only once in a while.

All you need from the graphics command set of a language is a key to get in each door. From the built-in predicates, you can build more complex routines or rules. In Turbo Prolog, you can make the dot and line predicates serve as clauses within larger rules that can accomplish exactly what you need. Then you can save those rules for introduction into other programs.

Table 11-1. Standard Predicates for Dot and Line Graphics

graphics (ModeParam,Palette,Background)
text

dot (Row,Column,Color)
line (Row1,Col1,Row2,Col2,Color)

Getting Into Graphics Mode   To start doing graphics, you must get Turbo Prolog and the PC into graphics mode. The "graphics (Mode-Param,Palette,Background)" predicate does just that. The "graphics" predicate clears the screen, puts the cursor in the top left corner, sets the resolution, chooses the available foreground colors, and sets the background color. But it doesn't draw anything. You use the "dot" and "line" predicates to do that. When you are done with graphics and want to return to text, you simply avail yourself of the "text" predicate. This single predicate without arguments resets the screen to text mode. (If you use it while in text mode, it doesn't do anything at all.)

The first thing you'll need to do with the "graphics" predicate is make sure that all three arguments are instantiated at the point in the program where it will be called. You can either place constants into the holes explicitly, or you can rig up logical structures that assign the right values at the right times. You instantiate these values just as you would any others in Turbo Prolog. Figure 11-1 shows the "graphics" predicate setting up to do graphics. You should now examine each of the arguments for the "graphics" predicate.

ModeParam   The IBM PC offers a number of different display styles. The original monochrome display offers the 80 columns by 25 lines of black-and-white (or amber or green) characters used so far in this book. The character set does include some graphics shapes for making rudimentary forms. There are also alternative monochrome display cards (special printed-circuit boards) that offer differently

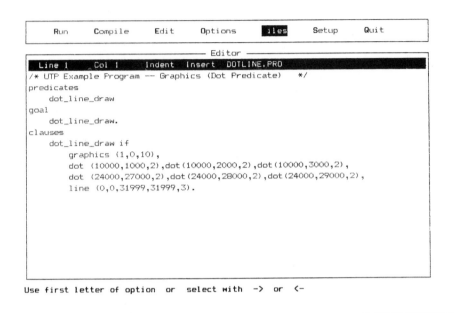

```
    Run      Compile     Edit     Options     iles     Setup     Quit

                          ─── Editor ───
  Line 1    Col 1      Indent  Insert  DOTLINE.PRO
/* UTP Example Program -- Graphics (Dot Predicate)    */
predicates
    dot_line_draw
goal
    dot_line_draw.
clauses
    dot_line_draw if
        graphics (1,0,10),
        dot (10000,1000,2),dot(10000,2000,2),dot(10000,3000,2),
        dot (24000,27000,2),dot(24000,28000,2),dot(24000,29000,2),
        line (0,0,31999,31999,3).




Use first letter of option  or  select with  -> or  <-
```

Figure 11-1.   The "dot" predicate

shaped letters and higher resolution than the original IBM equipment. Many IBM PC-compatible computers have this style of display adapter already built in.

By plugging in other display cards, you can even add color to your screens (although you'll also need a color monitor to see a color display). The two most popular color-display standards from IBM are the CGA (Color Graphics Adapter) and the EGA (Enhanced Graphics Adapter). Many other companies make display adapters that imitate these, and some make boards based on other standards. Both the CGA and the EGA have a variety of graphics modes (that is, even a single card will be able to produce several different styles of display). The basic reason for this multiplicity of styles is that when you set up a color display, you must

Table 11-2.   Graphics Modes and "ModeParam" Values

ModeParam Value	Description	Resolution Columns	Rows	Number of Colors	CGA or EGA
1	Medium	320	200	4	CGA
2	High	640	200	b/w*	CGA
3	Medium	320	200	16	EGA
4	High	640	200	16	EGA
5	Enhanced	640	350	13	EGA

*Black and white, or monochrome.

trade the number of colors in the palette (the colors you'll be able to choose to draw with) against the resolution (the number of dots on the screen).

Turbo Prolog works with some of the more common modes of both the CGA and the EGA. Table 11-2 shows these modes along with their resolution and number of colors.

Palette   As you can see in Table 11-2, the CGA supports only modes 1 and 2. You can have a high-resolution black-and-white display or you can have four colors. The CGA's mode 1 lets you use four colors, but one of those colors is reserved for the background. For the foreground's three colors, you have a choice of two palettes, as shown in Table 11-3.

Table 11-3.   CGA Medium-Resolution Palette Choices (Foreground Colors)

Palette Value	Color1	Color2	Color3
0	Green	Red	Yellow
1	Cyan	Magenta	White

Background   Once you have chosen both a graphics mode (for the "ModeParam" argument) and colors (for the "Palette" argument), you need to select a background color. This is not taken care of by "Palette." Table 11-4 shows the possibilites for the background color. You always have a choice among 16 colors for this, and the values are the same as you saw for the windowing predicates in Chapter 7.

Making Some Marks

Once you have settled into graphics mode and have chosen your colors, you're ready to actually put something on the screen. Your two initial tools are the "dot" and "line" predicates.

dot (Row,Column,Color)   Use of the "dot" predicate is fairly straightforward. This predicate can work in either of two ways. It can put a dot of a given color on the screen, or it can read the color value at the point indicated by "Row" and "Column." It will not read the color of the dot there, because that spot may have the same color as the background and may not appear to you as a dot. Still, every point on the screen has a color value.

Table 11-4.   Background Color Choices for "graphics" Predicate

Value	Color	Value	Color
0	Black	8	Gray
1	Blue	9	Light blue
2	Green	10	Light green
3	Cyan*	11	Light cyan
4	Red	12	Light red
5	Magenta	13	Light magenta
6	Brown	14	Yellow
7	White	15	High white*

*Cyan is a greenish-blue color, similar to turquoise. "High white" is a high-intensity white.

To draw a dot of a given "Color" value, you must instantiate all three arguments of the predicate. "Row" and "Column" place the dot on an imaginary grid on the screen. That grid has its zero points at the top left corner. Now you have a chance to enter any coordinate integer value from 0 to 31999 for either argument, no matter what screen mode you are in. You'll actually see a dot only if it has a color value different from the background's.

To read the color value of a spot on the screen, instantiate "Row" and "Column" to legal values (0 to 31999). The "dot" predicate will then succeed by binding "Color" to the appropriate color value.

The program in Figure 11-1 will show both uses of "dot" (as well as the "graphics" and "text" predicates) in action. Figure 11-2 shows a black-and-white rendering of the result of that use. The dots are in the upper-left and bottom-right sectors of the screen.

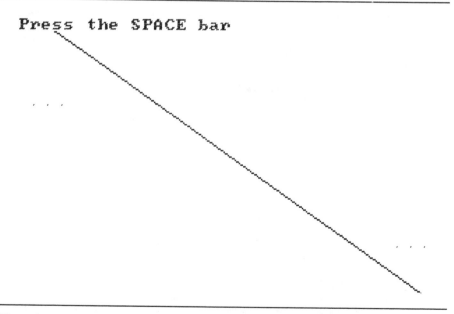

Figure 11-2.   Result of using "graphics" and "text" predicates

line (Row1,Col1,Row2,Col2,Color) Unlike "dot", the "line" predicate can only be used to draw on the screen, not to read a color value on the screen. That's understandable, since a line isn't like a dot in that it doesn't necessarily have a single color value.

The "line" predicate needs five instantiated variables. Four of these are row and column specifications that set the endpoints for the line. The final one sets the line's color. To succeed, this predicate draws a line between (and including) the two endpoints. Again, as with the "dot" predicate, the legal "Row" and "Column" values range from 0 to 31999. The program in Figure 11-1 also employs the "line" predicate. Figure 11-2 shows the program's running result.

Graphics mode does not prevent you from using the "write" predicate you have learned about. Figure 11-3 shows some writing added to a graphics program. Figure 11-4 shows the result.

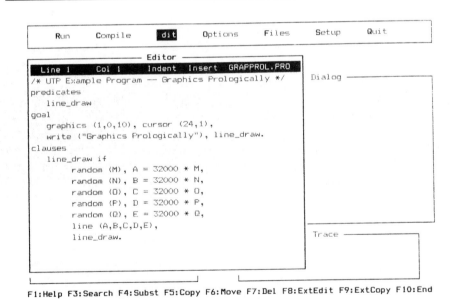

Figure 11-3. Writing added to a graphics program that draws random lines

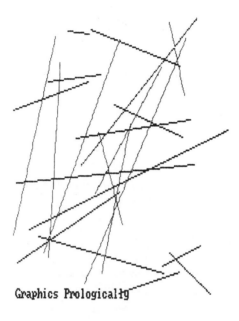

Graphics Prologically

Figure 11-4.   Result of writing graphics program in Figure 11-3

If you have a Hercules graphics board or a Hercules monochrome display adapter, you won't be able to use the standard "graphics" predicates — Turbo Prolog doesn't support them on that hardware.

Build Your Own Graphics Functions

You can make more complex graphics rules out of the two basic graphics commands. Similarly, you can use the mathematics predicates and operators in concert with the two basic graphics commands to make rules that will succeed by drawing any other shape. Other do-it-yourself rules could perform such functions as filling a given area.

Graphics in Windows

You can also put graphics in windows. In fact, you can put graphics in a number of windows in the same program as well as on the screen.

Turtle Graphics

Turtle graphics is the other major method for putting lines and figures on the screen in Turbo Prolog. The idea of a "turtle" that creates graphics is the foundation of the computer language Logo and has been adopted by a number of other languages.

The turtle is an imaginary robot "drawing tool" on the screen. It takes its instructions from the program in the form of the predicates in Table 11-5. The predicates tell it whether to move forward or back, turn right or left, press a pen down (against the screen, as if the screen were

Table 11-5.   Turtle Graphics Predicates

Pen Control

pencolor (Color)	(integer) — (I)
pendown	
penup	

Movement

forward (Step)	(integer) — (I)
back (Step)	(integer) — (I)

Rotation

left (Angle)	(integer) — (I) or (O)
right (Angle)	(integer) — (I) or (O)

drawing paper) or to hold the pen up. Turbo Prolog's turtle is even more talented than just that. It can also obey instructions concerning what pen color to employ.

Breathing Life Into the Turtle   When you enter graphics mode by calling the "graphics" predicate, the turtle is motionless in the center of the screen (centered both horizontally and vertically), with its pen up and its nose pointed toward the top of the screen. You won't see the turtle at any time. All you'll see is the trail left by its pen. If you choose to use only the "dot" and "line" predicates, you won't see even a hint of the turtle. But you can intermix turtle graphics and dot and line graphics if you wish.

The turtle awaits your orders. Figure 11-5 shows a program that gives the turtle something to do.

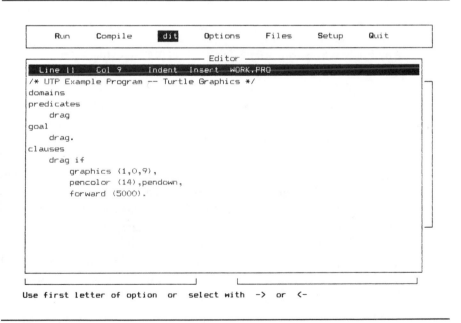

Figure 11-5.   Working with the turtle

Pen Control   The first step after entering graphics mode in this program is to put the pen down. If you wanted a graphics image that began somewhere other than the center of the screen, you could first move the turtle to another starting position (with its pen up), put the pen down, and draw.

But in this program, the turtle will start drawing immediately. Before it starts, you should set the color that the drawing will use.

pencolor (Color)   The "pencolor" predicate sets the color of the turtle's drawing pen to the previously instantiated value of "Color." For mode 0 of the CGA (which is what was set in the sample program), the color choices are limited by the palettes to the integer values shown in Table 11-3.

pendown   After choosing the pen color, you direct the turtle to put the pen down against the screen. The "pendown" predicate (no arguments) is satisfied by setting the system so that succeeding moves by the turtle leave a trail of the chosen pen color on the screen.

penup   The "penup" predicate doesn't have any arguments, either. Any turtle moves that are made after this predicate has been called will not leave any trace on the screen.

forward (Step), back (Step)   At this point in the program, the turtle is ready to run (graphics mode has been entered with the "graphics" predicate) with a certain color pen (from the "pencolor" predicate) and with the pen against the screen (from the "pendown" predicate). All that remains is to move the turtle and to see the trace. The two movement predicates are "forward" and "backward." The directions are in relation to the way the turtle's nose is pointing. Initially its nose is pointing toward the top of the screen. Later, you'll learn to change that direction.

Each movement predicate requires a single instantiated variable: "Step." The value of "Step" can be any integer from 1 to 32000. The size of each step depends on the graphics mode. If a step either forward or backward would move the turtle off of the screen, it isn't allowed; the trace is not made and the predicate will fail.

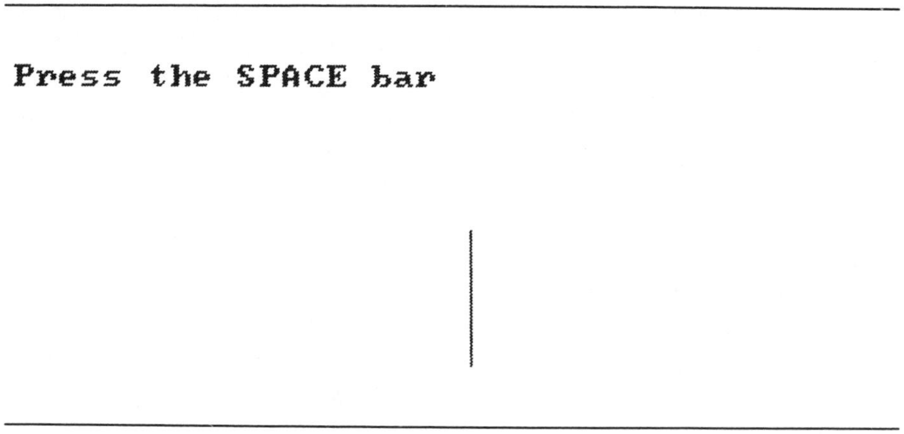

```
Press the SPACE bar
```

Figure 11-6.   Graphics effect of program using "pendown" and "forward" predicates

Figure 11-5 shows a program that will draw a straight line using the "pendown" and "forward" predicates. Figure 11-6 shows the graphics effect of that program.

left(Angle), right(Angle)   You will soon be tired of making straight lines. The "left" and "right" rotation predicates will give you more variety. Each of these can work in two ways: by rotating the turtle or by reading the angle of the turtle.

If "Angle" is instantiated (to an integer), the turtle will be rotated that many degrees in the indicated direction. The "right" predicate rotates the turtle clockwise; "left" rotates it counterclockwise. Any rotation that is more than 360 degrees will simply move the turtle through more than a complete rotation. After the rotation, any moves will be made along the line of the nose's new direction.

If "Angle" is free, the "left" or "right" predicate will bind it to the current angle. This angle is measured relative to a basepoint of straight up. For instance, a value of 180 for "Angle" would mean that the nose pointed straight down toward the bottom of the screen.

Figure 11-7 shows the turtle program with several turns added. Figure 11-8 shows the graphics effect of the program. Notice that this graphics program also produces writing generated with the standard "write" predicate. The cursor position for writing is not the same as the current turtle position.

Sound

You can employ sound in your Turbo Prolog programs, although the hardware of the IBM PC itself is not designed to produce particularly complex or interesting music. The PC does have a speaker, however, and

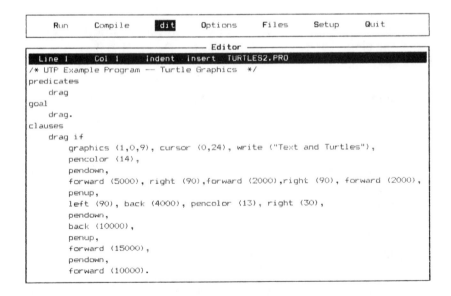

Figure 11-7.   Turtle program with several turns

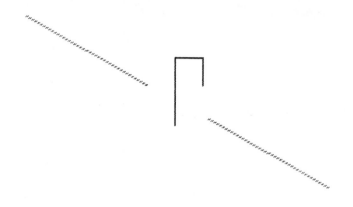

Figure 11-8.   Graphics effect of turtle program

Turbo Prolog is able to exert some control over that speaker. In fact, it can actually play notes through it. If you don't want to use the sound ability of Prolog, or if the "beep" predicate that is described in Chapter 10 is enough sound for you, you can skip the rest of this chapter.

Two Predicates

The only two standard predicates that produce sound are "beep" and "sound." The "beep" predicate doesn't allow you much control at all. The "sound" predicate allows you direct control of both the length and the pitch of the note.

beep   This predicate just makes a quick "beep" of the kind that many programs make when you strike the wrong key. Probably the most

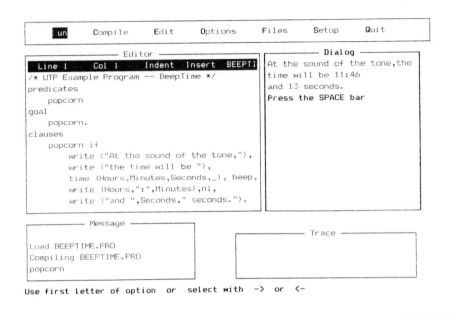

Figure 11-9.   Program using "beep" predicate

frequent use you'll make of the beep is just that: to warn of input errors. The "beep" predicate is used in the program in Figure 11-9.

sound (Duration,Frequency)   If you want to play actual notes, this is the predicate to use. To use "sound" you have to instantiate both the "Duration" and "Frequency" arguments with integer (bound) values.

The "Duration" value will be interpreted as hundredths of a second. The "Frequency" value will be intepreted as Hz (cycles per second). You can go as low as 41 Hz or as high as about 17,500 Hz. A little modification could easily make a rudimentary hearing-test program out of this code.

The ability to dictate the frequency in Hz means you can use

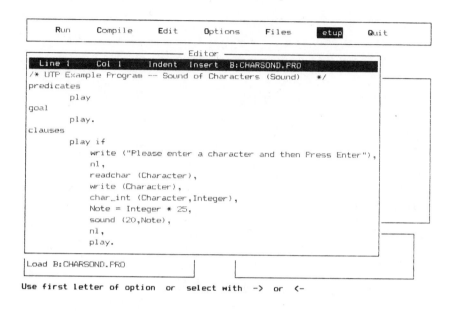

Figure 11-10.   Program using "sound" predicate

standard tables of the frequencies of diatonic scales to produce music.
Figure 11-10 shows the "sound" predicate at work. You can expand on
this program to play entire strings or files. To do that, you may want to
use some of the type-conversion predicates.

User-Defined Sound Rules

As in any other sphere of Turbo Prolog work, you can build rules that
behave as customized predicates. For the production of sound, you could
use the "sound" predicate and such other standard predicates as "time",
the various "read" predicates, and the mathematical predicates to construct more complex sound rules.

12

Advanced Programming Techniques

Turbo Prolog provides a number of features that let you build programs that are more complex than the ones shown so far in this book. This chapter will briefly describe those features and show a few of them in action. If you want more details on them, read the technical descriptions in the "Programmer's Guide" section of the Borland manual, check out one of the more advanced Turbo Prolog books, and take a look at GeoBase (described in Chapter 13). GeoBase employs quite a few of the techniques described here.

There isn't one "best way" to structure these sorts of advanced topics. They often refer to each other, and most are optional in any given program. This chapter presents the compiler directives first in order to give you a sense of control over compilation details; it then examines the other ways to compile a program: to disk, with "include" files, or in modules.

This chapter is useful for two purposes: to understand GeoBase better and to write more complex programs for yourself. If you just want to play with GeoBase before trying to understand its inner workings, then skip to Chapter 13. If you don't plan to write longer programs but would still like to experiment with the basic predicates and operators, you won't need this chapter yet. But the information here will at least let you know what else Turbo Prolog offers and what depths you have left to explore.

Compiler Directives

When you try to compile a program, Turbo Prolog first checks to see if the program code follows the syntax rules of the language. Then it examines the arguments for any misuse of domains. Turbo Prolog is a Prolog compiler, but its system of pull-down menus and windows allows you to develop programs interactively. Each time Turbo Prolog finds either a syntax or domains error, it will pinpoint that error with the cursor (in the Editor window), give you a message explaining the problem, and put you back into Editor mode so you can fix the problem. After each fix, you have only to press the F10 key again to reattempt the compilation.

Once you have made it past the syntax and domains hurdle, you have a program that compiles. Whether it will do what you want it to, when you want it to, is another matter. If it has an internal goal, you'll soon see some outward signs of its progress. But even then you can't be sure what the code will do if you change the internal goal. In addition, if the program depends on an external goal, you need to provide "test" goals immediately. Any sort of testing should include both standard and extreme cases. This is a regular practice in programming with any language.

While you are studying your program to see what it does and why, you can make good use of the various *compiler directives*. These are instructions (listed in Table 12-1) that you add to the program source file to tell the compiler how to handle the compilation. Some directives allow complex, multiple-file compilations, and others just help you figure out what a program is doing. They are *not* predicates. They are instructions to the Turbo Prolog system.

Tracing Directives and Predicates

If your program is not answering your goals in the way you expected, you can use tracing to find out what it is doing and why. The simplest way to do this is to add a "trace" directive to the program source file. But that is not the only way to get a trace. There are other options, as shown in Table 12-2.

trace

You have seen the basic "trace" directive used several times in this book. This single word sits at the very beginning of a program (after a comment is acceptable, but before the domains section). When this directive is

Table 12-1. Compiler Directives

check __cmpio	Checks if any predicates use compound flow patterns.
check __determ	Checks if any predicates have nondeterministic clauses.
code = nnnnn	Sets the maximum size in memory for the code. The count is in paragraphs. Each paragraph equals 16 bytes. The default size is 1K paragraphs (the nnnnn figure equals 1024 in that case).
diagnostics	Prints compiler diagnostic data.
include "filename"	Allows you to compile programs that extend over several files. The named file will be included in the compilation and can itself contain an "include" directive.
nobreak	Normally, Turbo Prolog scans the keyboard periodically to see if any keys have been pressed. This lets you use CTRL-BREAK to escape from programs that may be looping upon themselves. This directive eliminates such checking. Use it and you may be confronted with a program that can only be ended by restarting DOS.
nowarnings	Stops Turbo Prolog from sending you warnings.
shorttrace	See Table 13-2.
shorttrace p1,p2,...	See Table 13-2.
trace	See Table 13-2.
trace p1,p2,...	See Table 13-2.
trail = nnn	Specifies the size of the trail (in bytes). The trail is the area used to register the binding and unbinding of reference variables. The default size is 0.

added, the program is examined through single steps, calling one predicate, making one match, or writing one line at a time. At the end of each step, it stops, describes what it has done, and waits for further instructions from you. Table 12-3 shows the various types of messages you get from a "trace" directive.

The "trace" directive places the cursor at the point of action in the Editor window and shows the goals and subgoals it is trying to match in

Table 12-2.   Trace Directives, Operators, and Predicates

trace	Turns tracing on for the entire program.
trace p1,p2,... trace (on)	Turns tracing on for particular predicates.
trace (off)	This is a predicate, not a directive. It turns the tracing on or off (depending on which argument value is used). Can only be used if the "trace" or "shorttrace" directive is at the top of the program code. Notice that if the "shorttrace" directive is at the beginning of the program, then that is the type of tracing this predicate will turn on and off. It can be used many times to turn tracing on only where it is needed.
shorttrace	Turns tracing on for the entire program, but uses the compiler's optimizations and therefore returns less detailed trace information in some circumstances.
shorttrace p1,p2,...	Turns "shorttrace" on for particular predicates.
ALT-T	This key combination can be used for trace toggling. By pressing ALT and T, you can turn tracing on or off while single-step tracing through a program.

Table 12-3.   Messages During Trace

CALL	Appears each time a predicate is called. Shows both the predicate and the present values of its arguments.
RETURN	Appears when a clause has been satisfied and the logic of the program is returning to a previous predicate. An asterisk after the RETURN means that there are other clauses that could match the input arguments, and that this point needs to be and has been marked for future backtracking.
FAIL	Appears when a clause has failed; i.e., the clause cannot be matched or Turbo Prolog cannot perform its chore.
REDO	Appears when the program is backtracking. Shows the name of the reCALLed predicate and the present value of its arguments.

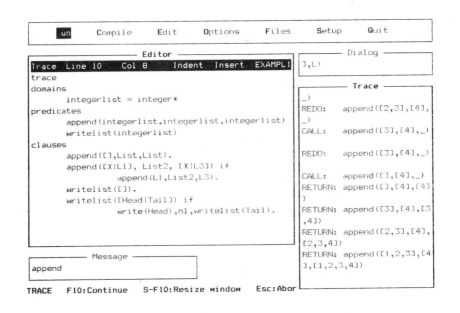

Figure 12-1. Trace program from Library/Example disk

the Trace window. Figure 12-1 shows this sort of tracing on a program from the Library/Example disk. The Trace window has been enlarged to show the messages gathered from each step. After each message was deposited in the Trace window, the F10 key was pressed to view the next step. This figure is, in essence, a form of time-lapse photography that shows how the two lists were appended.

shorttrace

This directive is used the same way as "trace," but it provides you with somewhat less information. That's because it lets you see what happens

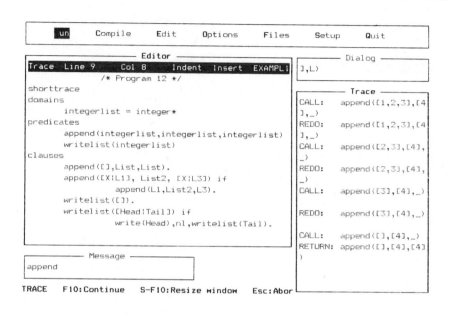

Figure 12-2.   Using the "shorttrace" directive

with the implemented compiler optimizations. When Turbo Prolog compiles something, it normally uses special *optimizing* routines to add speed and to cut corners where it can do so without changing the meaning of the program. One of the most obvious of these is the elimination of tail recursion. Try the "trace" directive on a recursion and then try "shorttrace" (see Figure 12-2). You can see that fewer Trace window messages were generated by the same process of appending two lists.

Other Tracing Options

Both "trace" and "shorttrace" offer a specialization. You can choose which predicates to trace and leave all others alone to run normally. To

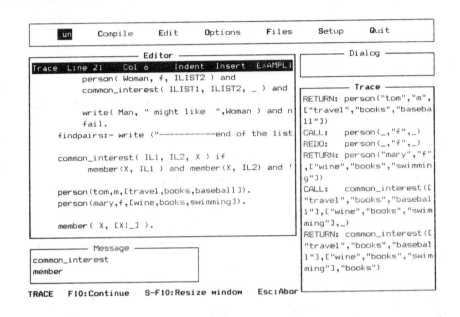

Figure 12-3. Using "trace" directive for specific predicates

do this, type the names of the predicates after the directive, and separate each name from the next name with a comma. Figure 12-3 shows an example of this in the EXAMPL16.PRO program. To create this output, load the program and add the following line above the domains declaration:

```
trace person, common_interest
```

Run the program and enter the goal

```
findpairs
```

Press the F10 key ten times. The Trace window should now be full of information.

The "trace" Predicate

The last example of tracing and tracing control that you'll look at here concerns a "trace" predicate. This has the same spelling and basic use as

```
                     /* Program 18 */
trace
predicates
     solve(real,real,real)
     reply(real,real,real)
     mysqrt(real,real,real)
     equal(real,real)
clauses
     solve(A,B,C) :-
               trace (off),
               D = B*B-4*A*C, reply(A,B,D), nl.

     reply(_,_,D) :- D < 0, write("No solution"), !.
     reply(A,B,D) :-
               D = 0, X=-B/(2*A), write("x=",X), !.
     reply(A,B,D) :-
               mysqrt(D,D,SqrtD),
               X1 = (-B + SqrtD)/(2*A),
               X2 = (-B - SqrtD)/(2*A),
               write("x1 = ",X1," and x2 = ",X2).

     mysqrt(X,Guess,Root) :-
               trace (on),
               NewGuess = Guess-(Guess*Guess-X)/2/Guess,
               not(equal(NewGuess,Guess)),!,
               trace (off),!,
               mysqrt(X,NewGuess,Root).
     mysqrt(_,Guess,Guess).

     equal(X,Y) :-
               X/Y > 0.99999  , X/Y < 1.00001.
```

Figure 12-4.   Listing for placing "trace" directive at top with tracing turned on just for part of a single rule

the "trace" directive. However, because it is a predicate, you place it in the clauses section instead of at the beginning of the program. The "trace" predicate has a single argument that may have one of two values: on or off. To use it, you must also have the "trace" or "short-trace" directive at the top of the program. Putting in the predicate as well is one more way to keep the tracing confined to only the areas where you need it. That isn't very significant here, but imagine stepping through a huge program in which you could choose to turn the tracing on just before the part that baffled you and then turn it off after.

Figures 12-4 and 12-5 show this in action. This time, Borland's Example Program 18 is used. You just want to see what happens in a small part of the calculating, so put the "trace" directive at the top, turn tracing off near the beginning (as shown in Figure 12-4), and then turn it

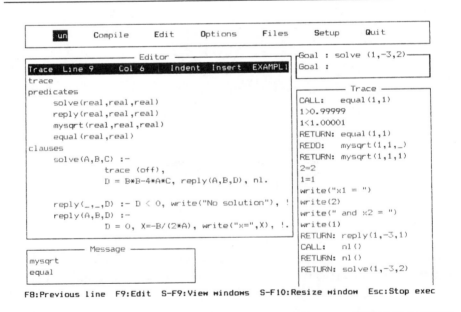

Figure 12-5. Tracing turned on

on for the part you want to understand (shown in Figure 12-5). To run the program, enter the goal

```
solve (1,-3,2)
```

and press F10 until the final solution appears as in Figure 12-5. Quite a bit of tracing comes through, even though the traced area is so small. That's because the traced area calls other predicates, which return subgoal answers to it. These other predicates look like they are outside the trace area, but they aren't —they are called before the "trace (off)" predicate is called.

Exceptions in Tracing

Not all predicates are equal in the eyes of the tracing mode. The CALLs and RETURNs of "write" predicates, for instance, are not noticed by the Trace window because it has an undetermined number of arguments. You can see this in Figures 12-1 and 12-2, as well as in Figure 12-5. The other predicates and operators that are exceptional cases for tracing are shown in Table 12-4.

Table 12-4.   Operators and Predicates That Receive Special Trace Treatment

COMPARISON OPERATORS		PREDICATES
Operator	**Meaning**	asserta
=	Equal to	assertz
<>	Not equal to	bound
><	Not equal to	findall
>	Greater than	free
>=	Greater than or equal to	not
<	Less than	readterm
<=	Less than or equal to	retract
		write
		writef

```
                        /* Program 23 */
check_determ
domains
    person      = p(name,age,telno,job)
    age         = integer
    telno ,name,job = string
predicates
    readperson(person)
    run
goal
    run.
clauses
    readperson(p(Name,Age,Telno,Job)):-
        write("Which name ? "),readln(Name),
        write("Job ?"),readln(Job),
        write("Age ?"),readint(Age),
        write("Telephone no ?"),readln(Telno).
    run:-
        readperson(P),nl,write(P),nl,nl,
        write("Is this compound object OK (y/n)"),
        readchar(Ch),Ch='y'.
    run:-
        nl,nl,write("Alright, try again"),nl,nl,run.
```

Figure 12-6.   The "check__determ" directive in place

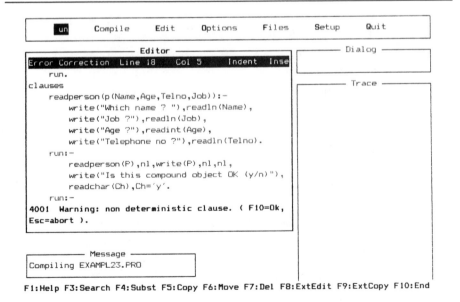

Figure 12-7.   Message from compiler with nondeterministic clauses

Determinism and check __determ

A predicate has *nondeterministic* clauses if those clauses are capable of finding multiple solutions when backtracking occurs. Although some Prologs have memory-use problems with nondeterministic clauses, Turbo doesn't — it checks for such clauses before running. A special directive is available if you want to be even more sure that a nondeterministic clause won't ruin your program's performance.

The "check __determ" directive can be inserted at the beginning of the program, just as you have inserted the "trace" directive in numerous programs in this book. If "check __determ" is inserted, Turbo will warn you each time it runs into nondeterministic clauses.

You can deal with such nondeterministic clauses in one of two ways. First, you can just press the F10 key to ignore the warning and continue running the program (searching to match a particular goal). Press any other key, and the system will end the program's run.

Second, in many cases you can transmute the nondeterministic clauses into deterministic clauses by inserting a "Cut" (!) command. Because "Cut" forbids backtracking, if it is placed in the right position, it ends the nondeterministic problem by definition. Figure 12-6 shows the "check __determ" directive in place in Borland's Example Program 23. Figure 12-7 shows the message that this compiler, prompted by the "check __determ" directive, then sends along, with examples of nondeterministic clauses that the cursor points to in the Editor window. The message goes off the right side of the Editor window. Figure 12-8 shows the same program in a cleared-up form. A "Cut" command has been inserted to transform the difficult clauses, and "check __determ" no longer finds a problem. The program will compile correctly and await a goal.

Flow Patterns

Another problem that can arise comes from the several possible uses of many of the predicates. For instance, you have seen already that a number of built-in predicates have one action when bound variables are used and another when free variables are used. Others that have more than one variable have even more potential uses, along with their increased combinations of bound and free values. User-defined predicates can have the same abilities.

In Turbo Prolog, this is referred to as having *compound flow pat-*

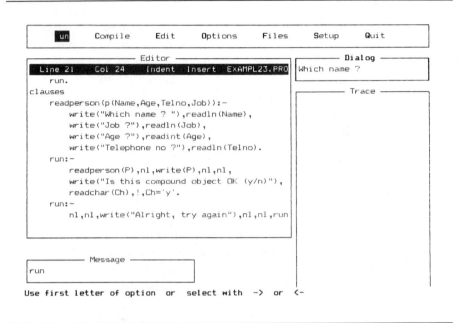

```
   un      Compile      Edit      Options      Files      Setup      Quit

──────────── Editor ────────────          ──────── Dialog ────────
Line 21    Col 24    Indent  Insert  EXAMPL23.PRO   Which name ?
    run.
clauses                                            ──────── Trace ────────
    readperson(p(Name,Age,Telno,Job)):-
        write("Which name ? "),readln(Name),
        write("Job ?"),readln(Job),
        write("Age ?"),readint(Age),
        write("Telephone no ?"),readln(Telno).
    run:-
        readperson(P),nl,write(P),nl,nl,
        write("Is this compound object OK (y/n)"),
        readchar(Ch),!,Ch='y'.
    run:-
        nl,nl,write("Alright, try again"),nl,nl,run

──────── Message ────────
run

Use first letter of option   or   select with   ->   or   <-
```

Figure 12-8. Example Program 23 with "cut" inserted

terns. The flow moves in these directions: a bound variable (or parameter) provides input to the computer (from the program), whereas a free variable (or parameter) provides output from the computer (to the program). This mixed input/output (I/O) pattern requires longer program code, and it therefore is sometimes useful to know where such predicates are for tracing and testing. By injecting the "check_cmpio" directive at the beginning of the program, you can have the compiler alert you to such flow patterns.

Putting It All Together

The "diagnostics" directive will give you a static table that contains a summary of the information provided by the compiler directives men-

```
                    /* Program 29 */
diagostics
domains
    list=symbol*
    scores=integer
predicates
    member(symbol,list)
    run
    continue(list,scores)
    yes_no_count(symbol,list)
    guessword(scores,list)
    word(list,integer)
    read_as_list(list,integer)
goal
    makewindow(1,7,0,"",0,0,25,80),
    makewindow(2,7,135,"Counting",1,20,4,34),
    makewindow(3,112,112,"YES",5,5,7,30),
    makewindow(4,112,112,"NO",5,40,7,30),
    makewindow(5,7,7,"",14,20,10,34),
    run.
clauses
    run:- word(W,L),
        shiftwindow(1),clearwindow,
        write("The word has ",L," letters"),
        shiftwindow(2),clearwindow,
        shiftwindow(3),clearwindow,
        shiftwindow(4),clearwindow,
        continue(W,0),fail.
    continue(L,R):-
        shiftwindow(5),clearwindow,
        write("Guess a letter :"),
        Total=R+1,readln(T),yes_no_count(T,L),
        shiftwindow(5),clearwindow,
        guessword(Total,L),continue(L,Total).
    yes_no_count(X,List):-
        member(X,List),shiftwindow(3),write(X),
                        shiftwindow(2),write(X),!.
    yes_no_count(X,_):-
        shiftwindow(4),write(X),
        shiftwindow(2),write(X).
    guessword(Count,Word):-
        write("Know the word yet? Press y or n"),
        readchar(A),A='y',cursor(0,0),
        write("Type it in one letter per line \n"),
        word(Word,L),read_as_list(G,L),
        G=Word,clearwindow,window_attr(112),
        write("Right! You used ",Count," guess(es)"),
        readchar(_),window_attr(7),!,fail.
    guessword(_,_).
    word([b,i,r,d],4). word([p,r,o,l,o,g],6).
    word([f,u,t,u,r,e],6).
    member(X,[X!_]):-!.
    member(X,[_!T]):-member(X,T).
    read_as_list([],0) :-!.
    read_as_list([Ch!Rest],L) :-
        readln(Ch),L1=L-1,read_as_list(Rest,L1).
```

Figure 12-9.   The "diagnostics" directive in place in Example Program 29

tioned previously ("check_determ" and "check_cmpio"), as well as domain information and code size. Figure 12-9 shows the "diagnostics" directive in place in Borland's Example Program 29. Figure 12-10 shows

```
   Run      ompile      Edit      Options      Files      Setup      Quit

 ───────────────────────────── Diagnostics ─────────────────────────────


Predicate Name  Dbase Determ Size  Doml -- flowpattern
──────────────  ───── ────── ─────  ──────────────────
goal             NO    YES    102   --
member           NO    YES     72   symbol,list -- i,i
run              NO    YES    222   --
continue         NO    YES    189   list,scores -- i,i
yes_no_count     NO    YES    198   symbol,list -- i,i
guessword        NO    YES    289   scores,list -- i,i
word             NO    NO     128   list,integer -- o,o
word             NO    YES    879   list,integer -- i,o
read_as_list     NO    YES    184   list,integer -- o,i
──────────────  ───── ────── ─────  ──────────────────
Total size              2263

Press the SPACE bar

Use first letter of option  or  select with  ->  or  <-
```

Figure 12-10.   Compiling Example Program 29 using "diagnostics" directive

the result of compiling this program with the "diagnostics" directive — a great deal of information in the Message window. In fact, the entire screen is used as a message window so that you can see the extent of the diagnostics table. None of the predicates are in a database. They are all in the regular clauses area. All except one are determinate. They take up 76 to 913 bytes, and they have a variety of domains and flow patterns.

You should also know that you can use all or any combination of the compiler directives at one time. They have been presented separately to emphasize their particular actions. Just put them all before the domains section. An exception is the "include" directive, which can go anywhere that one of the program section or division words can go.

Suppressing Warnings and Escapes

If "diagnostics" is the opposite of what you want, and instead you want to limit the warning messages because you're sure of what you're doing, there are two compiler directives that will help you.

nobreak

In regular running, Turbo Prolog checks the keyboard for CTRL-C or CTRL-BREAK before each new predicate call. If it finds either of these, it ends the program run. In a looping program, this may be the only way to get out. For instance, Example 41 in the Turbo Prolog manual can only be stopped with CTRL-BREAK. If you add the "nobreak" directive at the beginning of this program, as shown in Figure 12-11, the only way you'll

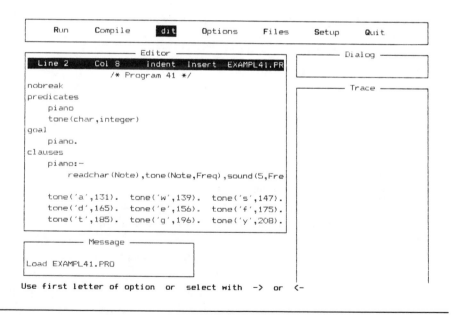

```
        Run       Compile      dit      Options     Files    Setup    Quit

                         ─ Editor ─                          ─ Dialog ─
   Line 2    Col 8    Indent  Insert  EXAMPL41.PR
                     /* Program 41 */
 nobreak                                                     ─ Trace ─
 predicates
     piano
     tone(char,integer)
 goal
     piano.
 clauses
     piano:-
         readchar(Note),tone(Note,Freq),sound(5,Fre

     tone('a',131).   tone('w',139).   tone('s',147).
     tone('d',165).   tone('e',156).   tone('f',175).
     tone('t',185).   tone('g',196).   tone('y',208).

         ─ Message ─
 Load EXAMPL41.PRO

 Use first letter of option  or  select with  ->  or  <-
```

Figure 12-11.   Adding a "nobreak" directive

get out is to reboot the operating system — CTRL-BREAK won't do the trick. Anything you had stored in RAM and not on disk will be lost. Nonetheless, you may want to use "nobreak" at times, because the break procedure slows the program down.

nowarnings

You are familiar with such warnings as "Variable occurs only once in a clause" and "Variable not bound on return from a clause," which appear during so many compilations. You won't see them if you use the "nowarnings" directive. Of course, the program will still have those conditions. You just won't be warned of them. If you're sure of what you're doing, eliminate the signposts, and you'll gain some speed.

Making Room

The "code" and "trail" directives tell the system how much memory to keep available for the program code and the register of reference variables, respectively. These are explained briefly in Table 12-1. You don't need to worry about them until you move into fairly advanced applications.

Including Other Files

In many instances, you may want to include other files in a compilation. These files could contain code from another programming language, or they could be other Turbo Prolog files that you don't want to rewrite. The "include" directive allows you to use that code "as is" in some cases.

The "include" directive doesn't have to be placed at the beginning of a program as other directives do. Instead, it can be placed anywhere a keyword (a section delimiter such as "clauses," "goal," or "global predicates") could go. You use it to tell Turbo Prolog to compile other files into this single object code. An included file can contain a goal, domain and predicate declarations, and clauses. You write it like this:

```
include "DosFileName"
```

where "DosFileName" is the disk name of the file you want to include.

Here's an example of an "include" directive at work. The program in Figure 12-12 doesn't have all the information necessary — the "paid_enough" predicate isn't fully worked out. But instead of building more source text into this file, you can refer to another file that has been made before. This file (the program shown in Figure 12-13) details the

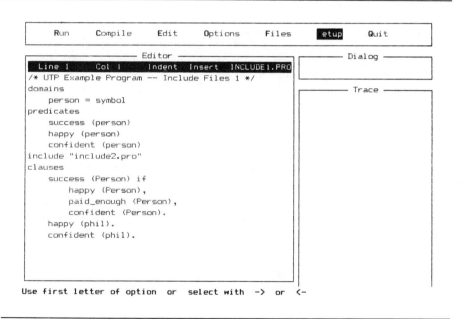

Figure 12-12.   Program with "paid_enough" predicate not fully worked out

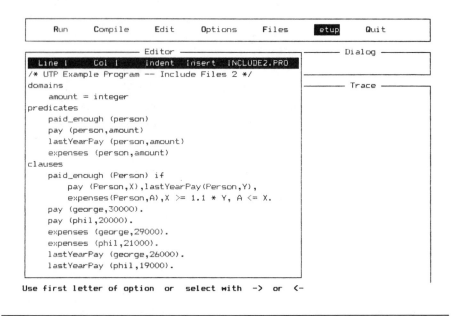

```
  Run      Compile     Edit      Options     Files    etup     Quit
┌───────────────────── Editor ──────────────────┐ ┌─── Dialog ───
│ Line 1     Col 1     Indent  Insert  INCLUDE2.PRO│ ├──────────────
│ /* UTP Example Program -- Include Files 2 */    │ │
│ domains                                          │ ┌─── Trace ───
│     amount = integer                             │ │
│ predicates                                       │
│     paid_enough (person)                         │
│     pay (person,amount)                          │
│     lastYearPay (person,amount)                  │
│     expenses (person,amount)                     │
│ clauses                                          │
│     paid_enough (Person) if                      │
│         pay (Person,X),lastYearPay(Person,Y),    │
│         expenses(Person,A),X >= 1.1 * Y, A <= X. │
│     pay (george,30000).                          │
│     pay (phil,20000).                            │
│     expenses (george,29000).                     │
│     expenses (phil,21000).                       │
│     lastYearPay (george,26000).                  │
│     lastYearPay (phil,19000).                    │
└──────────────────────────────────────────────────┘
Use first letter of option  or  select with  -> or  <-
```

Figure 12-13.   File detailing the "paid—enough" predicate

"paid—enough" predicate. Because the first program has the "include" line referring to the second program, the combination of the two should compile properly.

Try it yourself. Get the first program on the screen (as shown in Figure 12-12) and then press C for compile. You'll see the compilation begin, and you'll even see Turbo Prolog automatically load the second program (the *include file*) into the Editor window. The first time I tried this, the compiler ran into a domain-type error. George was listed as making $45,000 a year, which is too big an integer for Turbo Prolog to handle.

Turbo therefore jumped back into editing mode. I changed "45000" to "30000" (remember not to use commas in the middle of numbers such as this), and then press F10. Normally this key attempts a failed compilation once again. It does so here, too, but it automatically saves the fixed version of the include file you just worked on. Then it jumps back to the first file, starts compiling it, calls the include file in, adds it to the mix, and finishes. You're ready to run, as shown in Figure 12-14.

```
success (george) and success (phil)
```

you will get two "False" responses. Why? Try to trace it. Add the "trace" directive to the beginning of the INCLUDE1 program. Then recompile

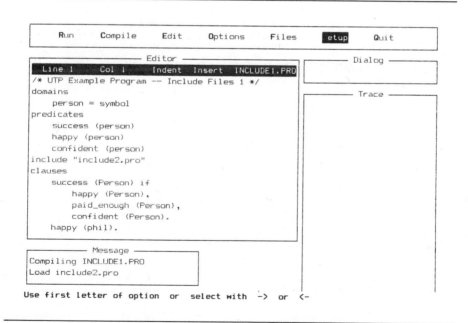

Figure 12-14.   Recompiled program with "include" file

and rerun. Pose a goal, and step through the program with the F10 key. You'll not only see a trace on the INCLUDE1 program, you'll see the trace jump to the include file (include2.pro) and continue there (as shown in Figure 12-15).

Referring to Another File

The "include" predicate lets you specifically state which other file to pull into this compilation. The called files can themselves contain an "include" directive that calls yet another file. However, you should not

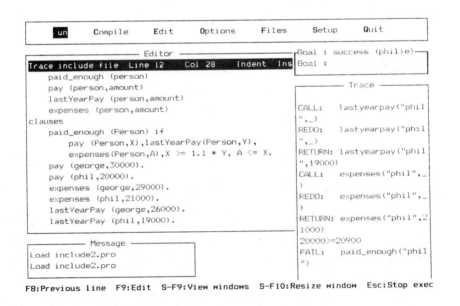

Figure 12-15.   Trace on the INCLUDE1 program

have "include" directives that go in a circle (eventually calling again on one of the files already included).

Using the "include" directive isn't the only way to work with multiple files for a single compilation. There is also modular programming. But before getting into that, you should examine some of the options, as yet undiscussed, that are available for single-file compilation.

Compilation Alternatives

When you use the standard compilation procedure, you are compiling your code directly into RAM and running it from there. This is very fast, but it limits the size of your program severely. To get access to more data and code and to make programs that aren't completely dependent upon the Turbo Prolog development system of menus and windows in order to run, you can compile to disk.

Compiling to Disk

All of the programs used so far in this book have been compiled to memory (RAM). When you compile a program to disk, you are able to run it later without starting the Turbo Prolog development system. All you have to do is type the name of the program and press RETURN.

EXE

The simplest way to compile to disk is to choose the EXE option under the Options menu (as shown in Figure 12-16). The moment you choose it, the menu will disappear again, so you just have to have faith that you picked the right part of the menu.

After choosing EXE, you tell Turbo Prolog to compile. It will create an OBJ file and then link that file to make an EXE file. *Linking* is the process of adding standard code to the code you have developed. The file

Figure 12-16.   .EXE selection of Options menu

that does the linking is PLINK.BAT. When you compile an EXE file to disk, you don't need to even think about linking. That is taken care of automatically by the compiler. For an EXE compile to work properly, you need to make sure that several files are in the proper directories.

The file COMMAND.COM (part of the operating system) is in the DOS directory specified by the setup menu. The PLINK.BAT file must be in the OBJ directory specified by the setup menu. The LINK.EXE file must be in the OBJ directory specified by the setup menu or in a directory specifed by a path in the PLINK.BAT file. You can either move the files to the proper directory or change the setup menu specifications.

You must also ensure that you have enough memory (RAM) in your computer to hold the entire linked program. If that is in question, and you still want to make an independent EXE version of your program, you should choose the OBJ option of the Options menu.

OBJ

If you choose to compile to an OBJ file, you'll need to follow up your compilation with a linking. To do that, all you have to do is properly invoke the PLINK.BAT file.

Choose the OBJ option under the Options menu. Then press C to compile. After compiling, check the directory of the area that has the OBJ file. There should also be a SYM file that holds the symbol table. Get to the directory that holds the PLINK.BAT file, and then type "plink" followed by a space and the name of the OBJ file you want to link. You can also add two other parameters: the path for the EXE program and the path for the Turbo directory.

When you run the link operation on the OBJ file, you turn it into an EXE file or program. This sort of program can be run just by typing its name and pressing RETURN. To specify where the EXE file should be on disk, you just skip a space after the OBJ file description and then type the pathname you want used. The PLINK.BAT file needs the INIT.OBJ and PROLOG.LIB files. If these aren't in the same directory as PLINK, you need to skip another space after the EXE path specification and type the path to the part of the disk where these can be found. Table 12-5 summarizes these options.

Table 12-5. PLINK.BAT Parameters

The linking file is invoked with this syntax:

plink.bat %1 %2 %3

%1	Refers to the name of the project or module to be linked.
%2	Refers to the drive and path to which the EXE file will be written.
%3	Refers to the drive and path to which PLINK.BAT will look for the INIT.OBJ and PROLOG.LIB files.

Modular Programming

There is yet another way to compile. It lets you use source files from a variety of languages, on a variety of disk paths. *Modular programming* builds a final program (or "project") out of a few or several independent "modules." All of the modules in a project have to share a single internal symbol table. Therefore, each module must know the project for which it is intended. Each module needs a "project" directive along with a project name on the first line of the code.

Program Modules

You can create programs of modules that are written, edited, and compiled separately. There are three advantages to using this approach on long programs; two are generally true in many programming languages, and the third is specific to Prolog.

Simplify Debugging

The longer a program is, the harder it is to debug. There are more and more combinations of things that can interact in a way you don't want them to and that you may not notice. One answer to this problem is to work in modules. Each module is practical and small, and each handles a single task. A module can be thoroughly tested and debugged before it is added to the entire integrated program. Then when you need to modify or update a program, you can probably modify only a few modules instead of the entire program. This is true in many computer languages.

Interface to Other Languages

Modular programming also eases the task of including program code that was written in other languages. Turbo Prolog can combine with modules from other languages and link them into a Pascal, C, or FORTRAN program and assembler. Borland expects to update Turbo Pascal in 1987 so that Turbo Prolog modules can be included in Pascal programs.

Retain Local Variables

All predicate and domain names are local in Prolog (unless you use Turbo Prolog's special "global" declarations). That means that you can reuse a predicate or domain name in a different module, put the modules together, and the various parts of code will remain discrete and not interfere with any other part. Different things may have the same names in different modules, but they will not be mixed up by the code or seen to be the same thing. This is particularly impressive when you realize that Turbo Prolog keeps the programmer's own variable names when compiling. (Not all Prologs do.) This makes it easier to look at compiled Turbo Prolog programs and understand what is happening.

Requirements for Modular Programming

There are four things you must do to make a modular program work: set up a project definition, declare global variables, ensure that at most one module has an internal goal, and make sure the proper files for linking are in the proper directories (described previously in the "Compiling to Disk" section). The module with the goal is the main module. After you have defined the project and declared the global variables, you can start compiling each module one by one using either the OBJ or EXE option. If you use the OBJ option, don't link those files until the last module is compiled. When you come to the last module, you can either use the OBJ option, quit Turbo Prolog, and call the linker yourself (PLINK.BAT); or you can choose the EXE option, watch the final module compile, and then link to all of the others.

Project Definition

To use modular programming, you have to specify which modules will be used in the final, compiled program. You create this file by choosing the Module List option of the Files menu (as shown in Figure 12-17), giving the project name to that list, and then editing the list to contain all of the module names. The name must not include the extension (file-type

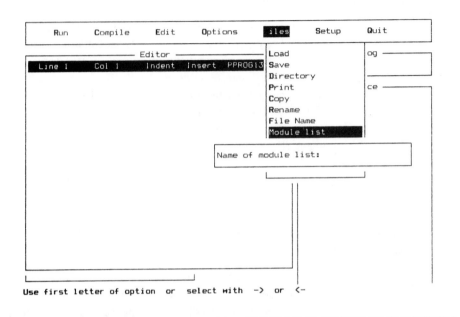

Figure 12-17.   Module List option of Files menu

designation) and must be followed by a plus sign (+). The project file will
have the extension ".PRJ."

The project definition does two things. First, it allows the compiler
to set up a symbol table with the project name. This table will be shared
by all the modules and will be stored as a disk file (with the project name
and file type SYM) in the OBJ directory. Second, the PLINK.BAT file
can refer to the PRJ file at link time to see what files need to be linked
together.

To let each module know what SYM file it should use, you must put
the compiler directive "project" at the beginning of that module's code
and follow the directive with a space and the name of the project.

Global Predicates
And Variables

These have been mentioned several times before in this book. The declarations allow Turbo Prolog to check for syntax and domain errors, even across modules. Although the locality of Prolog variables is often handy, there are times when you'll want one module to mean the same thing as another module when it refers to a particular variable name. You can make it do so by declaring the variable to be *global*.

There are two parts to such a declaration: the predicate and the domain.

Global Predicates

Predicates can be declared global in a *global predicates* section. However, you can only have one such section in all of the modules (for compilation) put together. One difference between these declarations and regular predicate declarations is that the flow patterns of global predicates have to be specified in advance. A global predicate may have more than one flow pattern, and several patterns can be shown on a single line. The predicate is followed by the arguments, a hyphen, and then the syntactically legal patterns enclosed within parentheses. Each argument must have either an "(i)" (input or free) or an "(o)" (output or bound). Here's an example:

```
global predicates
    glob_pred_1 (dom1,dom2,dom2) - (i,o,o)
```

Global Domains

Domains need to be globally declared unless they are standard. This is done in the global domains section. These declarations look the same as other domain declarations. Here's an example for the previous predicate:

```
dom1 = symbol dom2, dom3 = integer
```

Using an "include" Directive
For Global Declarations

Once you have written your global declarations, the easiest way to make sure each and every module to be compiled has access to them is to make a separate file of them and put an "include" directive into the text of each module.

Program Divisions

There are more possible program divisions than have been presented so far in this book. Several of these are employed in GeoBase, the application described in Chapter 13. These divisions, in the order in which they appear, are as follows:

- Compiler directives

- Domains

- Global domains

- Database

- Predicates

- Global predicates

- Goal

- Clauses.

Most of these divisions are optional. As you have seen, a program can consist entirely of a goal, or it can have a single, built-in predicate in a clauses section and depend on an external goal. Nevertheless, these other divisions let you declare other sorts of information that can be very practical in long and complex programs.

Compiler Directives

These have been discussed earlier in this chapter.

Domains

You are already familiar with this section, which describes the type of data used by the predicates.

Global Domains

This section allows you to specify domains that will work for more than one module.

Database

Another sort of file that Turbo Prolog can work with is a *dynamic database.* The standard list of clauses (facts and rules) is a database, and Turbo Prolog has a built-in engine for searching that database. The matching and backtracking that take place automatically when a goal is posed are an efficient and thorough way to search a database. However, it is sometimes very useful to add or subtract facts and rules while posing goals. In effect, these are external predicates that you want considered when you query the database. This sort of dynamic (changeable) database is declared in a separate section at the beginning of a program and can be saved in a separate file by using the "save" predicate. This and the other predicates that handle dynamic databases are listed in Table 12-6.

The database declaration comes before the other predicate declaration. It declares the predicates for the database that can be made of typed-in clauses or of clauses brought in from a disk file by the "consult" predicate.

Three standard predicates let you build a dynamic database: "as-

Table 12-6.   Predicates Handling Dynamic Databases

---

asserta (<fact>)   dbasedom — (I)

Adds a fact to the database that is stored in RAM. The fact is placed before any other clauses of the same predicate.

assertz (<fact>)   dbasedom — (I) (O)

Adds a fact to the database that is stored in RAM. The fact is placed after any other clauses of the same predicate.

retract (<fact>)   dbasedom — (I)

This is opposite to the "asserta" and "assertz" predicates. It deletes the first fact in the database that matches the "<fact>" in the argument.

consult (DosFileName)   string — (I)

Pulls a database file of predicates into memory. The file will be a text file: if any of the lines in it don't meet Turbo Prolog syntax standards, the "consult" predicate will fail. Often the text file will be one that was put on the disk with the "save" predicate.

save (DosFileName)   string — (I)

Saves the clauses on the disk under the "DosFileName." This text file will have one clause on each line and can be edited directly. It can also be called into memory by a "consult" predicate within a program.

---

serta", "assertz", and "retract". The first two add facts to the database; the last one deletes a fact. The "asserta" predicate puts the new fact before all of the previous facts of the same predicate, while the "assertz" predicate puts the new fact after the old ones. The order matters, because Prolog searches from top to bottom, left to right, in a list.

Predicates

In this section you can officially declare all of the user-defined predicates that will be found in the clauses section. By declaring them, you allow

Turbo Prolog to know such things as what sort of data the predicates will use and how many arguments they possess. This lets the compiler check for errors in syntax and types.

Global Predicates

You can also declare predicates that will be good for more than one module. Only one global predicates section can be used for a compilation. In other words, any other files that are included cannot have their own global predicates section if one has already been read by the compiler.

Goal

The standard Clocksin and Mellish Prolog works entirely with external goals. You have to run the program and then tell it the goal you want to achieve. Turbo Prolog lets you choose to use an internal goal, so that the system will not wait for another goal but will work toward the specified goal immediately.

Clauses

Clauses are the facts and rules that Prolog searches through in its quest to satisfy a goal.

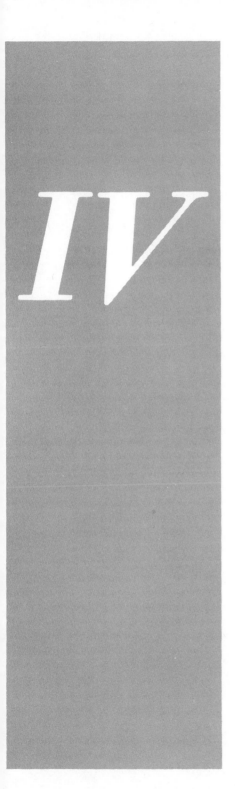

Using Turbo Prolog has introduced you to Prolog in general and specifically to the basics of Turbo Prolog. By now you are probably ready for more challenging Prolog problems, so this section introduces "GeoBase," Borland's powerful natural-language query database. GeoBase is both interesting and fun, and because it was written in Turbo Prolog, it should give you an idea of the power of applications written with this language.

13

Using
GeoBase

When you buy Turbo Prolog, you get more than a software development tool. You also get GeoBase, an example of an application program written in Prolog. GeoBase is a natural-language database; that is, it combines a database (information about United States geography) with an interface that can interpret questions written in everyday English. In a sense, GeoBase comprises two of the most important applications of Prolog: expert systems and natural languages.

Not only do you get this application written in Turbo Prolog, you get the complete, commented source code. That makes GeoBase a wonderful laboratory for your Prolog research. After compiling, running, and asking questions of the program, you can inspect the code, modify it, improve it, or chop off pieces of it for other programs you want to write. GeoBase makes use of many of Turbo Prolog's capabilities and lets you experiment with such advanced features as EXE compiling and database modification.

If you don't want to use GeoBase, skip this entire chapter. But remember that this working code and data wait for your inspection.

What You Need to Compile GeoBase

Figure 13-1 shows the files you'll need to compile and run GeoBase. If you compile to disk, you'll be able to run GeoBase later from a single file.

You'll find three major obstacles when compiling and running a large program like GeoBase: too little disk space, wrong directory paths, and too little RAM space.

Too Little Disk Space

Format new disks, and copy only the files listed in Figure 13-1 to those disks. You'll then have room for any modified versions of the files you might want to make and for the files that the compiler will generate. You've probably noticed how crowded both the System/Program disk and the Library/Example disk are, with little room left for anything new.

PROLOG.LIB
PROLOG.EXE
PROLOG.SYS
PROLOG.ERR
PROLOG.HLP
PLINK.BAT
INIT.OBJ

GEOBASE.PRO
GEOBASE.INC
GEOBASE.HLP
GEOBASE.DBA

Figure 13-1.   Files needed to compile GeoBase

This obstacle and the following one are more easily overcome if you have a hard disk, although you'll have to be even more careful of the paths you select on a hard disk system.

Directory Paths

You may run into error messages that say a certain file cannot be opened. This normally means that the file isn't on the disk that Prolog expects it to be on. You just have to use the setup menu to change the directory settings, and in the worst case, exit to the operating system to copy files into more convenient places.

RAM Constraints

You'll need a lot of memory to run GeoBase. First, try it with your system as is. Then if you have trouble with error messages, you'll need to quit Turbo Prolog and get more free memory. You can either remove some RAM-resident programs that you're using (such as SideKick or Ready!) or buy a memory board with more memory chips to add to your PC.

Inspecting the PRO File

To try GeoBase, get Turbo Prolog running and load the GEOBASE.PRO file into the Editor window. Use the setup menu to enlarge the Editor window so that you can see the entire width of the program's code.

Figure 13-2 shows what you'll see when the title section of GeoBase

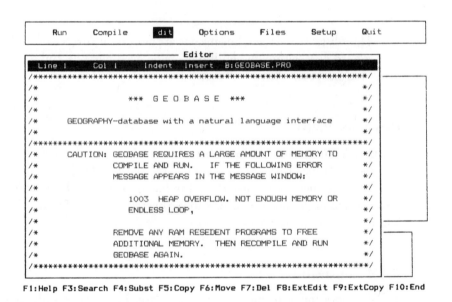

Figure 13-2.   Title section of GeoBase in Editor window

```
┌───────────────────────── Editor ─────────────────────────┐
│ Line 37    Col 1     Indent  Insert  E:GEOBASE.PRO        │
│ code=2500                                                 │
│                                                           │
│ DOMAINS                                                   │
│   LIST = SYMBOL*                    /* The domain LIST is a list of words │
│                                                           │
│ DATABASE                                                  │
│   /* The Language Database */                             │
│   relat(SYMBOL,LIST)                /* Relation name and a list of attribu │
│   schema(SYMBOL,SYMBOL,SYMBOL)      /* Entity network: entity-assoc-entity │
│                                                           │
│   entitysize(SYMBOL,SYMBOL)         /* Which attribute gives the size of a │
│   relop(LIST,SYMBOL)                /* Example: relop([greater,than],gt] * │
│   assoc(SYMBOL,LIST)                /* Alternative assoc names */          │
│   synonym(SYMBOL,SYMBOL)            /* Synonyms for entities */            │
│   ignore(SYMBOL)                    /* Words to be ignored */              │
│   min(SYMBOL)                       /* Words stating minimum */            │
│   max(SYMBOL)                       /* Words stating maximum */            │
│   big(SYMBOL,SYMBOL)                /* big, long, high .... */             │
│   unit(SYMBOL,SYMBOL)               /* Unit for population, area ... */    │
│                                                           │
│   /* The Real database */                                 │
└───────────────────────────────────────────────────────────┘
 F1:Help F3:Search F4:Subst F5:Copy F6:Move F7:Del F8:ExtEdit F9:ExtCopy F10:End
```

Figure 13-3.   Portion of GeoBase code

is in the Editor window. Proceed into the Editor, and use the cursor keys
to move down through the code. Note the declaration sections at the
beginning; also note the comments explaining what each line is there to
do. Figure 13-3 shows part of this code. You can't even see all of the
code's horizontal width.

Next you will see the clauses that access the database itself (which
is a different file). Some of these are shown in Figures 13-4 and 13-5.
Finally, you'll come to the "INCLUDE" line (shown in Figure 13-6) that
refers to another of the important files for GeoBase.

```
─────────────────────────── Editor ───────────────────────────
 Line 67   Col 1    Indent  Insert  B:GEOBASE.PRO
/***************************************************************/
/*               Database Access                              */
/***************************************************************/

PREDICATES
  member(SYMBOL,LIST)              /* membership of a list */

CLAUSES
  member(X,[X!_]).
  member(X,[_¦L]):-member(X,L).


PREDICATES
  /* Access to database */
  db(SYMBOL,SYMBOL,SYMBOL,SYMBOL,SYMBOL)
  ent(SYMBOL,SYMBOL)


CLAUSES

/* ent returns values for a given entity name. Ex. if called by
```
F1:Help F3:Search F4:Subst F5:Copy F6:Move F7:Del F8:ExtEdit F9:ExtCopy F10:End

Figure 13-4.   Clauses that access GeoBase database

```
─────────────────────────── Editor ───────────────────────────
 Line 105  Col 1    Indent  Insert  B:GEOBASE.PRO
CLAUSES

/* ent returns values for a given entity name. Ex. if called by
   ent(city,X)  X  is instantiated to cities.
*/

  ent(continent,usa).
  ent(city,NAME):-       city(_,_,NAME,_).
  ent(state,NAME):-      state(NAME,_,_,_,_,_,_,_,_).
  ent(capital,NAME):-    state(_,_,NAME,_,_,_,_,_,_).
  ent(river,NAME):-      river(NAME,_,_).
  ent(point,POINT):-     highlow(_,_,_,_,POINT,_).
  ent(point,POINT):-     highlow(_,_,POINT,_,_,_).
  ent(mountain,M):-      mountain(_,_,M,_).
  ent(lake,LAKE):-       lake(LAKE,_,_).
  ent(road,NUMBER):-     road(NUMBER,_,_).


/* The db predicate is used to establish relationships between
   entities. The first three parameters should always be instantiated
   to entityname-assocname-entityname, the last two parameters
```
F1:Help F3:Search F4:Subst F5:Copy F6:Move F7:Del F8:ExtEdit F9:ExtCopy F10:End

Figure 13-5.   Additional clauses that access GeoBase database

```
   Run      Compile     Edit     Options    [iles]    Setup     Quit

 /* Relationships about mountainss */
 db(mountain,in,state,MOUNT,STATE):-    mountain(STATE,_,MOUNT,_).
 db(state,with,mountain,STATE,MOUNT):- mountain(STATE,_,MOUNT,_).
 db(height,of,mountain,HEIGHT,MOUNT):- mountain(_,_,MOUNT,H1),str_int(HEIGHT,

 /* Relationships about lakes */
 db(lake,in,state,LAKE,STATE):-        lake(LAKE,_,LIST),member(STATE,LIST).
 db(state,with,lake,STATE,LAKE):-      lake(LAKE,_,LIST),member(STATE,LIST).
 db(area,of,lake,AREA,LAKE):-          lake(LAKE,A1,_),str_real(AREA,A1).

 /* Relationships about roads */
 db(road,in,state,ROAD,STATE):-        road(ROAD,LIST),member(STATE,LIST).
 db(state,with,road,STATE,ROAD):-      road(ROAD,LIST),member(STATE,LIST).

 db(E,in,continent,VAL,usa):-          ent(E,VAL).
 db(name,of,_,X,X):-                   bound(X).

 INCLUDE "geobase.inc" /* Include parser + scanner + eval + Menusystem */
```

Use first letter of option or select with -> or <-

Figure 13-6. "INCLUDE" line referring to geobase.inc file

Compiling and Running GeoBase

All you have to do now is leave the Editor and press C to compile the program in memory. Be prepared to wait a little while for results. The GEOBASE.PRO file has to call in the other code, and thus there's a lot of compiling to do. Also, if you haven't already done so, you may have to go to the setup menu before compiling, enter the Directories option, and change the PRO directory to the B drive or to whatever drive houses the GEOBASE.PRO file.

Compilation Options

You can also use the Options submenu to choose a different compilation method for GeoBase. As explained in Chapter 12, compiling GeoBase to disk as an OBJ or EXE file allows you to use it independently of the

Turbo Prolog development environment — you'll be able to run it as an independent program. Type 0 to get the Options submenu, and then move the highlighting to either OBJ, EXE, or Project.

Compiling to Disk

When you compile to memory, your program can only run in tandem with the compiler. You can compile any program, including GeoBase, to a disk file that will run by itself without the further aid of the compiler. If you choose this option, make sure the disk containing the OBJ and EXE directory settings (in the setup menu) has enough room for new files.

If you have a lot of free RAM in your computer, you can directly compile an EXE file. This is easy, because the compilation automatically calls the linker. However, if you don't have enough memory, you can use the OBJ option, call the linker yourself by waiting for the OBJ file to write to disk, quit Turbo Prolog, and then type

```
plink geobase
```

When you run the compiler, you'll see the same compilation messages that you'll see when compiling to memory (described in the next section), but at the end you'll also see messages about the final files generated. Once you have a GEOBASE.EXE file, you can run GeoBase simply by typing

```
geobase
```

and pressing RETURN.

Compiling to Memory

The first thing the program will do is load the GEOBASE.INC file. After about 15 seconds, you'll see a sequence of predicates scroll by quickly in the Message window. Then, after almost a minute, you'll see the main menu and window appear. This is shown in Figure 13-7. (Note: Do not use the Save the Database on File option yet.)

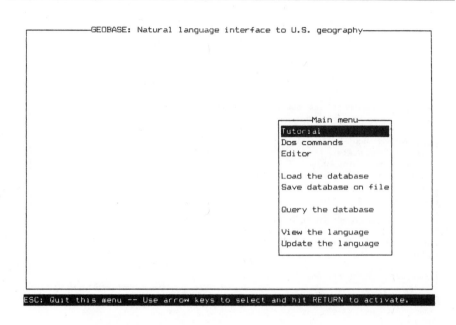

```
 ┌─────GEOBASE: Natural language interface to U.S. geography──────┐
 │                                                               │
 │                                                               │
 │                                                               │
 │                                                               │
 │                                                               │
 │                                 ┌────Main menu────┐            │
 │                                 │Tutorial         │            │
 │                                 │Dos commands     │            │
 │                                 │Editor           │            │
 │                                 │                 │            │
 │                                 │Load the database│            │
 │                                 │Save database on file│        │
 │                                 │                 │            │
 │                                 │Query the database│           │
 │                                 │                 │            │
 │                                 │View the language│            │
 │                                 │Update the language│          │
 │                                 └─────────────────┘            │
 │                                                               │
 └───────────────────────────────────────────────────────────────┘
  ESC: Quit this menu -- Use arrow keys to select and hit RETURN to activate.
```

Figure 13-7.   Main menu and window for GeoBase

The next sections of this chapter detail the options presented by the main menu.

Tutorial

If you choose to see the tutorial at this point (by moving the cursor to the Tutorial option and pressing RETURN), GeoBase will quickly refer to the GEOBASE.HLP file. The first screen (as shown in Figure 13-8) explains the sorts of questions GeoBase can answer and what syntax is needed.

You can use the key commands shown at the bottom of the screen or you can use the standard Editor window commands to move through this Help screen. There is more information as you scroll down. Remember

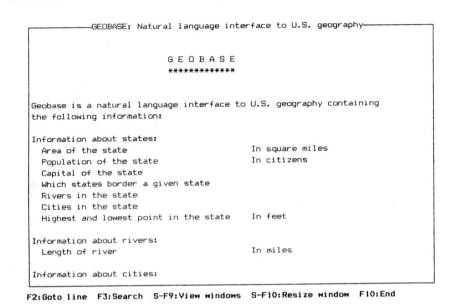

```
┌──────────GEOBASE: Natural language interface to U.S. geography──────────┐
│                                                                         │
│                          G E O B A S E                                  │
│                          *************                                  │
│                                                                         │
│                                                                         │
│  Geobase is a natural language interface to U.S. geography containing   │
│  the following information:                                             │
│                                                                         │
│  Information about states:                                              │
│    Area of the state                      In square miles               │
│    Population of the state                In citizens                    │
│    Capital of the state                                                  │
│    Which states border a given state                                     │
│    Rivers in the state                                                   │
│    Cities in the state                                                   │
│    Highest and lowest point in the state    In feet                      │
│                                                                         │
│  Information about rivers:                                               │
│    Length of river                        In miles                       │
│                                                                         │
│  Information about cities:                                               │
└─────────────────────────────────────────────────────────────────────────┘
F2:Goto line   F3:Search   S-F9:View windows   S-F10:Resize window   F10:End
```

Figure 13-8.   Help screen for GeoBase

that even this screen is part of the program code. You can delve into the code to see how the Editor key controls were implemented within a user-defined window.

The rest of the GeoBase tutorial explains where the information for question parsing is kept within GeoBase. This lets you add your own rules to the set or change the rules already there. Figure 13-9 shows part of this section.

DOS Commands

This option on the main menu lets you get out to the DOS prompt to use the standard DOS utilities. Just like the OS option in Turbo Prolog's

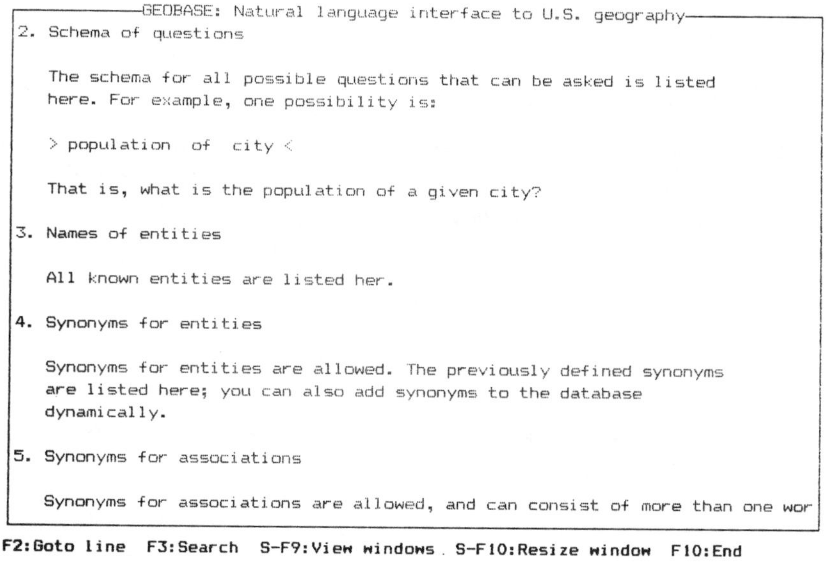

```
        ┌────GEOBASE: Natural language interface to U.S. geography────┐
        │2. Schema of questions                                        │
        │                                                              │
        │   The schema for all possible questions that can be asked is listed
        │   here. For example, one possibility is:                     │
        │                                                              │
        │   > population  of  city <                                   │
        │                                                              │
        │   That is, what is the population of a given city?           │
        │3. Names of entities                                          │
        │                                                              │
        │   All known entities are listed her.                         │
        │                                                              │
        │4. Synonyms for entities                                      │
        │                                                              │
        │   Synonyms for entities are allowed. The previously defined synonyms
        │   are listed here; you can also add synonyms to the database  │
        │   dynamically.                                               │
        │                                                              │
        │5. Synonyms for associations                                  │
        │                                                              │
        │   Synonyms for associations are allowed, and can consist of more than one wor
        └──────────────────────────────────────────────────────────────┘
F2:Goto line  F3:Search  S-F9:View windows  S-F10:Resize window  F10:End
```

Figure 13-9.   Part of the question-parsing section of GeoBase

Files submenu, you return to the program simply by typing

```
exit
```

If you use the DOS Commands option to escape to the operating system, then be careful which drive you are on when you return by using the Exit command. The drive you return from will be the default drive, which Turbo Prolog searches for such files as the database. If the database is on another disk drive it won't be found, and you'll have to either go back to DOS again or retreat to the main Prolog menu to change the directory setting.

Editor

Choose this menu item to get an Editor window ready for text processing.

View the Language

If you choose this option, you'll be presented with another menu, as shown in Figure 13-10. This menu lets you look at natural-language definitions and rules already within the program.

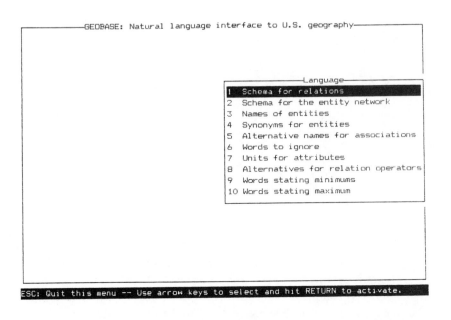

Figure 13-10.   Menu presented by View the Language option

Update the Language

This choice offers another submenu (as shown in Figure 13-11). With this menu you'll be able to add new synonyms, new alternative associative words, or new words to be ignored within the question text. You can back out of the menu one level at a time by pressing ESC.

Load the Database

Before you ask questions of the program, you need to load the database into memory. When you load the database, be prepared to wait a little

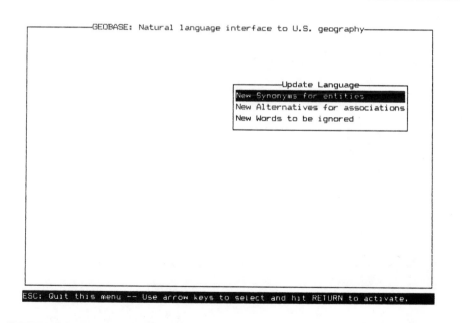

Figure 13-11.   Submenu for updating the GeoBase language

while for any action other than disk noise. And be prepared for a possible "out of memory" statement. To beat the "out of memory" problem, you can back out of Turbo Prolog and start again without the memory-resident programs.

You don't have to load the database to use the program in its most fundamental way: asking questions. All you need to do is choose the next option.

Query the Database

This choice does not require extra memory or take very long to process. As soon as you press RETURN, you'll be asked for a query. First try some

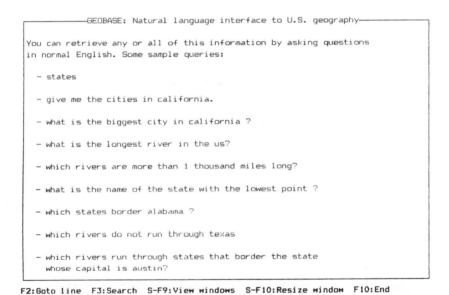

```
───────────GEOBASE: Natural language interface to U.S. geography───────
┌────────────────────────────────────────────────────────────────────┐
│You can retrieve any or all of this information by asking questions    │
│in normal English. Some sample queries:                               │
│                                                                       │
│  - states                                                            │
│                                                                       │
│  - give me the cities in california.                                 │
│                                                                       │
│  - what is the biggest city in california ?                          │
│                                                                       │
│  - what is the longest river in the us?                              │
│                                                                       │
│  - which rivers are more than 1 thousand miles long?                 │
│                                                                       │
│  - what is the name of the state with the lowest point ?             │
│                                                                       │
│  - which states border alabama ?                                     │
│                                                                       │
│  - which rivers do not run through texas                             │
│                                                                       │
│  - which rivers run through states that border the state             │
│    whose capital is austin?                                          │
└────────────────────────────────────────────────────────────────────┘
  F2:Goto line  F3:Search  S-F9:View windows  S-F10:Resize window  F10:End
```

Figure 13-12. Sample queries for the database

of the example queries that Borland suggests, as shown in Figure 13-12 (these are taken from the tutorial). As with any other position in GeoBase, you can back out by pressing the ESC key.

Save the Database

Be very careful with this option. If you absent-mindedly choose the option and you haven't loaded a database to modify, you could save a database that is 0 bytes long and banish the previous database to a BAK file. GeoBase won't be able to run without the data in the database, and it won't find that data if the file has a BAK extension. Worse yet, if you do it twice, you could entirely erase the database. This proves the utility of backup disks.

Modifying the Database

Try posing questions until you find several that the language cannot understand. Then add definitions to the language routines that will allow them to deal with the questions. Come back again and ask the same questions and compare the responses. How much can you perfect Geo-Base's ability to understand English?

Appendixes

A *ASCII Codes*

ASCII Value	Character	Printable	Turbo Prolog Special Effect
1	CTRL-A	No	No
2	CTRL-B	No	No
3	CTRL-C	No	Halt execution
4	CTRL-D	No	No
5	CTRL-E	No	No
6	CTRL-F	No	No
7	CTRL-G	No	No
8	CTRL-H	No	Backspace
9	CTRL-I	No	Tab
10	CTRL-J	No	No
11	CTRL-K	No	No
12	CTRL-L	No	No
13	CTRL-M	No	Carriage return
14	CTRL-N	No	No
15	CTRL-O	No	No
16	CTRL-P	No	Toggle printer echo
17	CTRL-Q	No	Resume print
18	CTRL-R	No	No
19	CTRL-S	No	Pause or stop print
20	CTRL-T	No	Toggles tracing
21	CTRL-U	No	No
22	CTRL-V	No	No
23	CTRL-W	No	No
24	CTRL-X	No	No
25	CTRL-Y	No	No
26	CTRL-Z	No	Signals end of file
27	ESC	No	Escape
28	none	No	No
29	none	No	No
30	none	No	No
31	none	No	No
32	SPACE	Yes	Blank space character

ASCII Value	Character	Printable	Turbo Prolog Special Effect
33	!	Yes	No
34	"	Yes	No
35	#	Yes	No
36	$	Yes	No
37	%	Yes	No
38	&	Yes	No
39	'	Yes	No
40	(	Yes	No
41	)	Yes	No
42	*	Yes	No
43	+	Yes	No
44	,	Yes	No
45	—	Yes	No
46	.	Yes	No
47	/	Yes	No
48	0	Yes	No
49	1	Yes	No
50	2	Yes	No
51	3	Yes	No
52	4	Yes	No
53	5	Yes	No
54	6	Yes	No
55	7	Yes	No
56	8	Yes	No
57	9	Yes	No
58	:	Yes	No
59	;	Yes	No
60	<	Yes	No
61	=	Yes	No
62	>	Yes	No
63	?	Yes	No
64	@	Yes	No

ASCII Value	Character	Printable	Turbo Prolog Special Effect
65	A	Yes	No
66	B	Yes	No
67	C	Yes	No
68	D	Yes	No
69	E	Yes	No
70	F	Yes	No
71	G	Yes	No
72	H	Yes	No
73	I	Yes	No
74	J	Yes	No
75	K	Yes	No
76	L	Yes	No
77	M	Yes	No
78	N	Yes	No
79	O	Yes	No
80	P	Yes	No
81	Q	Yes	No
82	R	Yes	No
83	S	Yes	No
84	T	Yes	No
85	U	Yes	No
86	V	Yes	No
87	W	Yes	No
88	X	Yes	No
90	Y	Yes	No
90	Z	Yes	No
91	[	Yes	No
92	\	Yes	No
93	]	Yes	No
94	^	Yes	No
95	—	Yes	No
96	`	Yes	No

ASCII Value	Character	Printable	**Turbo Prolog Special Effect**
97	a	Yes	No
98	b	Yes	No
99	c	Yes	No
100	d	Yes	No
101	e	Yes	No
102	f	Yes	No
103	g	Yes	No
104	h	Yes	No
105	i	Yes	No
106	j	Yes	No
107	k	Yes	No
108	l	Yes	No
109	m	Yes	No
110	n	Yes	No
111	o	Yes	No
112	p	Yes	No
113	q	Yes	No
114	r	Yes	No
115	s	Yes	No
116	t	Yes	No
117	u	Yes	No
118	v	Yes	No
119	w	Yes	No
120	x	Yes	No
121	y	Yes	No
122	z	Yes	No
123	{	Yes	No
124	¦	Yes	No
125	}	Yes	No
126	~	Yes	No

Bibliography

General Texts

Clocksin, W.F., and C.S. Mellish. *Programming in Prolog*. 2d ed. New York: Springer-Verlag, 1984.

This book is the bible of the field. If you're only going to look at one more book, make it this one. It does an excellent job of stepping through a standard version of Prolog, demonstrating its features and some of the theoretical underpinnings.

Burnham, W.D., and A.R. Hall. *Prolog Programming and Applications*. New York: Halsted Press (division of John Wiley & Sons), 1985.

This book is the next most valuable source. Although thin, it contains a complete walk-through of the predicates and syntax of Prolog.

Bharath, B. *An Introduction to Prolog*. Summit, Pa.: TAB Books, 1986.

This entire book is written in question-and-answer form. Although this may be a little hard to follow, and the syntax is micro-Prolog style, the information is lucidly presented along with demonstrative clauses and rules. Not many complete programs are included. Extensive appendixes cover what Prolog products are available for microcomputers, background information on expert systems and AI, and some of the theory of logic. One long appendix contains an introduction to the Prolog86 implementation of Prolog.

micro-Prolog in the Schools

de Saram, H., *Programming in micro-Prolog*. New York: Halsted Press (division of John Wiley & Sons), 1985.

Both this and the next book are strongly oriented toward micro-Prolog, the most popular microcomputer version of Prolog until Turbo Prolog appeared. The syntax of micro-Prolog differs substantially from that of

Turbo Prolog, but its fundamental predicates are the same and have the same meaning. This book is a bit "cute," with a cartoon character trying to match clauses and example programs such as "Fox, Chicken, and Grain." Hugh de Saram borrows heavily from his experience of teaching Prolog to schoolchildren in England.

Ennals, R. *Beginning micro-Prolog*. New York: Harper & Row, 1984.

This book is also derived from the experience of teaching Prolog to schoolchildren. It includes answers to exercises and would make a fine text for a high school class that was using micro-Prolog. Unfortunately, the syntax differences between micro-Prolog and Turbo Prolog make it useful mainly as a teacher's supplement for any class using Turbo.

Logic Programming: History and Theory

Clark, K.L., and S.A. Tarnlund, eds. *Logic Programming*. New York: Academic Press Inc., 1982.

This is the most famous book in logic programming. It includes contributions from Colemerauer (the man credited with inventing Prolog) and other major Prolog luminaries, including Pereira, Kowalski, and Mellish. The technical level is fairly high.

Van Caneghem, M., and D.H.D. Warren, eds. *Logic Programming and Its Applications*. Norwood, N.J.: Ablex Publishing Corp., 1986.

This is a compilation of research papers that range from "Optimizing Tail Recursion" and "Teaching Logic as a Computer Language in Schools" to "A Prolog Simulation of Migration Decision-Making in a Less Developed Country." Theory and applications are both present.

Campbell, J.A., ed. *Implementations of Prolog*. New York: Halsted Press (division of John Wiley & Sons), 1984.

This is a book about the state of the art in Prolog research. It has papers about the history of the language (from those who were involved), current issues in Prolog, theoretical questions, and future directions.

General Background

Feigenbaum, E.A., and P. McCorduck. *The Fifth Generation: Artificial Intelligence and Japan's Computer Challenge to the World.* Reading, Mass: Addison-Wesley, 1983.

Borland claims that Turbo Prolog brings the genius of the fifth generation and artificial intelligence to your PC. This is the book that introduced the American public to the concept of fifth-generation computers.

Trademarks

Apple®	Apple Computer, Inc.
AT™	International Business Machines Corp.
GeoBase™	Borland International, Inc.
Hercules™	Hercules Computer Technology
IBM®	International Business Machines Corp.
Macintosh™	Macintosh is a trademark of McIntosh Laboratory, Inc., licensed to Apple Computer, Inc., and is used with express permission of its owner.
MS-DOS™	Microsoft Corp.
MultiMate®	MultiMate International Corp.
PC-DOS™	International Business Machines Corp.
ProKey™	RoseSoft, Inc.
SideKick™	Borland International, Inc.
Turbo Pascal®	Borland International, Inc.
Turbo Prolog™	Borland International, Inc.
WordStar®	MicroPro International Corp.

Index

:- symbol, 115

The manuscript for this book was prepared and submitted to Osborne/McGraw-Hill in electronic form. The acquisitions editor for this project was Jon Erickson.

Text design by Judy Wohlfrom, using Bodoni for both text body and display.

Cover art by Yashi Okita. Cover supplier is Phoenix Color Corp. Text stock, 50 lb. Glatfelter. Book printed and bound by R.R. Donnelley & Sons Company, Crawfordsville, Indiana.

Turbo Prolog Command Card

MAIN MENU

To choose one of the main menu selections, either press the key of the first letter of the selection or use the cursor keys to move the highlighting to the desired selection and then press RETURN. This holds for submenus also.

Escape

To get out of most situations	ESC

Help

Help	F1 (always)

EDITOR

Delete Keys

Delete character above cursor	DEL or CTRL-G
Delete character to left of cursor	BACKSPACE
Delete cursor's word to right	CTRL-T
Delete cursor's line	CTRL-Y or CTRL-BACKSPACE

Cursor Movement

Up one line	Up arrow or CTRL-E
Down one line	Down arrow or CTRL-X
Left one character	Left arrow or CTRL-S
Right one character	Right arrow or CTRL-D
Left one word	CTRL-left arrow or CTRL-A
Right one word	CTRL-right arrow or CTRL-F
To beginning of cursor line	HOME or CTRL-Q-S
To end of cursor line	END or CTRL-Q-D
Up one page	PGUP or CTRL-R
Down one page	PGDN or CTRL-C
To beginning of marked block	CTRL-Q-B
To end of marked block	CTRL-Q-K
To beginning (top) of file	CTRL-PGUP or CTRL-Q-R
To end of file	CTRL-PGDN or CTRL-Q-C
Go to a certain line number	F2, type the line number, and press F2 again
Display cursor's line number	SHIFT-F2 (version 1.0 only)
Turn on automatic indenting	CTRL-Q-I (second press turns it off again)

Text Entry

Enter Editor window	E
Enter Auxiliary Editor window	F8
Leave Editor or Auxiliary Editor (end editing)	F10 or ESC
Toggle between insert and overwrite modes	CTRL-V or INS

Running Programs

Toggle trace mode	ALT-T
Toggle echo to printer (prints output as well as sending it to screen)	CTRL-P
Pause program output to screen (press again to resume)	CTRL-S
Permanently interrupt program execution	CTRL-C or CTRL-BREAK
Automatically retype previous external goal in Dialog box	F8
Call the Editor	F9
Select window for size change	SHIFT-F9
Recompile after compiling error message	F10
Change size of or move Dialog window	SHIFT-F10

Block Functions

Mark beginning of block	CTRL-K-B (or special function key)
Mark end of block	CTRL-K-K (or special function key)
Hide block markings	CTRL-K-H (second use redisplays markings)
Delete marked block	CTRL-K-Y or F7
Move marked block to cursor	CTRL-K-V or F6
Copy marked block to cursor	CTRL-K-C or F5
Repeat copy of marked block	SHIFT-F5
Read block from disk to cursor	CTRL-K-R or F9
Write marked block to disk	CTRL-K-W

Search and Replace

Search for (also called "Find") a given string	F3 or CTRL-Q-F
Repeat most recent search	SHIFT-F3 or CTRL-L
Search for and then replace a given string	F4 or CTRL-Q-A
Repeat most recent search and replace	SHIFT-F4 or CTRL-L

IF YOU ENJOYED THIS BOOK...

help us stay in touch with your needs and interests by filling out and returning the survey card below. Your opinions are important, and will help us to continue to publish the kinds of books you need, when you need them.

What brand of computer(s) do you own or use? _____

Where do you use your computer the most? ☐ At work ☐ At school ☐ At home

What topics would you like to see covered in future books by Osborne/McGraw-Hill? _____

How many other computer books do you own? _____

Why did you choose this book?
☐ Best coverage of the subject.
☐ Recognized the author from previous work.
☐ Liked the price.
☐ Other

Where did you find this book?
☐ Bookstore
☐ Computer/software store
☐ Department store
☐ Advertisement
☐ Catalog

Where did you hear about this book?
☐ Book review.
☐ Osborne catalog.
☐ Advertisement in:
☐ Found by browsing in store.
☐ Found/recommended in library
☐ Other

☐ Required textbook
☐ Library
☐ Gift
☐ Other

Where should we send your FREE catalog?

NAME _____

ADDRESS _____

CITY _____ STATE _____ ZIP _____

BUSINESS REPLY MAIL

FIRST CLASS   PERMIT NO. 3111   Berkeley, CA

Postage will be paid by addressee

Osborne McGraw-Hill

2600 Tenth Street
Berkeley, California 94710